HOW DR. DEATH BECAME DR. LIFE

STEVE WILLIAMS
with TOM CAIAZZO

SPECIAL FOREWORD BY
BARRY SWITZER

FOREWORD BY
JIM ROSS

SportsPublishingLLC.com

ISBN-10: 1-59670-180-3
ISBN-13: 978-1-59670-180-9

All photos courtesy of Steve Williams
Back cover photo location courtesy of Cathedral of St. John Berchmans, Parrish and School; 939 Jordan Street; Shreveport, LA 71101; (318) 221-5296

Publishers: Peter L. Bannon and Joseph J. Bannon Sr.
Senior managing editor: Susan M. Moyer
Acquisitions editor: Noah Amstadter
Developmental editor: Laura Podeschi
Art director: K. Jeffrey Higgerson
Cover design: Dustin J. Hubbart
Photo editor: Erin Linden-Levy

Sports Publishing L.L.C.
804 North Neil Street
Champaign, IL 61820
Phone: 1-877-424-2665
Fax: 217-363-2073
www.SportsPublishingLLC.com

Printed in the United States of America

CIP data available upon request.

CONTENTS

ACKNOWLEDGMENTS

This book is dedicated to all my fans. Without them, this story wouldn't have been possible. It is also dedicated to my mother, late father, and late sister; my brothers, Jeff and Jerry; my son, Wyndam; my daughter, Stormy, and her family; and my ex-wife, Tammy. Additional thanks is given to all my church and prayer group brothers and sisters, as well as the entire team of doctors and support staff at M.D. Anderson Cancer Center.

Tom would like to thank his wife, Janet, and son, Dante, for all their patience and understanding with the writing of this book.

Both authors wish to thank the following individuals for their contributions and help with this book: Jeremy Young; Barry and Becky Switzer; Jim Ross; Mike Geary; Dr. Jodi Knott; Kelly Mitchell; Keith Meador; Harley Race; Terry Funk; Bill Watts; Buddy Landell; Jim Duggan; Ricky Morton; Ted DiBiase; Missy Hyatt; Superstar Billy Graham; Michael Myers; Marchel Ray; Tommie Neathery; Matt Roberts; Mark Givens; Gerri Wollbert; Pastor Denny Duron; Delores Winder; Andy Vineberg; Chris and Mark Youngblood; and, Laura Podeschi, Andi Hake, Noah Amstadter, Peter Bannon, and all the wonderful folks at Sports Publishing.

We both give praise and glory to God, our creator and Father, as well as our Savior, Jesus Christ.

FOREWORD

I first met Steve "Dr. Death" Williams between his junior and senior years of college at the University of Oklahoma in the early 1980s. Of course, Doc's legend as a physically intimidating, two-sport star for the Sooners was well known to all of us Sooner fanatics who followed, with passion, the OU football and wrestling teams' exploits in the then-Big Eight Conference.

Doc was a dominating offensive guard for legendary coach Barry Switzer's powerhouse Sooner football team, earning All-Big Eight honors and playing in multiple bowl games for the crimson and cream. Former OU defensive backfield coach Bobby Proctor, who served the university with pride for many, many years and coached a fair amount of future NFL players while at Oklahoma, once told me that Dr. Death was "the scariest player that he had ever seen on the football field."

Coach Switzer, a hall of fame coach and one of the most charismatic and good-hearted human beings alive, told me that Doc was as tough as any football player he had ever coached, and, having led OU to three national championships and the Dallas Cowboys to a Super Bowl victory, that includes some pretty fair ball players.

As soon as football season would conclude, usually with a bowl game, Doc would head immediately to the wrestling room and start dominating on the mat. Many amateur wrestling experts have told me on numerous occasions that if Doc had focused strictly on wrestling, he would have been a gold medalist in the Olympic Games. These statements were made more valid as they came from men who won the Gold in the Olympics and who wrestled the good Doctor in the NCAA tournament. In Doc's spare time, he made All-America in wrestling on multiple occasions. Not bad for a part-timer!

However, to me, the "real" Dr. Death is the Steve Williams of today, the man I know and love like a brother and who is alive by the grace of God after defeating his toughest opponent ... cancer. God has blessed Steve's life in so many ways. Never once through all the challenging chemotherapy and radiation treatments did I ever hear Steve complain. Never once did I hear Steve ask, "Why me?" Steve put his faith totally in the Lord and trusted Him to pull this fiercely competitive athlete through the most challenging contest of Doc's life.

This is the story of a powerful man who conquered foes on the gridiron at the highest level. It is the story of a man who dominated both amateur and professional wrestling with the strength of a bull and who was intimidated by nothing. But most importantly, it is the story of a man's faith and belief in the good Lord to help pull him through what appeared to be certain death.

Dr. Death is really Dr. Life, and this story is one that will touch your heart and your soul. I know you will enjoy the story of the oftentimes controversial but blessed journey of my dear friend, Steve "Dr. Death" Williams.

Jim Ross
Voice of the WWE's Monday Night Raw

SPECIAL FOREWORD

Throughout one's life, most of us, over time, closely associate with four or five truly remarkable individuals outside of our families whom we can never forget. Steve "Dr. Death" Williams makes my list.

Steve Williams played offensive guard for the University of Oklahoma Sooners in the early 1980s. Over his career, he was part of a succession of the nation's best collegiate offensive lines—small groups of intensely dedicated and talented young men, each large in stature—who made it possible for our team to lead the nation in rushing for several of those seasons, win the Big Eight Conference, and New Years' Day Bowl championships.

In the time that I have been coaching, I have never seen any player physically tougher or stronger than Steve Williams. He was simply a force that no one, and no combination of "someones," could physically handle on the football field. He was so dominant. Likewise, on the football field he was truly a 300-pound "monster" who intimidated many, if not most, of those against whom he played.

He was an even better heavyweight wrestler. Unlike all of those against whom he competed, as a collegiate All-American, Steve was never able to practice and train for wrestling until our football seasons were over—which always lasted until early January.

My very close friend and former wrestling coach at the University of Oklahoma, Stan Abel, has told me on numerous occasions that Steve would have unquestionably been a several-time NCAA champion and perhaps even a two-time Olympic champion had he not, by circumstance, been forced into this most difficult *dual training regimen.*

This is true. Even if an athlete is finely tuned to perform at his best in one sport, this does not mean that he is properly trained and tuned for another sport. It takes different training techniques and strength and conditioning for an athlete to be able to perform his very best in those different sports.

Despite this significant limitation, Steve was one of the nation's very best in both sports. He competed at the very highest level. I always considered him to be one of the nation's superb, even elite, football players. But in wrestling, he was simply among the very best ever.

After Steve was already engaged in professional wrestling, he told me one time at a social occasion that he really enjoyed football and wrestling. He felt that the skills learned and applied (not the training regimens) complemented one another. But he also laughed and said, both in jest and as a matter of simple truth, that one of the big kicks he got out of life was knowing that, during the 1980s and 1990s, there was no room anywhere that he could walk into where there would be anyone he could not physically whip!

Some individuals might ask why I would place someone with the surly nickname "Dr. Death," which some non-sporting or non-wrestling fan might find offensive, so high on my list of really special people. The reason is simple: "Dr. Death" is show business and part of the intimidation associated with his particular role in it.

Steve Williams the man, like any of us, is measured by his heart much more than by his accomplishments. He is what some call a "pussy cat," although before his illness, he may well have looked very much like a Gorilla!

Steve Williams is one of those special people who loves others, who cares for others deeply, and who, at any weight or size, would still be a great person and great friend.

I have to say that Steve is now, at this very moment, fighting the toughest opponent he has ever played against or wrestled: the cancer that has invaded his body. Knowing Steve as well as I do and after having shared the trial with him, I know the cancer has not affected his heart and feelings for others. No matter who ultimately wins this particular bout, he is still and will always be the great Steve Williams to me.

Coach Barry L. Switzer
Norman, Oklahoma
October 16, 2006

ONE

THE FIGHT OF MY LIFE

I thought I was dead. Around four a.m., I woke up in a pool of blood. I ran into the bathroom and saw in the mirror that something was dreadfully wrong: my entire upper body and neck were covered in blood. My throat was also clogged, so I took a drink of water. Like a breached dam, the water shot out of my stoma, the opening in my throat created by my surgeon. I then realized what was wrong; my stoma had sprung a leak.

I was scared as heck and thought this was the end. After three months of chemotherapy and radiation, two major surgeries, and almost 15 months of emotional depression and physical deterioration to get rid of my cancer, I wasn't too sure that I would make it this time. All I knew was that I had a hole in my stoma the size of my thumb and I was bleeding.

All I could think about was getting through this ordeal. As I prayed for my survival, a miracle happened: the bleeding just stopped. I was elated. But my thoughts quickly turned to what might happen next. Would I start bleeding again? Would I pass out? Would I eventually stop breathing and die?

I threw on some sweats and grabbed my keys and wallet. Acting out of instinct and clearly being led by God, I hopped in my truck and headed to the M.D. Anderson Cancer Center in Houston, Texas, some four hours away.

You would think that I would have called an ambulance or at least gone to the local emergency room. But for whatever reason, those options never crossed my mind. Rather, I drove as fast as I could out of town, asking and praying to God, "Please keep me alive."

During the drive down, I prayed a lot. I called my older brother Jeff. He was living in Houston at the time, less than five miles away from M.D. Anderson. He kept my spirits up and told me that I was going to make it. We spoke three or four times during the drive. As I got closer to Houston I called him and told him to meet me at the emergency room. I also tried to call my daughter, Stormy, but there was no answer. I really didn't want to worry anyone else.

As soon as I saw Jeff, we hugged. He couldn't believe what I looked like: my head was so swollen that it was the size of a pumpkin. With tears in his eyes, he reassured me that everything would be all right. As I was admitted, one of the doctors made the comment, "I can't believe you're still alive."

After running some tests and checking my vitals, we learned some very bad news: they were going to have to cut two and a half feet of muscle out of my thigh to plug the hole in my throat. I thought, "Oh my God."

I couldn't imagine having a big chunk of muscle taken out of my thigh. I had suffered enough scars throughout my life. I was tired of people cutting into me. I also took great pride in my legs and had some of the best in the wrestling business. The thought of having muscle removed from my legs was crushing.

As I waited to be prepped for surgery, the only thing going through my mind was that I wanted to live. Jeff and I tightly held hands. I could see the fear in his eyes, but we both remained strong. I couldn't have endured the wait without him. Around that time, a hospital missionary visited, and together the three of us prayed for my life to be saved.

While the anesthesiologist was administering a cocktail of drugs to me, he tried to cheer me up by cracking some jokes. At that point I really needed a laugh. In turn, I joked with him, saying, "Aloha" in reference to his Hawaiian-style headband.

But my half-hearted jokes were just a front. I knew what was about to go down: they were going to cut my darn head open! I was told that due to my size, they were going to have to administer some heavy-duty anesthesia. He wasn't kidding; I didn't wake up for nearly two days.

After ten hours of successful surgery and many more of recovery, I finally woke up. The first thing I felt was tremendous pain in my leg. I called for a nurse to put a pillow under it, hoping it might alleviate some of the pain. My head, neck, throat, thigh—basically my entire body—were hurting. Nurses would come in every six minutes to give me morphine for the pain. It was so bad that I would watch the clock, anxiously waiting for the 5:55 mark.

Along with Jeff, my 82-year-old mother joined me in recovery. As a breast cancer survivor, she was able to relate to what I was going through. With her courage and unconquered spirit, I always knew that there was hope.

Because of the surgery, I couldn't talk for months. I was initially given a computerized voice synthesizer to communicate. I couldn't stand the thing. It made me sound like a robot. I eventually settled for a dry erase board, but I hated it too. Although it was an inconvenience, the board at least allowed me to communicate through writing. The first thing I wrote on that board was to my mother: "MOM, I LOVE YOU!"

I had been in excellent health until shortly after Christmas of 2003. For some reason, I kept getting sick, and my throat was in constant pain. I visited a few local doctors and they would treat me with antibiotics, but the pain would never completely go away. I simply thought I had a bad cold that for some reason I could not shake.

Right before the New Year, I was booked for a tour in China and Japan with Ricky Nelson's promotion out of Charlotte, North Carolina. Nelson's promotion was the second one ever to hold a wrestling card in China. I was so excited that I decided to just tolerate the pain and take my medicine. Heck, I was going to China! I was also pumped because I would challenge my old friend Terry Taylor for the NWA Heavyweight Title—a belt that I really wanted to capture.

Simultaneously, I had recently opened a professional wrestling school, American Championship Wrestling (ACW). With my partner and friend Jeremy Young, I ran some shows at home, hoping to revitalize the Mid-South wrestling scene. We had some sponsors, and the school was attracting interest. Things were looking bright in Shreveport.

About this time I really started noticing some major problems with my voice. I have always had a raspy voice, but soon I could barely speak. I also had difficulty swallowing, and my throat was constantly sore. I continued to take my antibiotics, tried to stay away from smoky bars, and looked for some natural stuff to help fight what I thought was just a sore throat and a cold.

When I returned home in mid-January 2004, my voice was becoming even more hoarse. With my 23-year-old daughter, Stormy, I decided to see a local throat specialist, Dr. Keith Christy, in Bossier City, Louisiana. He ran various tests and did a biopsy. Although he was not certain what was wrong, the tests indicated that I might have throat cancer. I was shocked by this potential diagnosis, and Stormy cried for what seemed like hours.

Before I left his office, Dr. Christy gave me a dose of antibiotics and prescribed a course of oral steroids. He also arranged for me to go to the M.D. Anderson Cancer Center in Houston, Texas. In the meantime, I was also advised to return to his clinic if I did not have total resolution of the symptoms.

I just couldn't believe what the doctor had said. In my mind, I still thought that it was just a bad sore throat. The idea that I might have cancer was inconceivable.

I guess you could say I was in denial. I was even looking forward to seeing a specialist, thinking that they would finally give me some stronger medicine to cure my sore throat.

A few days later, I drove to M.D. Anderson by myself. My brother Jeff met me there, and as we waited to see the specialists, we sat in the waiting area together and prayed for the best. They conducted numerous evaluations, studies, and tests. At the conclusion, specialist Dr. Erich Sturgis informed me that I did indeed have cancer.

Dr. Sturgis, one of the best neck and head surgeons in the world, found that I had a slight irregularity of my right vocal cord, as well as some edema, or swelling, and possible partial paralysis. Also, the cancer was so advanced that I needed surgery immediately.

The type of cancer I had is called T4 cancer. T4 cancer is the most devastating one can get in the lymph nodes and throat. With T4, the cancer extends outside the larynx by invading the thyroid cartilage and into the esophagus or soft tissue of the neck. There was a tumor the size of a golf ball on the side of my neck.

I was blown away. I couldn't imagine having my head opened up from ear-to-ear and all my vocals removed. I asked if there were any other options. Dr. Sturgis said that I would also be a good candidate for radiation and chemotherapy. That sounded a little better I thought.

I thanked Dr. Sturgis and the other doctors for their time and told them I needed a few days to think about it. Because of the severity of my condition, they told me a decision would have to be made quickly. I absorbed all of the information, but I wanted a second opinion. I just felt that there had to be other options.

Terrified and confused, I hugged my brother and headed back to Shreveport. Ironically, the song playing on the radio was Tim McGraw's "Live Like You Were Dying." I started weeping like a baby. It hit me: at 42 years old, I might really be dying.

I thought about what the doctors had said. They weren't sure what had caused the cancer, but it could have been almost anything. I started smoking cigarettes after my first divorce, thinking that it would help me cope. I also chewed tobacco and dipped snuff from the age of 12 until I hit 30. As a jock, chewing tobacco was part of the practice field and locker room. It seemed like everyone was doing it, and at the time, I thought nothing about the health risks.

Today, I try to teach my son, Wyndam, about the harmful effects of tobacco products. What really upsets me are some vendors' advertising techniques. They will put beef jerky in cans to make it look like snuff. This advertising technique conditions kids to be attracted to tobacco. I am confident that, because of our discussions, Wyndam understands the dangers of tobacco products.

It is also possible that the sheer trauma from being a professional wrestler could have contributed to the cancer. The numerous clotheslines, lariats, punches, kicks, and shots to my neck and throat area could have spurred the cancer cells. To this day, nobody knows for sure what actually caused my sickness.

When I got back to Shreveport, my daughter and her family were waiting on me. I hugged them and then hugged my son. I did not want to let go. He is my life, and he and my family are the reason why I am alive today.

I called all over the world seeking a second opinion. I called throat cancer specialists in Japan, Europe, Hawaii, as well as others. I couldn't believe it: each doctor gave me the same advice: "Go to the M.D. Anderson Cancer Center in Houston. They are the best." It was amazing to know that the best cancer center in the world was indeed M.D. Anderson.

I called my mom and the rest of my family. I told them that after lots of thought and prayer, I was going to return to M.D. Anderson for treatment. Everyone was very supportive, and the encouragement was what I needed to conquer this cancer. I then made arrangements to stay with my brother Jeff and signed a contract for the biggest match of my life.

> DOTTIE YOUNG: I FELT SAD FOR STEVEN. AFTER ALWAYS SEEING HIM IN GREAT PHYSICAL CONDITION, ALWAYS DOING WHAT HE LOVED TO DO IN LIFE, I WANTED HIM TO GET BETTER SO HE COULD DO WHAT HE LOVED TO DO. SO HE COULD SPEND TIME WITH HIS SON, WHOM HE LOVES SO DEARLY. IT IS AWFUL TO WATCH YOUR CHILD GO THROUGH SOMETHING LIKE THAT. BUT I KNEW HE WOULD BEAT THIS CANCER. I HAVE WATCHED HIM OVER THE YEARS OVERCOME ALL ADVERSITY, AND KNEW HE WOULD DO THE SAME THIS TIME.

For three months, I went through 36 rounds each of the strongest available radiation and chemotherapy treatments. Let me tell you, radiation and chemotherapy work very differently. Radiation is a "local" treatment, which means it is a therapy focused on a specific area of the body. Chemotherapy is "systemic," meaning it attacks the cancer by treating the entire body. Due to their differences, radiation and chemotherapy provided a strong one-two punch in attacking my cancer.

Fighting that horrible Houston traffic, I would go for treatments every day, Monday through Friday at 4 p.m. Each session lasted 20 minutes. I went to all of those sessions with God in my heart and my mom by my side.

My family's support and my faith in God gave me the belief that, no matter what, I was going to beat this cancer. I have never backed down from any challenge in my life, and I wasn't going to start then.

The sessions began with me lying on a MRI table. They placed a nylon mask over my face and a specialized outfit over my head and upper body. The nurses would then fasten me down so I couldn't move. I received treatment for only 20 minutes, but it seemed like an eternity.

Every day after my treatments, I would get into my truck and cry. I was so scared and in so much pain that I even flirted with suicide. I would tell my mom that I couldn't take it anymore, but she would hug me and reassure me that everything would be all right. I prayed often, asking God to help me get through my battle against cancer.

From eight in the morning to three in the afternoon, I would do what I could to keep busy. Every day I would go to the gym and work out. I was lucky that I was still able to exercise. I also went to the mall looking to buy things for Wyndam, or just watching people going about their business. Throughout my whole career, I've been a big people watcher.

Jeff posted messages on my personal website and other message boards about my battle with cancer. He also e-mailed and telephoned all my friends and family in the states and overseas. The responses from people were so overwhelming. I spent every spare moment answering hundreds of e-mails and returning phone calls.

People came out of the woodwork to offer support. Though Vince McMahon never contacted me, numerous folks from the WWE did. The conversations with Stone Cold Steve Austin, Mick Foley, Kurt Angle, and Chris Benoit were so encouraging. I would also get correspondence from my high school and college wrestling and football buddies and coaches, fans and friends in Japan, church members, and countless others. Every call and e-mail raised my spirits. I was truly blessed to have such a network of support.

On weekends, I couldn't wait to get out of Houston and go home to visit with my family. I am a proud grandfather, and it was such a joy to see and spend time with my grandkids. Stormy is a great mother and she has been with me from day one as I fought this cancer. And of course I couldn't wait to see Wyndam.

On one occasion, I was at home spending some time with my son when I started to cough. Pieces of the tumor came out of my mouth and nose. Combined, they were about the size of my hand. Due to the radiation and chemotherapy, the tumor was breaking up and coming out. Although he was scared, Wyndam was supportive and knew that I was going to beat the disease.

I also sought much advice regarding natural cures. I was going to do everything in my power to get healthy. I was told that alternatives such as acupuncture and herbal medicine might be effective cures. Maybe I was being duped, but I purchased product after product hoping for a cure. I even bought some special water from Africa that was supposed to cure cancer—about five cases are still sitting in my garage.

I would leave no stone unturned in my fight for survival.

TWO

MIRACLE FROM GOD

When you visit the same place nearly every day for three months, you meet many people. I got to know lots of other cancer patients. These wonderful folks became part of my family. They all knew who I was; I was perceived as their leader, and I accepted the role. I cheered them up with encouragement, laughter, and prayer.

And then there was Susan. Just like me, this 98-pound woman would get cancer treatments every day. She looked so feeble and was always in pain. Susan was a wrestling fan and knew me as a big, tough wrestler. I always acted like everything was fine, though deep down I was scared to death. Some days she would have the energy to talk, and some days she wouldn't. But no matter what, I gave her a big hug every day. Though she said I made her day, she actually made mine.

The people working at the hospital also became part of my family. Because I spent so much time there, I got to know everyone on a first-name basis. In fact, many on the staff were old wrestling fans. They knew of Dr. Death from the years I had wrestled locally at the Sam Houston Coliseum. On one occasion, I brought about 100 pictures to the hospital to autograph and by the end of the day, the pictures were all gone.

Throughout my stay at Jeff's house in Houston, his two children, Mason, 12, and Taylor, 14, were also loving and supportive. They respected me and did whatever they could to help. We hugged a lot, and they made me laugh—and I needed to laugh. Jeff's beautiful wife, Martha, was also very caring and generous. She graciously accepted me into their home as part of their family.

During this time, my mother had come down from Colorado to take care of me and be by my side. She stayed with us at the house. My mom is a tough cookie, but due to her age, it was very uncomfortable for her to walk up and down the stairs, so Jeff turned his first-floor dining room into a bedroom! That brother of mine is an angel.

Although they welcomed me with open arms, I could tell that my stay was quite an adjustment. After my first chemotherapy treatment, the poison that was being put into my body started running out of me. The doctors gave me pills for the nausea, but I failed to read that they were to be taken before and not after the treatment.

Well, the day after my first radiation treatment, I was on the toilet all night long. I had the worst gas you could imagine. One time, I literally passed gas for five minutes straight. My stomach was hurting and the noise woke up Jeff's oldest son, Wes. He shouted, "Hey, be quiet!" He didn't know what it was. I made such loud noises as my body released the poisons. It was quite embarrassing.

Because I had taken such good care of my body and had always been so healthy, the treatments minimally fazed me. The entire Williams' family, though, saw the emotional and physical changes I was going through. They saw firsthand the emotional and physical pain I suffered, but even with that pain and some minor hair and weight loss, I still fared better physically than most people who go through the same treatment.

The physical changes, mood swings, depression, and the fact that I could die were realities everyone had to deal with.

Finally, after three months of treatment, I was ready to "ring the bell." At M.D. Anderson, when you complete the final day of radiation and chemotherapy treatment, you get to ring this bell as a symbol that you have finished all of your treatments. When I rang that bell, it was incredibly emotional. I was so glad that my whole family was there to witness the remarkable event. We must have gone through 50 boxes of Kleenex.

At the time, the doctors couldn't immediately tell if the tumor was completely gone, but the initial X-rays came back negative. Many more tests were taken, but it would take a while to determine if I was cancer-free. Regardless, I was the happiest man in the world. I could now once again pursue my passion: professional wrestling.

During those three months of treatment, I worked the phones and sent e-mails to my connections to secure some wrestling bookings in Japan. I knew that, by the grace of God, I was going to pin the cancer and get back in the ring. A few days or so after I rang that bell, I was on a plane to Japan. It was time to once again do what I love.

It was also time to start making a living. To be candid, I was going broke. I did have health insurance that covered most, but not all, of my treatments. I even had to sell my retirement condo in Hawaii just to pay my other bills.

I had been a workaholic my entire life. The wrestling business is brutal, and for years, I worked 30 days on and four days off. I would also work three five-week tours with only a week off in between in Japan. Having spent almost half my life there, it was so refreshing to get another opportunity to see all my fellow workers, friends, and fans. I love Japan. I have the utmost respect for the Japanese and am in awe of their culture.

After spending a couple of days in Japan wrestling and promoting for the IWA, I felt great. I made sure not to do anything risky that would damage my throat. About 10 years ago, I was wrestling the current director of talent relations for the WWE, Johnny Ace. During our match, I told him, "Duck my clothesline," but he didn't. I hit him right in his throat and severely damaged his vocals. He had to have surgery to repair his voice so he would no longer sound like Pee Wee Herman. Having learned from that experience, I was extremely careful while wrestling this time around.

I felt like I was back on top and my life seemed to be getting back in order—or so I thought. The night before my shoot fight against a Russian, I called Stormy from my hotel room to find out about the test results. She gave me some awfully dire news: I wasn't cancer free. I couldn't believe it.

I didn't even finish the tour. I rushed back to the states. I called Jeff and asked him to meet me at M.D. Anderson. The doctors explained to us in detail the dreaded results. It was scary. In fact, the cancer was so aggressive that it spanned from the side of my neck to my vocal cords.

> STORMY MAXWELL: I TOLD DAD THAT THE TREATMENTS DIDN'T GET RID OF THE CANCER. WE CRIED, BUT DAD TOLD ME THAT EVERYTHING WAS GOING TO BE OKAY AND HE WAS GOING TO BEAT IT. I REALLY DIDN'T UNDERSTAND WHY THE CHEMOTHERAPY DIDN'T WORK. EVEN TO THIS DAY, TELLING DAD THAT HE STILL HAD CANCER WAS THE HARDEST THING I HAVE EVER DONE.

I was really worried. Jeff and I looked into each other's eyes and started bawling. We couldn't believe it. I had no choice left but to have the major surgery that was initially recommended by Dr. Sturgis some three months before. If not, I would die. No ifs, ands, or buts about it.

My family was equally shocked but supportive. Stormy couldn't understand why God kept putting me in these situations. But I am a man's man, and have fought through adversity my entire life. Though I was scared—very scared—I still wasn't going to quit.

> JEREMY YOUNG: DOC AND I SPOKE ON THE PHONE AND I COULDN'T BELIEVE THAT THE TREATMENTS DIDN'T WORK. WE SPOKE FOR A WHILE AND I JUST KEPT REASSURING HIM THAT EVERYTHING WOULD BE OK.

I also knew that I was in good hands. The doctors and staff at M.D. Anderson are the best in the world. When you have throat cancer, you don't just meet with a single doctor. Patients require a multidisciplinary team approach. Some members of my team included: Dr. Erich Sturgis (head and neck surgeon); Dr. Yu Peirong (plastic surgeon); Dr. George Blumenschein (chemo and radiation doctor); and Dr. Jodi Knott (speech pathologist). Every one of these professionals treated me like a champion, and though I was scared stiff, I was confident that everything was going to be okay.

It was time to defeat the cancer once and for all. On September 7, 2004, with my brother Jeff and mother once again by my side, I was placed in a supine position on the operating room table. Under the care of Dr. Sturgis, I underwent examination under anesthesia with direct laryngoscopy and biopsy of a right rue vocal cord mass. Also, when the frozen section came back positive for invasive squamous cell carcinoma, the second most common skin cancer, Dr. Sturgis removed as much of the tumor as possible to improve my airway.

After they cut my head open from ear-to-ear in the nine-hour operation, they removed my vocal cords, thyroids, and deltoid muscle and nerves. They also replaced damaged muscle

JODI KNOTT: AS STEVE'S SPEECH PATHOLOGIST, I HAVE HAD THE PRIVILEGE OF WORKING WITH HIM THROUGHOUT HIS "JOURNEY." I REMEMBER THE DAY THAT STEVE WAS TRANSFERRED TO THE HEAD AND NECK CANCER INPATIENT FLOOR. AFTER READING HIS MEDICAL HISTORY, I REALIZED I WAS GOING TO BE WORKING WITH "DR. DEATH," THE CELEBRITY WWE WRESTLER. I WAS SOMEWHAT APPREHENSIVE, KNOWING HOW THE WWE WRESTLERS WERE PORTRAYED ON TV. TO MY SURPRISE, STEVE WAS THE MOST GENTLE, POSITIVE-MINDED, STRONG-WILLED, HUMOROUS PATIENT I HAD EVER WORKED WITH!

STEVE HAD SOME COMPLICATIONS AFTER HIS LARYNGECTOMY (REMOVAL OF THE VOICE BOX) AND TOOK ALL OF THEM IN STRIDE WITH THE MOST POSITIVE OUTLOOK. HE ALWAYS HAD A SMILE ON HIS FACE AND A "THUMBS-UP." DESPITE THE FACT THAT STEVE COULD NOT TALK, HE DEFINITELY HAD A WAY OF GETTING HIS POINT ACROSS.

THE DAY THAT STEVE HAD HIS VOICE PROSTHESIS PLACED AND WAS ABLE TO REGAIN HIS VOICE WAS SUCH A WONDERFUL EVENT. I FELT IT WAS A MAJOR MILESTONE IN HIS RECOVERY.

THROUGHOUT STEVE'S REHABILITATION, HE WAS ALWAYS GRACIOUS ENOUGH TO SIGN AUTOGRAPHS, PROVIDE VIDEOS FOR EDUCATIONAL LECTURES, ALLOW MEDICAL PHOTOGRAPHS FOR EDUCATIONAL TEACHING, AND SPEAK TO OTHER PATIENTS THAT HAVE HAD LARYNGECTOMIES. HE PROVIDES GREAT MOTIVATION FOR OTHER PATIENTS AS WELL AS STAFF AT M.D. ANDERSON CANCER CENTER.

in my neck with tissue from my thigh. Since my larynx was removed, a stoma was matured through the skin using 3-0 PDS, 3-0 Vicryl, and 3-0 nylon sutures. At the conclusion of the procedure, an eight-cuffed tracheal tube was inserted through the newly formed stoma. A stoma is basically an artifical hole in my throat which allows air to go through my lungs. Without it, I wouldn't be able to breathe.

I couldn't speak for months. My only form of communication was a dry-erase board that left me frustrated to no end. During the two-month recovery period, I was also on a liquid-only diet. My weight went from 290 down to roughly 205 during the early stages of recovery. I went from a size 44 waist to a loose 38!

> JEFF WILLIAMS: DURING THIS TIME, I BOMBARDED THE INTERNET WITH INFORMATION, SENT OUT E-MAILS, AND CALLED ALL HIS FRIENDS ASKING FOR PRAYER AND SUPPORT. THE WORLD NEEDED TO KNOW ABOUT DR. DEATH. SINCE HE COULDN'T TALK, I WAS HIS VOICE. PEOPLE WOULD CALL HIS CELL PHONE, OFFERING SUPPORT AND EVEN INSIGHT ABOUT CANCER. I WOULD ANSWER AND RELAY THE MESSAGES. PROMOTERS, FANS, AND FELLOW WRESTLERS FROM JAPAN EVEN CALLED. STEVE WAS AND IS IDOLIZED BY THE JAPANESE, AND THEY WERE CONCERNED AND WANTED TO HELP. HERE I AM, TRYING TO COMMUNICATE WITH THESE PEOPLE AS THEY ARE SPEAKING TO ME IN JAPANESE. THOUGH I COULDN'T UNDERSTAND ANYTHING, YOU COULD FEEL THEIR COMPASSION AND LOVE. MORE IMPORTANTLY, STEVE KNEW WHAT THEY WERE SAYING. EVERYTHING WAS SO UPLIFTING.

In addition to the encouragement from my family, an outpouring of support came from friends and fans from all over. Jeff continued to keep the world updated on the status of Dr. Death through e-mails, phone calls, and my personal website. I again couldn't believe the responses. Their encouragement lifted me from the daily depression, especially in the early weeks of recovery.

My old Oklahoma Sooner quarterback and former U.S. Congressman, J.C. Watts, called me. So did legendary running back Billy Sims. Jeff also got an e-mail from my old football coach at the University of Oklahoma,

Barry Switzer. Coach wanted to see me, and Jeff made all the arrangements.

When Jeff told me Coach Switzer was coming to visit, I was excited beyond belief. When Coach entered my room, he wasn't alone. Coach Switzer surprised me by bringing along my college wrestling coach, Stan Abel, and the manager of my college wrestling team, Jon Cooperstein. Mom, Jeff and his family, my younger brother Jerry and his family, Stormy and her family, and Wyndam were also there.

This special visit is one of the many reasons why Coach Switzer is so great, both as a person and football coach. He is a player's coach. He was right there with them, which is why he had the most excellent teams. You wanted to play well for Coach Switzer because he was such a great man. Though he was a tough coach and ran a tight ship, he was just such a loveable and special person.

Coach Abel was equally both a first-rate person and coach. At the University of Oklahoma, he coached 15 NCAA champions and 74 All-Americans—including me. He is also a distinguished member of the National Wrestling Hall of Fame. Jon is also an outstanding person and would even give you the shirt off his back.

Though I still couldn't talk, they spent six hours with me. I wrote on the dry-erase board while Coach Switzer and the others made me laugh and boosted my spirits. After their visit, I felt once again that I was going to make it. They gave me that shot in the arm, that pep talk, to help me get back on my feet.

John Tenta also came for a surprise visit. John is better known on the wrestling circuit as "The Earthquake." Unbeknownst to me, he was at M.D. Anderson receiving cancer treatment himself. He read about me on the Internet and decided to pay me a visit. When I saw that big ol' man walk into my room, he made my day.

Though John was a professional wrestling superstar, few know that he was an excellent collegiate wrestler. In fact, he wrestled in the heavyweight division at LSU during the same time I was wrestling at OU. When our two schools collided, I was scheduled to wrestle him, but because he got hurt before the match, it never took place. That was lucky for him, because I would have whipped him real good. We had a great visit, and it was really uplifting to see The Earthquake.

When finally discharged from the hospital, I was so grateful to go home and be with my family, especially Wyndam. But I still had a hard time eating. I couldn't keep my weight up and looked pathetic. I was still on a liquid diet and had been told to drink Ensure, a dietary supplement drink, which I couldn't stand.

At the hospital, they wanted to puncture a hole in my stomach to make eating easier, but I rejected the surgery. I was sick and tired of being cut open, and I just wanted to go home. Unfortunately, though, since I was losing so much weight and wasn't eating, I was admitted for another surgery. This time they put a tube in my gut so I could properly eat.

When I was finally released and sent home for what I hoped would be for good, I sat in my living room for an hour watching that bag of fluid drip into my body. Though family and friends called and visited, depression often set in and I again started to wonder if I was going to make it. Still, I never gave up, always looking to my son for inspiration and my God for guidance.

As a funny guy and practical joker, I also needed to laugh. Laughter is the best medicine. I found myself watching a lot of TV, especially the Kelly and Regis show. To this day they make me laugh. I really needed their humor, and they jump-started me every morning.

Just because the major surgeries were finished didn't mean everything was back to normal, however. In fact, my recuperation was just beginning. I had to learn so many new things: how to eat, how to talk, how to breathe, how to care for my stoma, etc. Each step took patience and time. I have never been a patient person, but I really had no choice.

I also had no choice but to face the reality that I had a hole in my throat.

As a professional wrestler, one's appearance means a lot in the business. I always took pride in how I looked. During this entire ordeal, however, I never cared what anyone said. I just wanted to live. Many people wear a scarf or something to cover the hole. I haven't worn anything. I am not ashamed of the opening in my throat. I am not going to hide it from people; I hope to be an inspiration to others.

Nothing comes out of my nose—discharge, phlegm—it all comes out of my stoma. So the area must be kept very clean. I use this little brush along with warm water to clean out the entire area. I clean it twice a day, in the morning and right before I go to bed.

When I talk, I have to stick my thumb in the stoma. My pathologist taught me to use my left hand, but due to a messed-up collarbone and a barreled chest, it was awkward and difficult. I felt more comfortable using my right hand. To talk, I take my right thumb and, with some pressure, I stick the tip of it in the stoma. Due to the trauma of the surgery, it was painful at first. Now it doesn't hurt at all.

Some people become uncomfortable when I do this, and some even laugh. Wyndam, now 14, gets mad when people stare or look at me funny. He often tells me when people are talking about me. I have to often remind my son that it doesn't matter what people say, at least they are talking about me. I tell him that the most important thing is that I am alive and with him.

In November of 2005, I met with my plastic surgeon, Dr. Hue, and my speech pathologist for consultation to close my stoma so I could talk hands-free. The meeting raised suggestions but offered no guarantees. I jokingly told the doctors to go back to the drawing board. Then, in February of 2006, I had a meeting with another plastic surgeon, Dr. Reese. He made no guarantees, but Dr. Reese said that after seven operations, I might be able to talk hands-free. My jaw dropped.

My life has changed dramatically. For more than a year, I have suffered emotionally, financially, mentally, and physically. I am having a hard time finding a job and making a living to support Wyndam and myself. In order to pay for treatment to save my life, I had to sell my tanning business and all my investment property. Everything that I had financially accumulated in my lifetime has nearly been depleted. I can't even collect disability from social security because I am one credit short. Unfortunately, I still have a $30,000 medical bill to pay.

I need to work and get back into wrestling. People ask me why I don't quit and just retire. From the football field to the wrestling mat to beating cancer, I have never quit anything in my life. I have always been at the top of my game and still believe that I can contribute to the wrestling business.

I used to run 24-7, but now I take it day by day. I put all my energy into my family. I am doing everything possible to be a better father to Stormy and especially Wyndam. I don't have a social life. I don't have time to argue anymore. I now take nothing for granted and slow down for everything. Wyndam wrote me a poem that completely blew me away and brought tears to my eyes:

He was a man beat down from a world of strife,
Dr. Death soon died and became Dr. Life.
I knew the man they call Dr. Death,
His life was filled with such unrest,
From high to low I saw him fall,
That's when he began his transformation for all,
From drugs, cancer, to losing his wife,
I saw him turn into Dr. Life.

-Wyndam Williams

For me, being alive today is unequivocally a miracle from God. After all the rounds of radiation treatments, chemotherapy, and surgeries, as well as relying on a stoma to communicate, I have survived the odds. I am now cancer-free and plan on staying that way. Though I may look different, I feel great. God has given me a second chance. I now believe he wants me to take his message to the people—to give my testimony to others from the wrestling ring.

THREE

GET BUSY LIVING

I knew the WWE was bringing the LEGENDS program to Dallas, Texas, in December 2005 for a live *RAW TV* taping on the USA network. After being away from professional wrestling for some three years due to my throat cancer, I really missed being part of the business, as well as being with the "boys." I thought it would be therapeutic to be back at an arena and, more importantly, see some of my old wrestling buddies who were scheduled to be at the show—Hacksaw Jim Duggan, Ted DiBiase, Harley Race, Arn Anderson, Dusty Rhodes, Ric Flair, etc. I also wanted to talk to Johnny Ace about getting back in the business.

The American Airlines Arena was only a three-hour drive from my home in Shreveport, Louisiana. Like I had done so many times before, this time without my wrestling gear (white skull & bones boots, Sooner red trunks, etc.), I packed my red Corvette and headed to Dallas. After three miserable years away from the ring, I was so excited to get back to the arena and again be a part of something that had been my life since I was a senior in college.

When I arrived at the arena, I was treated with a tremendous amount of class and respect. The first person I saw was Hacksaw Jim Duggan. I actually heard him cutting a promo. "HOOOOO," Jim would scream while holding his trademark 2x4 and giving the thumbs-up. There is no one better than good ol' Hacksaw when it comes to working the microphone. When he finished, I walked right in there and we hugged. Yes, wrestlers

After my fight against cancer, I attend a 2005 LEGENDS Convention in Tampa, Florida.

do hug, and I hugged a lot of guys that night. We are a tight-knit fraternity, and we always look out for each other. I also saw Ted DiBiase. Ted said, "How are you, Doc? It is great to see you."

"Great," I responded.

As the day went on, I ran into a lot of other people. I saw Dusty Rhodes, Superstar Billy Graham, Skandor Akbar, Jimmy Snuka, Red Bastian, Hillbilly Jim, Koko B. Ware, the Honkeytonk Man, Arn Anderson, Ricky Steamboat, and a few other superstars.

As an accomplished athlete, for guys to shake my hand and say, "Great to see you, Doc" and "Doc, you look great," the respect that I received was unreal. After what I had been through battling this cancer when people literally thought I was going to die, it was great to just have another chance to see the boys. I had beaten the odds, and there I was at the American Airlines Arena being part of the greatest sport on earth.

After hanging out for a while, I pulled up a chair next to Skandor Akbar, Jeremy Young, and Michael Hayes in the cafeteria. Though the food looked good, I wasn't too hungry. Drinking my triple-shot café latte from Starbucks, I just sat at the table with the boys. Then I saw the owner and CEO of the WWE, Vince McMahon. Making eye contact, Vince walked toward me. All of a sudden he stopped and went over to one of the writers. Almost immediately, the writer came up to me and said, "Vince wants you to be part of the LEGENDS show. He wants you to come out with the boys. Would you like to be part of the show?"

I said, "Wow, what a great opportunity. Sure, I would love to be part of the show."

The first thing that went through my head was, "Oh boy, I sure didn't dress well enough for the show." But that was quickly overshadowed by the fact that I was about to be part of a live WWE event. To walk down that "aisle" one more time–to say I was excited would be an understatement. I was also going to be on the payroll. Since I hadn't worked for nearly three years and had nearly lost everything fighting cancer, it was an added bonus.

I told all the boys that Vince wanted me to be part of the show. Everyone patted me on the back and wished me good luck. Even the young guys like Triple H, KANE, Big Show, Kurt Angle, and John Cena came up to me and said, "It will be great to have you on the show."

I also saw the road agents, the refs, and some of the writers who knew me. I want to comment about the role of writers in professional wrestling. Writers contribute to the storylines and help produce the show. Many of them come from the entertainment world and have never stepped into the wrestling ring. When I started in the wrestling business, they didn't exist. But the business has changed so much over the last 20-plus years. I think to some extent writers are needed.

But wrestlers really know the business. They are trained to not only handle the mental and physical demands of the sport, but they are also very ingenious. To do what we do day in and day out, you must be in great shape. You must also possess creativity. Even though entertainment is on the marquee, I still believe that professional wrestling is a sport. Wrestlers should and need to be included with the storylines of their character.

I also bumped into my former tag-team partner and the current director of talent relations for the WWE, Johnny Ace. Johnny Ace is one heck of a guy, and I have so many memories with him both in Japan and in the states. Johnny said, "Did you get the news?"

"Yes," I replied.

Johnny said, "Well, it wasn't my call. I had nothing to do with it. Thank Vince." I told him that I had.

The show started, and we were ready to rock the house. Our first job of the evening was to go through the crowd and take a seat in the front row at ringside. We were to watch a two-out-of-three-falls match between Kurt Angle and Shawn Michaels. As we made our way to ringside, I could see that people recognized me and were chanting my name, "Doc!"

It was at that time I saw my old Oklahoma Sooner buddy, Bud Herbert. Bud said, "Hey, Doc, what's going on?" I had to do a double-take. I was so surprised to see him. We gave each other a big hug and exchanged brotherly handshakes.

From 1979 to 1982, Bud and I were football teammates under coach Barry Switzer at the University of Oklahoma. I remember it like it was yesterday. Bud had three interceptions in our 1980 Orange Bowl victory over Florida State University (FSU). He was an excellent cornerback and an even better person. It was so good to see a familiar face in the crowd.

Shawn Michaels and Kurt Angle put on an excellent performance. Throughout the entire match, I was cheering and getting into the action. In all my years of professional wrestling, I had never sat ringside. The closest I ever got was smashing someone's head on the steel barriers outside the ring.

After the match was over, all the LEGENDS went to the back and got ready for our second appearance. It was at this time the announcer, Lillian Garcia, was going to introduce us to the crowd one by one: Jimmy Snuka, Harley Race, Billy Graham, Dusty Rhodes, Arn Anderson, Ted DiBiase, me,

Jim Duggan, and Koko B. Ware. Waiting in the gorilla box, I was so pumped up! My emotions flowed like they had the evening of Giant Baba's Retirement Show in 1999. That night, I teamed with Akira Taue and Stan Hansen, and we whipped Gary Albright, Yoshihiro Takayama, and Takao Omori at the Toyko Dome.

When Lillian finally called my name, my reaction was somewhat mixed. You see, we were in Dallas, the hot bed of Texas Longhorn country. In five short days, my Oklahoma Sooners were going to play the Longhorns in their annual football classic. As a Boomer Sooner, I could only do what was right. So I decided to have a little fun.

As I made my way down the entrance ramp to the ring, I raised my fingers, exposing the "hook 'em horns" symbol. As I got closer to the ring, I turned those horns down! The cheers I had been getting quickly became boos—like any good heel such as myself would have it. The negative heat I received from the crowd evaporated as Jim Duggan garnered cheers galore as he followed me to the ring.

Once all the LEGENDS made it to the ring, Dusty Rhodes spoke to the crowd. He pulled us over and told the fans that we had "made wrestling what it is today," that we paid the price and paved the way for all the youngsters in the business. He is so right. Then, all of a sudden, I heard the music of Rob Conway. Conway rudely interrupted Dusty's presentation. This young punk came into the ring and, being all cocky, showed off his physique and insulted the LEGENDS, saying we were all washed up, that we were has-beens, and other hot air.

Well, let me tell you something, brother, you don't cut in on the legendary Dusty Rhodes. He is the "American Dream," and he deserves respect. Conway had no business interrupting our program, and of course, Dusty had to set him straight. With the crowd behind each punch, Dusty nailed him with a few rights and then some lefts. He followed them up with the signature bionic elbow. Hacksaw decided to join in and clocked Conway real good, laying him out.

All of a sudden, the crowd roared, and yes, we saw Jimmy Snuka going to the top rope. The rest is history. I tell you what, Conway is very lucky that I was in the back part of the ring, or I would have given him the "Oklahoma Stampede!"

I wonder if the young wrestlers understand that the LEGENDS made wrestling what it is today. Ted DiBiase, Harley Race, Cowboy Bill Watts, Dusty Rhodes, Ric Flair, Jimmy Snuka, me, and countless others paved the road for them. We were the ones who took all the hard knocks. We paid the price, going up and down the road, doing maybe nine to 10 matches a week. We developed the territories and built the fan base. Without the LEGENDS, professional wrestling wouldn't be what it is today!

In the back, we all congratulated each other, knowing that everything went perfectly. I had no idea that I was even going to be part of the show. I prayed and thanked God for the opportunity to be in Dallas. I gave God all the glory.

I stayed around for a while to visit with the boys some more and then realized it was getting late. I had to get back home to make sure Wyndam was in bed for school in the morning. Right before I left, I saw Johnny Ace. I said, "Thanks, man. I hope we can work some things out in the future."

Johnny said, "After the first of the year we will get together."

I then hopped into my red Corvette and headed back to Shreveport, going what seemed like 120 mph. My partner and friend, Jeremy Young, followed me home in tow. Using cell phones, we talked about all the action and events from the evening.

During some downtime, I had a chance to reflect on the evening. I thought about Vince McMahon and appreciated what he did for me in Dallas. As the owner of the number-one wrestling promotion in the world, he still found it in his heart to give me an opportunity to perform. I was fighting for my life and battling cancer, one of the worst diseases known, and

> JEREMY YOUNG: DOC WAS SO PUMPED UP FROM THE EVENING THAT WE WERE LIKE TWO TEENAGE KIDS, DRIVING WAY TOO FAST AND TALKING WAY TOO MUCH ON OUR CELL PHONES. WE STOPPED AT A GAS STATION TO GAS UP, AND SURE ENOUGH, DOC COULDN'T WAIT TO GET BACK ON THE ROAD TO SEE WHO WOULD GET HOME FIRST.

"Play Like a Champion Today": I have taken this Oklahoma Sooner advice to heart.

Vince still asked me to be part of the show. Vince didn't have to show me that respect, but he did.

My interaction with Kurt Angle also stood out. I truly admire Kurt. He is an accomplished mat wrestler and an Olympic gold-medal winner. He is a shooter, a go-getter, and a pure athlete. He knows what it takes to be a champion. I see a lot of "Dr. Death" Steve Williams in Kurt Angle.

I always played football and wrestled like a champion. At the University of Oklahoma, a big sign hangs from the door as you head out to the football field. It reads: "Play Like A Champion Today." You tap that sign and go out there and lay it all out on the line. Whenever I do anything in my life, from washing my car to cleaning my house to fighting for the world heavyweight title, I do it like a champion. Kurt Angle wrestles like a champion.

In 1998, I tore my hamstring and thigh muscle at the WWE's "Brawl for All" against Bart Gunn. To get back in wrestling shape, I went to Dory Funk's Dojo. While there, I was the first guy to do a 10-minute broadway (a match that ends in a time-limit draw) with Kurt Angle. As jocks, we clashed together so well and our match came out very good. Kurt has the work ethic to be one of the greatest wrestlers in the history of our business.

When I got home, I was so wired. There was no way I was going to go to sleep. My mind was still occupied from the day's events and I started reminiscing about my wrestling days in the UWF, Mid-South, ECW, WCW, WWE, and Japan. So I went downstairs to my office where I keep all my wrestling memorabilia and photos. Looking at the pictures on the wall, like the ones with Terry Gordy, Antonio Inoki, and Giant Baba, amongst many others, brought back a lot of wonderful memories. It was the perfect ending to a perfect day.

> JEREMY YOUNG: DOC IS STILL ONE OF THE BIGGEST NAMES IN THE WRESTLING BUSINESS AND HE KNOWS ALL THE INS AND OUTS OF WRESTLING. WHEN HE WALKED INTO THE ARENA, EVERYONE TREATED HIM LIKE A LEGEND. IT WAS AMAZING SEEING ALL THESE WRESTLERS SHOW RESPECT TO DOC.

A few days later, Jeremy Young told me that the WWE was going to be in Texarkana, Texas. It was a short drive from the house. Since I didn't have any scheduled medical visits, I thought it would be good to see the boys once again. I also wanted to help Jeremy meet some people so he could maybe get a spot with the company. When I arrived at the arena, I saw Arn Anderson. Arn came up to me and said, "Hey, Doc. How would you like to go out to the ring and say hello to everybody?"

I told Arn, "Sure, it would be great." I was introduced to the crowd and, for the first time, gave my testimony to the fans.

A couple of days passed and the phone rang. It was none other than my friend, JR, Jim Ross. I have known Jim since 1982 during our Mid-South days. He was Bill Watts' right-hand man and, bar none, the best announcer in the history of our business. JR is also a die-hard Oklahoma Sooner fan, so in my book, he gets points just for that!

Jim says, "Hey, Doc. How would you like to go down to Baton Rouge [Louisiana] and do a little fight scene on *Carlito's Cabana*?"

I said, "Sure man, it would be great." It was right before Christmas, and it was nice to know that I would have some money to buy presents for the family. After I got all the details from JR, I cleaned my Corvette like a champion and prepared for a trip on December 3 to the Civic Center in Baton Rouge.

When I arrived, the first person I ran into was the Big Show. Big Show said, "Boy, you are sure looking great, Doc. It looks like you even put on some more muscle." The Big Show is one of the nicest guys I have ever met. I have known him since our World Championship Wrestling (WCW) days. Standing nearly 7 feet tall and weighing more than 500 pounds, he is still the nicest and gentlest person you will ever meet.

I saw many of the other guys, such as Shelton Benjamin, Chavo Guerrero, Tajiri, and Chris Masters. I visited with some of the referees and writers. Triple H then came in and said, "You look great, Doc. I'm glad you are here tonight." I was very impressed with Triple H. He was very polite and treated me with respect. The writers then cued me in for the evening's program.

COACH introduced me to the ring. As I made my way down, I got a great pop from the crowd. Though it was a house show, the arena was packed. It was also a hot crowd. Those folks in Southern Louisiana love their gumbo, red beans and rice, and especially their wrestling! When I got to the ring, I talked about how I started my career in the Baton Rouge area. I gave my testimony on battling cancer, and said it was a "dream come true" to be back in the ring again.

Carlito's music then interrupted my promo. He came to the ring and told the COACH that "he thought he had a surprise guest" for him. He wanted to know, "Who is this guy?" Well, his comments got the good Doctor all fired up. I took Carlito's signature apple right from his greasy hand. He was stunned. I then began to stomp a mud-hole in him and stomped it dry. I gave him a hard left and then an even harder right. Carlito went down. The sound in the arena was now deafening, and the crowd knew what was next. I laid him out with my signature football tack-le. I sent both COACH and Carlito packing!

After my spot and once I said my good-byes, I started to head home. On the way out, I decided to stop and gas up at the convenience store that I used to frequent back in my Mid-South days. As I went in to pay for the gas, I decided to get a drink. It wasn't the same type of drink that I used to get when traveling along with Ted DiBiase, "Iron" Mike Sharpe, Buddy Landell, and Hercules Hernandez. As I got ready to pay at the counter, out of the corner of my eye I saw these two Oklahoma Sooner blankets. I thought to myself, "What are the chances of finding Sooner blankets in the heart of Bengal Tiger country?"

Then it hit me: after three years of not stepping in the ring, I had appeared in the WWE three different times at three separate locations in a span of less than two weeks. I had overcome all odds. God had indeed given me a second chance.

As an Oklahoma Sooner, I am a product of what some affectionately call the "MONSTER." I was bred to be a champion. Now, with God on my side, it's time to "get busy living." As Bill Watts used to say: "Lets Hook 'Em Up!"

FOUR

GROWING UP IN COLORADO

On May 14, 1960, I was born Steven Franklin Williams and weighed in at seven pounds. Named after my grandfather, I'm the fourth child of Dottie and Gerald Williams.

I grew up in Lakewood, Colorado. Located in Jefferson County, it is one of the largest suburbs of Denver. We lived in a big, four-bedroom brick house on a one-acre lot that my parents bought in the 1960s. It is the same house my mom lives in today.

The neighborhood, predominately middle class, was represented by a variety of different ethnic groups. I am of German ancestry and was raised a Protestant. My family attended the Mile High Church of Religious Science.

My mom and dad met in the Navy. Though they were both from Denver, they didn't know each other until they were stationed together to do hospital work at the naval academy in Annapolis. It was love at first sight. They became engaged on St. Patrick's Day, and exchanged nuptials in May.

My mom, Dorothy "Dottie" Colpin, an average-sized woman, was born in Bellevue, Pennsylvania. She is the best woman in my life. For as long as I can remember, Mom worked 40-plus hours a week as a bookkeeper for the Copper Kitchen restaurant. In spite of her busy work schedule, she managed to attend every one of my brothers' and my athletic events. She shuffled all of us to and from these events and was always there for us.

My dad, Gerald C. Williams, was the hardest working person I ever knew. He was my best friend. Dad was an entrepreneur, and in his lifetime

WITH MOM AND DAD, WEARING MY FIRST RING JACKET.

owned both a flower shop and his own tire store. He also worked for Storage Technology, a computer company, and held other jobs to secure extra money for his family. My dad had served on the city council. He was pro-community and cared very much for the people and city of Lakewood.

I loved to go fishing with my dad. He would take my brothers and me to a great many fishing places in Colorado. When I was eight years old, just the two of us camped and fished at a secluded lake for hours, away from everything. I was so excited to be there with my dad, and got up early to "get the fish" just like he taught me.

One time in the woods as I ran to use the bathroom, a branch from a tree ripped open my eyelid. I started to cry and scream because blood was everywhere. As my dad tended to me, I begged him to take me to a hospital and then home. Holding me tight, Dad said, "Steven, we aren't going anywhere." He calmly cleaned the cut and made a butterfly stitch to close the wound. After I calmed down, we went back to fishing.

My dad passed away from a heart attack at 65 years old. I was only 23 at the time. It was the worst day of my life, and I miss him dearly. He was a very genuine, down-to-earth person and my best friend. He made me a man and taught me a lot about life. He showed me the importance of raising a family and how to be a great dad. He was a great role model.

Though I was his baby boy, he was a disciplinarian and showed me no favors. The youngest of four children, I was a bar-none and wild kid. I thought I was invincible and could get away with anything. My parents had a local carpenter put a wooden fence around the backyard so I couldn't get out. After many attempts, as well as cuts and bruises, I eventually managed to climb that fence.

> DOTTIE YOUNG: I SHOULD HAVE KNOWN THAT STEVE WAS GOING TO BE A PROFESSIONAL WRESTLER, THE WAY HE WOULD CLIMB OVER THAT FENCE AND KEEP GETTING HURT AND CUT UP ON THE WAY OVER. WE WOULD WATCH HIM CLIMB AND CLIMB AND FALL AND FALL, AND NO MATTER WHAT, HE WAS DETERMINED TO GET OVER THAT FENCE. HE WAS ONE TOUGH LITTLE COOKIE.

I also got my share of whippings. My dad used to whip me bare bottom. I remember one time when I had just turned eight, my father was getting ready to whip me for something I had done. This time, however, I told my dad, "No!" I was tired of being beaten. You should have seen his reaction. Unfortunately, my request didn't stop his attempt. So, as my dad went to strike me, I grabbed his leg and I rolled over on him. I quickly snatched the belt from his hand and said, "I've had enough of this. I'm a man. Enough!" I am sure my dad was laughing inside, but I never got a whipping again.

> DOTTIE YOUNG: STEVEN WAS A VERY ADVENTUROUS KID, AND HE GAVE US A HEADACHE EVERY ONCE IN A WHILE.

After that episode, my dad did indeed start treating me like a man. He made me do so many chores as well as get a job that I yearned for a spanking. I would have to paint fences, do odds and ends around the house, mow lawns, and even deliver newspapers.

I didn't like being a paperboy. I would have to get up really early in the morning and ride my bike all over the neighborhood delivering newspapers. I especially hated doing it in the winter. Because I was so miserable, I did a horrible job. I slung people's newspapers on their roof, in the bushes, in the mud—just about anywhere except where they were supposed to be. Needless to say, I didn't deliver newspapers for very long.

> JERRY WILLIAMS: STEVE IS ONE OF A KIND. FROM THE TIME HE WAS A TODDLER, STEVE WAS UNIQUE. I REMEMBER WHEN HE WAS NINE MONTHS OLD, MOM PUT IN THE MIDDLE BEDROOM A "HALF DOOR" SO SHE COULD LET HIM PLAY SAFELY IN A MANAGEABLE AREA. IT DID NOT TAKE LONG FOR STEVE, HOWEVER, TO FIGURE OUT THAT ALL HE HAD TO DO WAS GET OVER THE HALF DOOR AND HE WOULD GAIN ACCESS TO FREEDOM. ALTHOUGH HE DID NOT WALK, THIS HERCULES OF A CHILD WOULD SUPPORT HIMSELF, LEANING AGAINST THE BED AND ROCKING IT BACK AND FORTH LIKE A BABY GORILLA UNTIL IT HAD MOVED ACROSS THE FLOOR AND UP AGAINST THE HALF DOOR. AT THAT POINT, HE WOULD USE THE BED TO CATAPULT HIMSELF OVER THE HALF DOOR TO THE OTHER SIDE. THE ONLY PROBLEM IS THAT HE WOULD LAND ON HIS HEAD AND START SCREAMING BLOODY MURDER. HE MUST HAVE BEEN SUCCESSFUL DOING THIS ROUTINE A DOZEN TIMES UNTIL DAD ADDED A THREE-QUARTER DOOR AND HIS EFFORTS WERE FINALLY CURTAILED.

My sister, Linda, was the oldest of all my siblings and almost 11 years older than I was. She served in the Peace Corps in Africa and traveled the world. She also worked as a fourth grade elementary school teacher in Ouray, Colorado. In her single years, she adopted a Korean girl named Kim, and later married a great guy, Mike Collins. She died prematurely at 54 from Marfan syndrome, a connective tissue disorder. She lived a very productive life. I miss Linda very much.

My brother, Jerry, nicknamed "Mad Dog," is my hero. He is ten years older than I, and I always wanted to be just like him. From the way he walked to the way he talked, Jerry was the man! He made good grades, and all the girls found him attractive.

He is also an outstanding athlete, excelling in football, basketball, baseball, and track. He seems unbeatable, and I have always looked up to him.

When I was 13 years old, I weighed close to 260 pounds. Yes, I was chubby, and everyone would call me "fatso" or "fatty." I was the biggest kid around. When Jerry got engaged and was planning to get married within six months, he wanted me to be in his wedding party. As a 13-year-old, it was such an honor to be in my hero's wedding party. However, I needed to lose weight so that I would look nice in my tuxedo. Jerry decided to make me an offer that I couldn't refuse: "Lose about 40 pounds, and I will give you $50 and my stereo." Wow, money and a stereo, and since Jerry was moving out, I would get my own room. Staring at my diverse collection of posters hanging on the wall, I could envision myself jamming to Jimmy Hendrix, Boston, Robert Plant, Three Dog Night, REO Speedwagon, and even the Little River Band. I excitedly accepted my brother's offer.

As most people know, losing weight isn't easy. For a young kid like me who loved to eat, it was especially difficult. Three gallons of fresh milk would be gone in a day or two. We also had two refrigerators that were both empty before the end of the week. My parents couldn't even keep the pantry stocked, especially with peanut butter. We used to go through peanut butter like it was water. Peanut butter was a major condiment: we would eat it with chips, fudge, chocolate, apples—just about anything.

> JERRY WILLIAMS: BEFORE I GOT MARRIED, STEVE WAS ONLY 13 YEARS OLD AND WEIGHED ABOUT 260 POUNDS. I BET HIM IF HE WOULD LOSE 40 POUNDS FOR THE WEDDING, I WOULD GIVE HIM MY STEREO. STEVE LOVED VERY STRANGE, WILD MUSIC. EVEN WITH THE WEIGH LOSS (40 POUNDS), I STILL HAD TO RENT A SIZE 56 EXTRA-LONG TUX FOR STEVE. MY BEST FRIEND, MARK COONEDY, WAS ALSO IN THE WEDDING PARTY. MARK, WHO PLAYED FOR THE GREEN BAY PACKERS, WAS A PRETTY BIG MAN, AND ALSO WORE A SIZE 56 EXTRA-LONG TUX. BUT MARK WAS 23 YEARS OLD AND STEVE WAS ONLY 13. THIS SHOULD GIVE ONE A FEEL FOR STEVE'S SIZE.

Linda, just back from the Peace Corps, was staying with us until she could find a job. She decided to put the entire family on a Weight

Watcher's diet, even though I was the only one who really needed to lose weight. Concerned with sugar intake, the first thing she cut out of our diet was ketchup, which broke my heart, because I *loooooved* ketchup. I put ketchup on everything from French fries to eggs.

To accommodate me, Linda decided she was going to make "homemade" ketchup. Let me tell you, that stuff was horrible. When it cooked, it produced a nasty stench that stunk up the whole house. It was nasty!

Looking back though, the diet wasn't too bad. At least we got to eat eggs, salad, fruits, and other reasonable dishes. We would only eat portions that were as big as our fists. To help matters, I knew it was only temporary, plus I had the additional incentive of the stereo and cash.

In the end, it all paid off: I lost 40 pounds. I couldn't believe how nice I looked in the tuxedo. We took lots of pictures and everyone was amazed at how much weight I had dropped. At the wedding reception, I had to make up for lost eating time. When I walked through the hall doors, I saw that buffet table loaded with meats, cheeses, cookies, and other deserts. It was go time. I literally lost control and tore into the buffet. I ate so much that my gut was literally bursting from the seams–so much for the diet and weight loss.

Though I come from a tight-knit family, I was probably closest to my brother Jeff. He is one year older than I am and was also a great athlete. He excelled in every sport he played, but he was a stellar football player. He ran like a gazelle and hit like a truck. Jeff was all-everything and even won the area's NFL "Punt, Pass and Kick" competition. We would later play football together, both in high school and at the University of Oklahoma.

Jeff and I were nearly inseparable, but we would also constantly fight. When we fought in the house, we broke lamps, vases, and anything else in our path. One time, Jeff was chasing me around the room and I tripped and fell. My eye met the end of a table. The gash was so deep that you could see my entire eyeball. All I can remember is my dad honking his horn, speeding, and running through red lights to get me to the emergency room.

We fought so much that our parents sent us to separate summer camps to keep us from killing each other. But all the fighting eventually made me tough as nails. Jeff and I would always argue over the couch. If I left to go to

THE TIGHT-KNIT WILLIAMS FAMILY SMILES FOR A GROUP PHOTO.

the bathroom, I lost my spot. When Jeff went to get something to drink, I reclaimed that spot. One day, while reclaiming my spot, we started to go at it like never before. Things were flying everywhere and we were tearing each other up. As fate would have it, Dad happened to come home early and saw us fighting. He got so mad that he took us out back and told us to put on the boxing gloves that he had acquired from Coach Hancock months earlier.

We put the gloves on and Dad watched us go at it. I was bigger than Jeff, but also scared. I just couldn't hit my older brother. Jeff, on the other hand, started wailing away, throwing punch after punch. As he was hitting me, I just started to laugh. With each chuckle, Jeff would get madder and madder. He eventually wore himself out. I never threw a punch.

We were also the two biggest kids in the neighborhood. Along with Danny Pearson, Nick Hammer, and Johnny and Joe Pennington, Jeff and I were part of the "Holland Gang." Our clique was named after the street we lived on. We played sports together and considered each other family. We also managed to find things to do to get ourselves in trouble. Let me tell you, we were some tough kids and acted as though we were invincible. We had the height, weight, and strength to pull it off.

> JERRY WILLIAMS: ONE OF THE STORIES THAT TOM HANCOCK, MY HIGH SCHOOL FOOTBALL COACH, LIKES TO TELL WAS WHEN STEVE AND JEFF WERE YOUNG BOYS WATCHING OUR HIGH SCHOOL FOOTBALL GAMES. DURING GAMES, COACH NOTICED THAT STEVE AND JEFF WOULD GET INTO FIGHTS OFF THE FIELD. AFTER ONE OF MY FOOTBALL GAMES, COACH HANCOCK PUT TWO PAIR OF OFFICIAL BOXING GLOVES IN MY DAD'S CAR. FROM THAT POINT ON, ALL FIGHTS WERE WITH OFFICIAL BOXING GLOVES, AND THEY WERE USED FREQUENTLY.

On several occasions, especially during the summer, we would sneak into our local elementary school. One summer when I was 13 years old, about two weeks before the start of the new school year, we broke the lock of an underground tunnel at Eiber Elementary. We, including my dog Heidi, made our way through the print shop and snuck into the gym. We played basketball, dodgeball, and kickball for hours. After all this activity, of course, we were hungry. So, like we had done in the past, we went into the cafeteria refrigerators and shoveled down cookies, fudge, cake, and an assortment of other foods.

Heidi, as all dogs do, got excited around the food. Somehow, she tripped the electric outlet behind one of the refrigerators, knocking out the power in the entire kitchen. We ran out of the building in hopes that no one had seen us. Unfortunately, someone had seen us when we were playing in the gymnasium. We were busted. We were criminally charged and had to appear in court. It made all the papers and everyone in the town heard about the incident. We were fined, placed on probation, and forced to do community service.

Jerry, Jeff, and I are all big guys. My mom and dad are of average size. We inherited our size from my mother's side of the family. Even though I was the only chubby one, I was still very athletic. The first trophy that I ever won was for catching a greased pig. Yes, a pig. When I was eight years old, I entered a greased pig catching contest at the local Fourth of July rodeo. I was one of around 20 kids ranging from all ages. I can remember running and digging through poop and slop, trying to grab that greasy pig. I was determined. With my bare hands, I grabbed the tag from around the pig's neck and was declared the winner of the contest. My family and I were so excited. As the winner, I was to receive a Shetland pony. I was ecstatic.

The people in charge told us that we had an hour or so to claim and pick up the pony or we would forfeit the prize. I had to get my picture taken and meet with a few other people from the contest before I could go claim my pony. There were a lot of people and a lot of confusion, and somehow I was separated from my family. I began to panic, running and screaming, looking for my mom and dad. I started to cry. Some employees at the event saw I was in distress and made a couple of announcements over the loudspeaker to help me locate my parents. When I saw my mom and dad, I ran to them. By the time I finally settled down and went to claim my Shetland pony, an hour had already passed. I went up to the officials to tell them that I was there for my prize. They sadly informed me that the time had already elapsed and I had forfeited my pony. I was heartbroken.

My family loved animals. Every Easter we would bring a new animal into the Williams family. We had rabbits, cats, dogs, chicks, and even a goat named Bam Bam. I raised him from a baby, but as he got older, Bam Bam became mean and would butt us if we got too close. He eventually became a problem and we decided to give him to the local petting zoo. It was hard to let him go, but I knew it was the right thing to do. As we left for our summer vacation to my Uncle's house in West Virginia, we dropped Bam Bam off. Upon our return, I asked Dad if we could go see him. We went to the zoo, but couldn't find our goat anywhere. We inquired about him and the zoo owner said, "The goat got so ornery, bucking all the kids, that we had no choice but to kill it." They butchered it and used it for meat. I was so mad that I wanted to butcher him!

FIVE

AMUSEMENTS AND RECRUITMENT

I wasn't the brightest kid on the block. Though I liked history, my favorite subjects in school were gym and lunch. I went to school to play sports and hang out with my friends. I liked school, but often found it very difficult. In elementary school I had to take special classes; it was hard for me to stay focused on things that I had little interest in. I would often find myself easily distracted by sights and sounds and had a hard time concentrating for long periods of time. Today, I would probably be diagnosed with Attention Deficit Hyperactivity Disorder (ADHD).

But I enjoyed working on cars. Though Lakewood High didn't have a vocational tech program, I registered for an auto mechanics class at the area technical school, which also counted for high school credit. Students registered for this class to learn how to become auto mechanics. I had no ambition to be one, but I registered for the class simply to work on my car.

My first car was a 1942 Willy Jeep, an old army-type Jeep and a classic. It had a steel frame and was built like a tank. I bought it for $389 and fixed it up real nice with new tires and wall-to-wall blue shag carpet. Though I was only 15, I was getting it ready to roam the streets as soon as I turned 16.

One day I decided to take my Willy for a spin, though it wasn't completely road-ready. Without a license and with my friend Nick Hammer, I pushed the ignition button and headed into town. I didn't make it but a few blocks when the steering wheel came off as I turned a corner, and we hit a telephone poll. The impact knocked us back about 20 yards. It didn't do any damage to the Jeep, but once my father found out, you can only imagine the damage done to me.

Not too long thereafter, on a Saturday afternoon, my mom and dad had left the keys in their car and gone out. Slightly hung over, I decided to go for a joyride. There I was, this 15-year-old kid, cruising the neighborhood. As I approached the corner, I inadvertently hit the gas pedal instead of the brake. I jumped the curve, mowed down two trees, smashed through a fence, and slammed into someone's flower bed. I quickly tried to back up and hightail it out of there. As I pressed the gas, flowers and dirt went everywhere. I wasn't moving. I was stuck. The owner of the house, who knew my family and me, came running out, yelling, "Stop! Stop! Shut off the engine!"

I was scared and the only thing going through my mind was jail. I got out of the car and started begging for the owner to cut me a break. I was crying like a baby. Then, out of the corner of my eye, I saw my older brother Jeff riding by on his ten-speed bike. I ran toward Jeff, screaming for his help. Jeff was laughing his butt off. I kept begging Jeff until he finally stopped and sarcastically said, "Good luck, Steven!" He took off laughing all the way home. Needless to say, the punishment I received from my parents was nothing to laugh about—I was grounded for an entire month!

I loved to drink and party. Every Friday night, the boys and I would go to Lakewood Park or another facility to shoot the breeze, chase women, and get drunk. Though we were all underage, I never had a hard time getting alcohol. I bought my first beer at 12 years old! I was the biggest guy around and would literally cart the keg to and from the party. One time, the police came to the park and raided our party. Man, I ran away as fast as I could, carrying that keg on my shoulder.

I also experimented with marijuana. I didn't do it often, because it affected my athletics. Sports were the number-one priority in my life. But some of the older kids got me stoned, and I kind of liked the thrill of the forbidden. When I was 12 years old, I bought my first bag of pot, or so I thought. I approached one of the stoners at school and asked him for a bag. The guy said, "Sure, dude, meet me after school and bring $40."

I said, "Okay, dude. I will see you then."

After we made the exchange, the boys and I went to the "Tunnel"—a place behind the school where everyone went to smoke. Excited about getting high, we opened the bag. To our surprise, it wasn't marijuana, but oregano! I was pissed, but it taught me to make wiser drug purchases in the future.

Learning from my older brothers, Jerry and Jeff, I excelled in every sport I tried. Jerry was a ski instructor, so of course I learned how to ski. I loved going down the beautiful Colorado Mountains. I was also good in baseball. I was a decent pitcher and center fielder. I received my first baseball trophy at ten years old for batting over .500 for the season.

And then there was football. Football was my passion. I grew up wanting to be a professional football player. Football was all I could ever think about, and I was very good at it. I started playing the sport at eight years old. Since I was bigger than all the kids my age and even many of the older ones, I spent only one year in pee wee, or little league. They quickly elevated me to the heavyweight league, where some of the older kids would pick on me and tease me. But their taunts only made me more determined. No one was going to intimidate me. I would hit them even harder.

I never intended to become a professional wrestler. In fact, I never attended a live pro wrestling event until after college. At times, usually before our Saturday football games, I watched local wrestling on TV. I would watch the old AWA wrestling show, which featured two of my favorites—Mad Dog and Butcher Vachon. Their in-ring antics would motivate me to bully my opponents on the football field.

When I was 10 years old and playing in the heavyweight division, one of the assistant coaches on my team decided to do the "Bull of the Ring" drill. The drill consisted of 12 to 15 players making a circle around one guy. The coach called a player from the circle to hit the player in the middle, tackling him to the ground. This time, I was the one in the middle. The coach kept calling different players' numbers. One by one, guys from the circle would nail me. I was getting hit left and right. I don't know what he

Where it all started: Lakewood Junior High.

was trying to prove. At the end, he had all the players dog-pile on top of me.

When I got up, I was so angry. I went straight to the coach and bluntly told him, "If you ever do that to me again, I will embarrass you in front of everybody." You should have seen the look on his face. Here was this big, 10-year-old kid scaring the crap out of a middle-aged man. My dad and older brothers made me tough. I was scared of no one, which made me second to nobody on the football field.

At Lakewood Middle School, I played fullback for the Cubs. Being the biggest and strongest kid on the field, I ran over everyone and drug people into the end zone. There would be often be four to five players hanging on me, trying to pull me down. One of my favorite plays we used to run near the goal line or if we needed 10 yards was called the "Water Buffalo Special." The quarterback would hand me the ball and I would just plow over the defense into the end zone. I would often drag a defensive player 10 yards with me.

When I was a senior in high school, I was the most highly recruited football player in the state. Lakewood High School has a long football tradition, going back to its most successful coach, Tom Hancock. In 15 seasons, Coach Hancock compiled a 137-36-3 record. His credentials led him to be inducted into the Colorado Sports Hall of Fame in 1969. The school also produced future NFL players, such as George Lewark, Pat Matson, and Mike Schnitker.

Under Coach Pete Levine, we were a football powerhouse. For four years, I played offensive guard and defensive tackle for our fighting Tigers. Coach Levine ran our program like a general and made sure we were disciplined. He pushed me to the max and helped me develop my skills, such as those needed to effectively perform in the "Wishbone" offense.

I'll never forget the last day of class as my junior year ended. Coach Levine pulled me over to the side. He reminded me that the next season I had a chance to be the best player in the state of Colorado and that all the major colleges were going to be interested in me. He reminded me not to come to summer camp overweight. If so, Coach stated that he was going to "tie a rope around [my] waist and run the weight off!"

We also ran the "Wishbone" offense, which would later help me at the University of Oklahoma. I will never forget my experiences with Coach Levine. His practices were hard and he demanded excellence, but he simultaneously treated me with dignity and respect.

During my senior year, I was chosen as the captain of our football team. I was very proud of my leadership role. I also respected many of those who made Lakewood a perennial winner on the football field, including my older brother, Jerry, who was the captain of the 1968 Lakewood State Champions. I wanted to motivate my team to be just as good, if not better than the 1968 champions. My first decree, just like my brother's, was for the whole team to get crew cuts. They all agreed. Come Monday morning, I showed up to school nearly bald. To my surprise, I was the only one who got the buzz! I was livid at the guys, and after a while the others decided to follow suit. I guess not everyone respects tradition.

I also loved mat wrestling. Like football, I enjoyed the contact as well as the competition. I had my first amateur wrestling match at 12 years old. It was held in the atrium of the local shopping mall. The place was packed, and kids of all different sizes and weight competed. I showed up wearing these old gray sweats and tennis sneakers. As I waited in line for the weigh-in, out of the corner of my eye I saw this big kid. He was wearing a brand-new green sweatsuit. He was also wearing shiny new wrestling shoes. Man, he looked good. But looks aren't everything, and I drew "Mr. Clean" in my first match. I pinned him in a record 23 seconds–so much for fancy outfits.

Coach Chuck Walters was my junior high wrestling coach and he taught me a lot about life and respect. He was a great motivator and teacher, and took a vested interest in me as both an athlete and person. He also made me a man.

As the big bully and tough guy, I also spoke like a man. I used the word "fuck" quite frequently. It was a major part of my vocabulary and I used it regularly as an adjective. One day, Coach Walters got tired of me saying it in practice. He had four to five guys hold me down. They subdued me as Coach proceeded to wash my mouth out with soap. Needless to say, I never cursed at wrestling practice again.

Throughout my entire junior and high school wrestling career, I was undefeated. Wrestling in the heavyweight division, I was known as the "Pinning Artist," because I pinned everyone I wrestled. Because of my fine high school wrestling record, on April 7, 1978, I was selected to represent the U.S. team in a match against the Pennsylvania All-Stars at the Pittsburgh Press Wrestling Classic. At the time, the event was heralded by many as the "Rose Bowl of High School Wrestling." And of course, I won my matches, pinning all my opponents.

In high school, I was a wrestling machine. Nobody could even come close to pinning me. This was due a lot to my work ethic and training, where I held school records for squatting (575 lbs), dead-lifting (800 lbs), and the bench press (375 lbs). It also had to do with my wrestling coach, Ed Linnabary.

Coach was an enthusiastic and passionate man for whom I had the utmost respect. Though his practices were hard and he demanded a lot, he also treated me like a son. He helped polish and transform my wrestling skills to the next level, while also instilling the values of determination, diligence, perseverance, and resolve.

Coach Linnabary is also the person who gave me the nickname "Dr. Death." The Japanese Wizard was one of my favorite moves. I would underhook my opponent's arm and literally throw him over my body. Though the move was successful, I would always end up shattering my nose in the process. Blood would be everywhere, so much so the officials would often have to temporarily halt the match.

Coach grew tired of opposing coaches who thought I was stalling, so for my protection, he gave me an old-time hockey mask. The first time I wore that thing, Coach made the comment, "Oh man, you look like 'Dr. Death.'" Soon thereafter the press, my teammates, and the fans picked up on it and started calling me Dr. Death.

Outside my family, Lyle Alzado was my idol. At 6-foot-3 and weighing 254 pounds, I thought he was the toughest person in the world. Growing up in the suburbs of Denver, Lyle played 15 seasons at defensive end for the Denver Broncos, my favorite football team. He was named All-Pro twice and compiled 97 sacks in 196 games. I never missed a game and relished every tackle and sack. On the football field, I wanted to be just like him.

In high school, I briefly met Lyle Alzado. At my senior year homecoming game, Lyle gave away the homecoming queen. It was great to finally see Lyle close up, and also to size myself up against him. Later in life, I got to know him a little more. When I was wrestling for Jim Crockett's NWA promotion from 1988 to 1989, Lyle was making a show, *Learning the Ropes.* The sitcom was produced in Canada and featured Lyle Alzado as a teacher named Robert Randall, who could not provide for his family with his job as a teacher and vice principal of a school, so he turned to wrestling part-time to pay the bills.

Lyle needed some real wrestlers to work on his show, as well as a stuntman who looked like him and could absorb the punishment of being in a ring. Several WCW stars appeared on the show, such as Ric Flair, Ronnie Garvin, and the Road Warriors. But Lyle chose ME as his stuntman, and I wrestled in the show as the "Masked Maniac."

Let me tell you, being a stuntman for the sitcom was one very painful experience. During one stunt, I blew out my knee landing on the canvas of a stiff ring after Ric Flair rolled out of the way. On another occasion, I got my head busted open when Tully Blanchard smashed a steel chair over it. I went to the hospital, got 39 stitches in my head, and quickly returned to the set to finish the session. It was the most painful $2,000 I would ever earn in my lifetime.

When Lyle Alzado died on May 14, 1992, it was a very sad moment in my life. Even to this day, I refuse to believe the rumors that he died from steroid abuse or AIDS. The official cause of his death was complications from brain cancer. I believe those results. Regardless, the painful fact remains that I lost my idol and friend way too early in life.

During my senior year, I was the highest recruited athlete in the state of Colorado. I was recruited by every major college in the nation including the major football powers, such as the University of Nebraska, University of Oklahoma, Southern Methodist University, University of Arizona, University of Arkansas, University of Colorado, Georgia Institute of Technology, and San Diego State University.

I was getting letters every day, and the phone line wouldn't stop ringing. Lou Holtz, the head football coach at the University of Arkansas personally wrote me a letter, dated September 14, 1977:

Dear Steve:

Just wanted to drop you a note to wish you luck this weekend. We're busy preparing for our game with Oklahoma State but I wanted to let you know we are thinking of you and hoping all is well. Good luck and go home a winner!

Sincerely, Lou Holtz

I will also never forget the compelling letters from two major University of Oklahoma alumni, H.E. Chiles, the chairman of the board for the Western Companies of North America, and Dr. William Castles, DDS. The University of Oklahoma really wanted Dr. Death.

In 1978, the NCAA policy was that recruits could make only six campus visits. My visit to the University of Arizona was interesting. The recruiter showed me one heck of a time, although no money ever exchanged hands. Flaunting food, alcohol, jewelry, and women, it was made explicitly and implicitly clear that Dr. Death would be "taken care of" if I signed with their school. The coaches and staff were very polite and they all treated me with respect.

I also got to know some of the players. A few members of the team also took me out that night to party. I was so drunk that I got into a fight. There was a guy sitting in his car saying something that I can't even recall. I went over to his car and had a few words and smacked him in the face. As the guy went to get out of his car, I held the door. Unfortunately,

FROM LEFT TO RIGHT, MY BROTHERS, JEFF AND JERRY WILLIAMS, AND I STAND WITH COACH GENE HOSHEA AND COACH PETE LEVINE.

I had these slick new dress shoes on, and as he pushed, I slipped on the gravel in the parking lot and fell facedown. After that, I'm sorry to say, I got up and beat the living crap out of the guy. There was blood everywhere. To escape the police, we took off back to campus. It took less than 24 hours for the city of Tucson to feel the wrath of Dr. Death

As a kid, I grew up a big-time Colorado Buffalo fan. Yet, because of what they did to my older brother, Jerry, I had no desire to attend the University of Colorado. In 1968, my brother was recruited and played fullback for Colorado under coach Eddie Crowder. Jerry was my hero. As a kid, it was such an honor to see my brother playing for my favorite college football team. However, due to desegregation and the influx of quicker and faster African-American players, Coach Crowder asked my brother to change positions. This request broke Jerry's heart as well as mine. Jerry refused and eventually quit the team. Nonetheless, he stayed in school and completed his degree in marketing, graduating in 1972. But the entire situation left me with bad feelings toward the University of Colorado and I vowed never to sign with them.

I was most impressed with San Diego State University. The recruiter from the Aztecs treated me like royalty. But the overall beauty of the campus was the school's main attraction. As a person who loves the beach, I was in awe of its ocean location. And then there were the girls. Let me tell you, there seemed to be so many pretty women on both the beach and campus that, when I got home from my recruiting trip, my neck hurt!

There was an outside weight room overlooking the beach, which I thought was extremely cool. I envisioned myself working out in the ocean breeze. Also, Jerry was now living in San Diego, so that made the school even more appealing.

I was all ready to sign a letter of intent with San Diego State. The only thing holding me back was that the university did not have a wrestling program. This was a major problem. Though I loved everything about San Diego State, my goal was to both play football and wrestle at the collegiate level; too bad for San Diego State.

Then there was the University of Oklahoma. Every since I was a freshman in high school, I envisioned myself playing for the Sooners. I really loved the University of Oklahoma. However, I really didn't want to use one of my six visits to go to Norman. Since Coach Levine was good friends with Coach Galen Hall and the other OU coaches, our high school team used to practice at and visit the University of Oklahoma every summer. Plus, my older bother, Jeff, was playing football there, and we attended all of his home games. I pretty much knew the university inside and out.

One day I pulled Jeff to the side and said, "Jeff, between me and you, if I don't take a recruitment visit to Oklahoma, do you think they will be mad at me? Will it affect my chances of getting a full ride?"

Puzzled, Jeff replied, "You have to be kidding me, Steve. If you don't take a trip, they won't pay any attention to you anymore.

I replied, "Come on Jeff, are you serious?" Jeff repeated his first statement with a tad more infliction. I decided to take a visit to Norman.

When I arrived on campus, it was nothing like my prior visits. This time I was treated like a member of the family. The entire Sooner staff treated me like a king. From the recruiters to the coaches, everyone showed me respect. I met and spoke in depth with coach Barry Switzer, immediately bonding with him. I was impressed with all the trophies, rings, and championships. The football field, weight room, athletic dorms, and even the cafeteria were out of this world. As I went to bed that night, I knew that the University of Oklahoma was in my future. What else could compare? Those guys were champions. They had excellent coaches and facilities. They went to major bowls. They received national attention and exposure. They traveled to great cities. My letter of intent went to the University of Oklahoma.

Even though I signed a letter of intent with the Sooners, the University of Arizona still showed interest, and the University of Oklahoma was aware of it. At my wrestling state finals, the University of Arizona sent a coach to watch my event. Coach Norris, the Oklahoma defensive line coach, was also supposed to be there, but for some reason he couldn't attend. Not to be outdone, the Sooners sent the head coach of their wrestling program, Stan Abel. Though I never had any intentions to break my promise to Oklahoma, it was pretty flattering to see both men jockeying to secure Dr. Death. In the end, Coach Abel witnessed me winning my match in 24 seconds to capture the state championship. He was blown away.

After the wrestling finals, I officially signed with Oklahoma to play football and wrestle. I accepted a full scholarship in football, but was a walk-on in wrestling. Yes, I am probably the only four-time, undefeated, state wrestling champion to sign on as a walk-on. I didn't want to take away a scholarship from the wrestling team. This was the right thing to do, and the university appreciated the loyal gesture.

My high school wrestling career concluded with a 77-4-1 record. I won 14 tournaments and was enshrined in my high school Hall of Fame.

I was a Colorado state champion both my junior and senior year, and still hold the following Lakewood high school wrestling records: Best Overall Record (1976,77,78), Most Takedowns (1977,78), Most Pins (1977,78), and Most Outstanding Wrestler (1976,77,78).

As graduation day approached, I focused on passing all my classes and getting ready for Norman. The day after my graduation, the plan was for my dad to drive me to campus. I was going to attend their summer camp and practices. However, I still had one more oat to sow: the graduation party.

I was the one in charge of organizing my high school graduation party. A few weeks before graduation, my buddies and I ransacked an old construction site. We got as much wood as possible. We built barricades, counters, tables, a platform, and a special square box for all the liquor and beer. I found a field where we could house the party and began to advertise the event. I must have invested $500. I charged $5 a head, which included all you could drink and a live band.

After the graduation ceremony, I rushed to the field and prepared for the biggest party that the Lakewood region had ever seen—and the people didn't let me down. I was literally running out of places to put the money. I stuffed money in every pocket on my body, and constantly made deposits in the trunk of my Impala. I even let many people in free, especially the pretty girls. By the time I quit monitoring the entrance, I had collected about $1,500.

Throughout the night, I also drank sloe gin fizzes. Come an hour or two into the evening, I was drunk out of my mind. I have no clue what time the party ended or how I even got home.

The only clear thing I recalled the next morning was my dad tapping me on the shoulder and saying, "Steven, it is time to go." I had such a hangover. Somehow, I managed to load everything into my money-packed Impala, and I headed to Norman, Oklahoma.

SIX

AN OKLAHOMA SOONER

I drove 12 hours non-stop. When I got on campus, I met with Stan Abel, the University of Oklahoma's head wrestling coach. I spent a few nights at Coach's house. The only things I had on me were my clothes and the money I had collected from my end of the year high school bash.

As a freshman, I was required to stay in the freshman dorms. My room was standard with a bunk bead. There was a community bathroom and a small kitchen. However, I preferred to eat in the cafeteria. It was out of this world, and thanks to the donations of the Beef Association, I ate steak four times a day.

My roommate that year was the quarterback of the football team, Kelly Phelps. Kelly and I hit it off right from the start. Though he was only my roommate as a freshman, he became one of my best friends. One of the vices we had in common was chewing tobacco. We often went out to the local convenience store to buy a pouch of Levi Garrett or any other brand we could find.

If I didn't like what Kelly was doing in the huddle or the way he was running the offense during practice, I would turn in protest. This didn't sit too well with Kelly, so, to get back at me, he would spit his tobacco juice on me while calling out the plays. Kelly knew I loved him, because I wouldn't have let anyone else get away with that garbage.

I was redshirted in football my freshman year because I was raw and they wanted to bring me along slowly. They saw my potential, and since

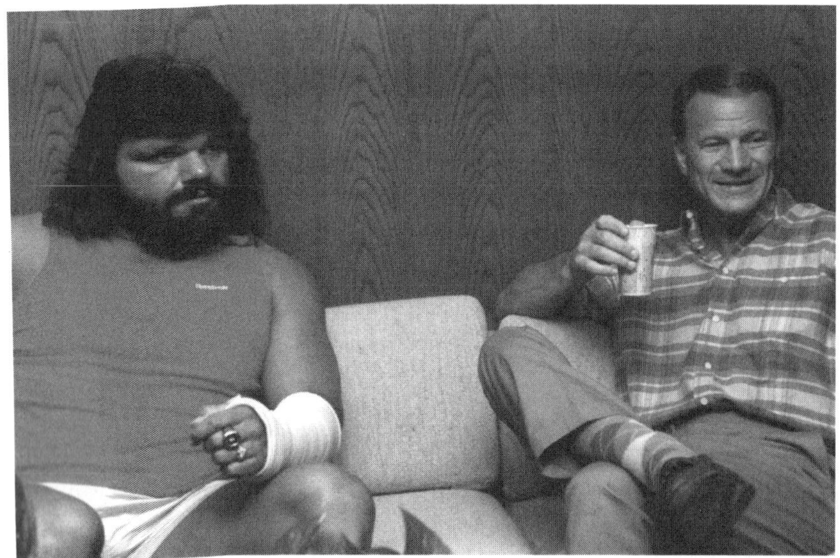

After Dick Murdoch broke my arm, I went back to Coach Switzer, who helped me mentally and physically train to capture the UWF Title.

the offensive line was already in place, they thought it would be best if I sat out a year to learn the offense. I was allowed to wear No. 76 and Coach Switzer still let me practice with the team.

During the 1978 regular season, we went 10-1 and tied for the Big Eight conference title. Our only loss was to Nebraska. They beat us 17-14 in front of 71,000-plus fans in rowdy Lincoln. But we got our shot at redemption in a rematch at the Orange Bowl. Though I wasn't playing, the team still invited me to go to Miami with them. We were redeemed, beating the Cornhuskers 31-24, as Billy Sims rushed for 134 yards and two touchdowns. The team even gave me an Orange Bowl ring.

When the football season concluded, I made my transition into wrestling. Unlike in football, I was a true freshman, wrestling as a heavyweight. I thought wrestling practice was more intense than football. Since I was so big, I didn't have any sparring partners on the team. So I recruited some of the heavyweights from football, such as offensive tackle Ted Colbert, to practice with during the season.

My first conference match at OU was a lesson in both humility and reality. We traveled to Nebraska to face a tough squad. In front of a hostile Cornhusker crowd, I was pinned by Tommy Williams. I didn't know what to think. As a high school standout, I was undefeated and pinned everyone that I faced. I couldn't believe that someone could pin Dr. Death. It affected my confidence and I began to question if I was even college-level wrestling material. But I didn't quit.

With the encouragement of my family and especially Coach Abel, I decided to work even harder. I vowed to get in better shape and to train as hard as I could to make sure that nobody would do that to me again. I ended my freshman year having won a heck of a lot more matches than I lost. In fact, I placed third in the Big Eight Conference wrestling tournament and sixth in the NCAA national meet.

As a student, my freshman year was also an experience. Coming from Lakewood High, which had about 30 students per class, I was blown away by the 400 to 500 students in each of my classes. My history course must have had some 600-plus people in it. The academics were a lot more challenging. I wasn't a dumb student, but it took time for me to learn the material.

> MIKE GEARY: FOR A CREATURE OF A MAN, DOC WAS A VERY LIKABLE AND FUNNY GUY. HE WAS VERY FUNNY. HE WASN'T A BULLY AND EVERYONE ON CAMPUS KNEW HIM. I WOULD TEASE DOC ABOUT IF HE EVER STUDIED AND WENT TO CLASS. "HEY DOC, DO YOU EVEN KNOW WHERE THE LIBRARY IS ON CAMPUS?"
>
> DOC WOULD JOKINGLY SAY, "NO!"

I really wanted to learn in order to have an education to fall back on after my professional football career. The football team had an academic advisor who worked with me, and I received lots of tutoring. I also learned early on that if I regularly attended class and genuinely made an effort, the professors would do whatever they could to help me pass the classes.

I didn't get homesick and sincerely enjoyed my freshman year. I was fortunate to have my brother Jeff attending OU. He was also on the football team. We spent lots of time together, and I knew Jeff was always there if I needed him.

One of the biggest adjustments was getting used to the outrageous Oklahoma weather. Coming from Colorado, I had never experienced the monstrous thunderstorms that hit Norman, or the continuous tornado watches and warnings. It was equally hot and humid in the summer. I had never sweated so much in my life.

During that time, I also started dating a couple of girls. Leslie Sword was very beautiful. I liked her a lot and we had some good times together. And then there was Linda. As an English graduate teaching assistant, she was much older than I. She was very attractive, but also took care of me. She cooked for me, let me stay at her apartment, helped me with my homework, and did other things that a young freshman in college only dreams of.

The summer after my freshman year, I decided not to go home. Rather, I stayed in Norman to train for the upcoming football and wrestling seasons. I was especially itching to get on the football field. Ever since I could play football, I had never missed a game. As a redshirt, I didn't play in 12. I hit the weights really hard. I wanted to make sure I was ready for the upcoming football season.

KELLY MITCHELL: DOC WAS THE TOUGHEST MAN I EVER MET. ON THE FOOTBALL FIELD, HE WAS A TERROR. THOUGH DOC DIDN'T MEMORIZE ALL THE PLAYS, HE WOULD MAKE IT UP WITH HIS SHEER STRENGTH AND WILL. EVERYBODY RESPECTED YET FEARED DOC. WITH A HEART OF A GIANT, HIS LOOK WAS NONETHELESS INTIMIDATING.

ONE TIME BEFORE PRACTICE, BARRY DITTMAN, A SENIOR AND STARTING LINEBACKER FROM HOUSTON, WAS SITTING IN THE LOCKER-ROOM WAITING TO GET HIS ANKLES TAPED AND WHATNOT FROM THE TRAINER. DOC, A FRESHMAN, CAME IN AND TOLD BARRY TO MOVE FROM "HIS" TABLE. BARRY, ABOUT 6 FOOT AND WEIGHING 205 POUNDS, WAS ONE TOUGH HOMBRE. A FEW OF US NEARBY PERKED UP AND WAITED FOR BARRY'S DECISION. WITHIN 60 SECONDS, BARRY GOT UP AND MOVED. DOC CLAIMED "HIS" TABLE. IN SHORT, NOBODY MESSED WITH DR. DEATH.

In between summer practices and training, I managed to secure a couple of part-time, local jobs. I worked as a loader for the Trans-Con Trucking Company and as a mechanic at a local bowling alley. College athletes didn't get paid and I needed some money to buy some wheels. As a car lover, I couldn't go another year without a vehicle. By the time the summer ended, I saved up enough cash to buy a blue Trans-Am.

My second year at OU, 1979, was very exciting. My four years playing football were about to begin. I had worked very hard in the off-season and had learned the Wishbone offense. It was still very difficult for me, especially since I had to work both sides of the line. It was tough enough to learn one set of plays, but two? The coaches would get so mad when I would mess up. But, with more practice and studying, I eventually got some of the plays down.

At 6-foot-2 and around 290 pounds, I was very fast for my size. I ran a 40 in 4.95, and Coach Switzer utilized my skills as a pulling guard. I battled all summer and fall with junior Terry Crouch for the job at left guard and didn't start right away. Terry was a big boy, standing 6-foot-1 and weighing close to 275. Nonetheless, I impressed enough people in fall practice to be listed in the *Sports Illustrated* preseason college football edition as one of Oklahoma's most formidable blockers.

> Mike Geary: Doc was naturally strong. He would easily bench 480 pounds 10 times. Combine that with his will, desire, and looks, he was without doubt the toughest man on the planet.

I played a lot as a swing-shift guard early in the season, rotating from the right and left guard spots. After an injury sidelined guard Don Key, I was inserted into the starting position, and there I remained.

It was a tremendous honor to finally accomplish my goal of starting for the great Oklahoma football program. It was equally a privilege to be part of an All-Star offensive line that included the Outland Trophy winner (1978, Best Interior Lineman), Greg Roberts. Greg was not only an outstanding person, but he also taught me a lot about playing on the line. Greg is one of the greatest offensive linemen I have ever seen in my life.

I also had the distinct honor to play with Julius Caesar (JC) Watts. JC is a natural leader and ran our offense with confidence. He is a remarkable person and treated me with class and respect. I was proud to be part of his team and marveled at his athletic ability on the football field. JC would receive wider fame when he made history in Oklahoma as the first black nominee for statewide office: in 1990, he was elected as Corporation Commissioner. He trumped that victory when he was elected to the U.S. Congress and consequently became the first black Republican in 120 years to be elected to a federal office in a Southern state.

And then there was running back Billy Sims. Billy was a stud. When he ran the ball, it was like poetry in motion. When he dove over the goal line, he flapped his arms, and you literally thought he was flying. Billy was the greatest running back I had the honor to both block for and play with, and I'm not the only one to think so. Billy Sims was recently ranked the best running back in Sooner history by *The Daily Oklahoman.*

In 1978, Billy won the Heisman trophy. The same year, he was also the AP and UPI College Player of the Year and won the Walter Camp trophy (player of the year). Billy was the first overall pick in the 1980 NFL Draft. Making the Pro Bowl from 1980 to1982, he played with the Detroit Lions for five years. He was a threat to score every time he touched the ball. In the prime of his career, Billy suffered an unfortunate knee injury, which ended his football career.

Billy is also a stand-up person. When I was going through my cancer treatments, he visited with me and was very sensitive to my plight. We hugged and exchanged stories. He even gave me an autographed football, which I still have in a glass case in my office. Billy is a true friend.

I also left my mark on the football field during my freshman year with chewing tobacco. I loved chewing tobacco, especially during games. To fluster the defensive linemen, I often spit my tobacco juice on their hands.

This infuriated the opposing linemen, but simultaneously produced a flag. Sometimes the linemen would jump offsides and sometimes they would just lose focus. Either way, I accomplished my objective.

In 1979, we went 10-1 and won the Big Eight conference. Our only loss was a 16-7 clash to our archrival, the Texas Longhorns. It always hurt when we lost a game, but it hurt even more if the loss was to the 'Horns. Nonetheless, we accepted an invitation to play Florida State in the Orange Bowl.

> KELLY MITCHELL: DOC AND I WERE BEST OF FRIENDS. MY MOM ONCE FOUND A BONG IN MY ROOM. MY MOM WAS ALSO MISSING LOTS OF BUTTER FROM THE REFRIGERATOR. DOC AND I WOULD GET THE MUNCHIES. WE WOULD RAID THE KITCHEN AND DEVOUR BREAD AND BUTTER. MY MOM GOT CONCERNED AND ASKED MY SISTER TO CHECK ON THE MISSING BUTTER. UNBEKNOWNST TO ME, SHE FOUND MY BONG. MOM THOUGH DOC AND I WERE SMOKING BUTTER WITH THE BONG. LATER, I TEASED MOM BY TELLING HER, "EVERYTHING IS BETTER WITH BLUEBONNET ON IT!"

When we arrived in Miami, I thought I was in heaven. I loved the beach, the people, the climate, and the bars. Coach Switzer, the other coaches, and the assistants made sure to keep a close eye on us. We had a full agenda. We practiced, studied film, met with the media, and traveled as a team to and from the hotel. But I also wanted to party, which led to some big trouble.

Barry Dittman, Mike Reilly, Kelly Mitchell, and I decided not to go to practice one day. Mike was from Florida and we were preparing to party big-time at Mike's place. We had a few drinks to get the party started a little early. This didn't sit well with Coach Switzer.

Kelly Mitchell was my new roommate. We would room together for the rest of my years at OU. He is a great guy and we shared many experiences together, from the football field to drinking beer and smoking pot.

Coach Switzer found us some four hours later at the hotel. We were drunk and we made up some story about how we missed the bus and decided to just go back to our rooms. Coach Switzer was not happy and even entertained the idea of dismissing us from the team. It wouldn't have

> KELLY MITCHELL: COACH SWITZER HAD US GET UP AT 5 A.M. TO RUN AROUND THE EMPTY HOTEL PARKING LOT. WE TRIED TO TAKE THE ELEVATOR DOWN FROM ABOUT THE 14TH FLOOR, BUT COACH HAD THE HOTEL TURN THEM OFF. AS WE CAME THROUGH THE STAIRWAY EXIT, COACH SWITZER WAS THERE WAITING ON US. COACH WATCHED US RUN AS HE DRANK HIS COFFEE AND READ THE PAPER. DELIVERY TRUCKS AND OTHERS WOULD STARE AT US, ADDING TO THE HUMILIATION. DOC WAS COMPLAINING THE ENTIRE TIME, AND EVEN SAID SOME THINGS THAT FORCED COACH TO GIVE DOC A TONGUE-LASHING. BY THE TIME IT WAS OVER, WE WERE ALL PUKING OUR GUTS OUT.
>
> BUT THE PAIN WASN'T OVER. WE THEN HAD TO GO TO PRACTICE. DOC'S FEET WERE SO BLISTERED AND SWOLLEN FROM ALL THE RUNNING, HE PRACTICED BAREFOOTED!

been the first time Coach kicked a player off the team. A few years earlier, he released fullback Horace Ivory before the 1976 Orange Bowl for sassing a graduate assistant coach.

We begged Coach Switzer not to dismiss us and said that we would do anything to make up for this indiscretion. Well, Coach opted to leave the decision of disciplinary action to our team captains. Fortunately, they let us back on the team. The conditions were that we apologize and that we run. Coach Switzer ran us for two hours non-stop all week before practice. By the end of each practice, I couldn't feel my legs.

Come game day, we all knew what needed to be done. To get us even more pumped, Coach Switzer showed the team the film *Raging Bull*. If this movie doesn't fire you up, then nothing will. Even though future professional wrestler and All-American Ron Simmons led the Seminole defense, they were no match for our Wishbone attack, and we thumped Florida State 24-7 in front of 66,000 fans. We finished the season 11-1 and I earned my second Orange Bowl ring.

Ron Simmons is one of the greatest athletes to ever come out of Florida State University. I played against Ron in two Orange Bowls. Ron was a nose guard and I was on the offensive line. We were like two big bulls ramming into each other on every play. He would pop me, and I would shake him off. I would then come back and pop him harder. He is one tough cookie.

During my sophomore year, Dr. Death had arrived! I worked out and trained harder for the wrestling season than ever before and had a stellar sophomore season.

On February 9, 1979, we gave Coach Abel his first victory ever against Oklahoma State. It was OU's first win against the Cowboys since January 11, 1969. In front of a record crowd of 10,000 at the Lloyd Noble Center, we beat the Cowboys at home, winning six of the ten weight classes. In my match, I wrestled 180-pound Rey Martinez. He was no match for me. With about 33 seconds left in the first period, I bear hugged Martinez to the mat, and my 290 pounds landed on his shoulder. I dislocated it. Martinez would soon default in the second period.

> MIKE GEARY: It was unprecedented to have 10,000 people in attendance to watch a wrestling match. But the people mainly came to the OU wrestling matches to watch Doc. Doc was funny, but had a look that would intimidate anyone. He would jump rope while the lighter wrestlers would be doing their matches. He would also stick his tongue out and make crazy faces to the opposing team's wrestlers. Even non-wrestling fans would come to the event to watch Doc's antics.

The highlight of the year was when I wrestled in the East vs. West tournament. I locked up and lost by one point in overtime to Bruce Baumgartner. It wouldn't be the last time I would lose to the Indiana State wrestling machine. Bruce is one of the most successful American super-heavyweight wrestlers of all time. He would go on to win four Olympic medals.

I also remember my match with Lou Banach from the University of Iowa. All week before our match, all I heard and read was that Lou was the "toughest" heavyweight around. Granted, Lou did compile a 92-14-3 record as a heavyweight wrestler and won two NCAA championships, but the proclamation that he was the "toughest" pissed me off.

"We Are the Champions": Celebrating at Nationals with Olympic champion Andre Metzger.

As we squared off in Iowa City, I played and toyed with him on the mat. Lou never had a chance. The Hawkeye fans were yelling and screaming at me because I just abused the guy. He was my puppet for the evening. When I pinned him, everyone unequivocally knew that Dr. Death was the toughest heavyweight around!

My sophomore football year had its ups and downs. Though we finished the season 9-2 and captured a Big Eight championship, we were hoping to become national champions. We started the season 1-0, thumping a non-ranked Kentucky Wildcat team, 29-7. Ranked number four in the country, we then hosted the non-ranked Stanford Cardinal. Maybe we were looking ahead to our Big Eight opener against Colorado in Boulder, but with future Super Bowl MVP and Hall of Fame quarterback John Elway leading the attack, Stanford upset us on our home turf 31-14.

> MIKE GEARY: DOC WAS ONE INTIMIDATING PERSON. IF YOU DIDN'T KNOW HIM, HE WOULD SCARE ANYONE. AND IF HE RAISED HIS VOICE, FORGET ABOUT IT. WELL, WHEN THE DOCTORS TOLD DOC TO PEE IN A CUP DOC BARKED, "NO!" THE POOR GUY ALMOST HAD A HEART ATTACK AND SIMPLY SAID, "OKAY, NEXT!"
>
> ANOTHER INCIDENT THAT DISPLAYS DOC'S INTIMIDATING PRESENCE WAS DURING HIS SENIOR YEAR. NEW RECRUITS FROM AROUND THE COUNTRY WERE COMING TO CAMPUS. DURING LUNCH, I CAME IN WITH A BUNCH OF THE RECRUITS. DOC WAS SITTING ALONE AT A TABLE EATING POUNDS OF GRUB. HIS HAIR WAS LONG AND LOOKING LIKE A CREATURE RIGHT OUT OF A SCIENCE FICTION MOVIE. HE PAUSED FROM HIS FOOD AND GLANCED AT ME. SOON THEREAFTER I SAT DOWN WITH THE RECRUITS TO EAT. I NOTICED THEY KEPT EYEBALLING DOC. ONE OF THE RECRUITS WHISPERED, "IS HE A SENIOR?" I SAID, "YES, WHY?" HE SAID, "WELL, WE HAVE ALL DECIDED THAT IF HE ISN'T, WE AREN'T COMING TO OU."

We couldn't do anything right that Saturday or at practice the following week, Coach Switzer made sure we wouldn't be embarrassed again. In our next game, we went to Boulder and destroyed them 85-42 in front of their fans.

I had lots of fun in the locker room. I would banter, joke, and yell at many of the guys. I often wore a Richard Nixon mask to practice that would make Coach Switzer chuckle. But I especially liked messing with the equipment manager, Jack Bear. Jack was one mean person. We used to go back and forth all the time. He yelled at me, and I yelled right back. He got so mad at me because I always asked for extra T-shirts and other OU football gear. He would scream, "I'm not giving you anything! You are stealing them anyway. The only thing you are going to do is sell them!" Regardless, I always managed to attain extra OU football shirts.

The NCAA also came down hard on drug testing about then. At this time in my life, I was 100 percent clean. Still, I didn't like the idea of them violating my privacy. When it was my turn to be tested, I simply refused. They never bothered to ask me to pee in a cup again.

We ended my sophomore football season with another trip to Miami, where we once again beat Florida State 14-13. I garnered my third Orange Bowl ring in three years, and we finished the year ranked No. 3 in the AP poll.

The victory party in Miami was spectacular. The food, accommodations, and events that the investors provided were out of this world. After enjoying the postgame obligations, Mike Reilly, Kelly Mitchell, Mark Lucky, a few others, and I decided to take advantage of the Miami bar scene. We drank the bars dry.

Unlike two years earlier, this time we were wiser and more cautious of Coach Switzer's schedule and curfew. We were somehow able to keep track of the time and managed to stumble back to the team bus before it departed. Though it was only a few miles from where we were, the bus ride to the hotel seemed to take forever. I also felt like we were on a rollercoaster. With my stomach churning, I threw up only a few minutes into the drive. Hoping not to get anything on the floor, I used my brand-new sports coat to catch the mess. Although I tried to be discreet, vomit oozed out of the jacket and leaked everywhere. I told the coaches I must have eaten too much barbeque.

SEVEN

PRO FOOTBALL

My junior year in wrestling was very productive, yet nearly tragic. On the mat, I improved in all facets. Coach Abel and the assistant coaches worked with me to take advantage of my size and skills. At times, I was unbeatable. But at our spring break wrestling tournament in Portland, Oregon, I almost died.

I was all alone in my hotel room getting pumped up for the matches. All of a sudden, I couldn't move and could barely breathe. I was having serious chest pains. I couldn't scream for help, so I just took baby breaths to survive. After what seemed like hours, I finally gained composure and managed to get hold of Coach Abel. He called an ambulance and, with Coach by my side, I was rushed to the local Portland emergency room. My parents were contacted.

Doctors ran a series of tests but weren't quite sure what was wrong. It was suggested that I had some inflammation around my heart. They put me on oxygen so I could effectively breathe, and I was advised to see my personal doctor.

After being stabilized, I flew home to Denver. My parents and an ambulance were waiting for me at the jet way. Our family doctor brought in a heart specialist, who ran test after test. My condition was finally diagnosed as Pericarditis–an inflammation of the membrane surrounding the heart. The doctors told me that all the wrestling, picking guys up and throwing them to the mat, with so much stress and strain had bruised my heart.

There was concern that the fluid was beginning to compress the chambers of my heart. The doctors recommended draining the fluid through a procedure called pericardiocentisis. The doctor carefully inserted a thin needle through my chest wall into the area of accumulated fluid. He then drained the fluid through the needle. The doctor left a tiny rubber drain in place for about two days to allow additional drainage. This fluid was sent to a lab for analysis, and the results were inconclusive, but the cause was more likely due to a viral infection.

I was given a series of medications and was told that recovery could be anywhere from two weeks to three months. It lasted about eight weeks. During the time off, my weight ballooned from 285 to roughly 325 pounds. I wasn't able to have any contact. I couldn't lift weights. I couldn't run. I couldn't participate in any athletic activity.

I also didn't watch my diet. I consumed everything in the house. Every evening, I ate an extra-large pizza with everything on it. That was very tough for me. Getting back into shape was the hardest part of the entire ordeal. But I had to lose weight if I wanted to play for Coach Switzer.

I figured one way to lose the weight was to find a physically demanding job during the summer. I went to Wyoming and caught on with an oil company, working the rigs, but that didn't last too long. It was very dangerous, and I felt that I might injure myself. I didn't want it to affect my football career, so I decided to go to Lakewood and stay with my parents. It was great being with my family, and I turned the few months there into a nice summer vacation. I enjoyed spending time once again in the mountains, a stark contrast to the old Oklahoma flatlands.

My junior season in football was a rebuilding year. With a new quarterback, Darrell Shepard, we had a decent regular season with a 6-4-1 record. It really hurt to lose to both Nebraska and Texas that season. We also tied Iowa State at home. It was not our best effort. Still, we concluded the season with a win against Oklahoma State and finished second in the Big Eight conference. Coach Switzer accepted a bid to play the University of Houston in the Sun Bowl. The mediocre season ended Coach Switzer's four straight Orange Bowl appearances.

The Sun Bowl is located on the University of Texas campus in El Paso. If you are driving on I-10, you can clearly see the stadium. As a border town, the Mexican city of Juarez was an American citizen's dream for drinking and fun. I spent the Christmas of 1981 in El Paso and Juarez with my good friend, Kelly Phelps, and his wife, Barbara (Barbie).

Juarez was a very depressing city. It was poor and dirty. I especially remember little kids begging for money on the street. I felt sorry for them and gave them way too much money for the packets of gum that they were selling.

On the other hand, the drinking in Juarez was very inexpensive. Kelly and I had a blast. Juarez was also the place where I was introduced to my first White Russian beverage. I really enjoyed this drink, which consists of vodka, kahlua, and milk. I drank so many White Russians that week, I felt like I could help President Reagan defeat communism in the Soviet Union.

We went on to defeat the University of Houston in the Sun Bowl 40-14. Our offensive line was dominating. We pushed their defense around, which led our ground game to rack up some 400-plus rushing yards. I was laying out defensive players left and right. After gaining 107 yards and two touchdowns, Darrell Shepard earned the MVP award. I attained my fourth straight bowl victory. We ended the season 7-4-1, ranking No. 20 in the AP poll.

That year in wrestling was my last opportunity to become a national champion. I trained as much as I could throughout football season and was physically ready for my final run. It was also about time that I helped the University of Oklahoma become national champions. We had the guys in place to win it all.

I got along with all the wrestlers as captain my senior year. We had lots of fun, and many of the smaller guys would always try me. One time I was walking on campus in front of the football dormitory, wearing my leather letterman jacket. All of a sudden, I felt this sharp pinching sensation on my left forearm. Lo and behold, I looked down and then up to see Mike Mangor with a pellet gun, laughing up a storm. That 131-pound turkey had just shot me from the third floor. I was furious. Out of the corner of my eye, I saw this concrete cinder block. With all my strength, I threw that block with hopes of nailing him in the head. It fell inches short from the third-floor window. You should have seen Mike scatter. He ducked me for days.

I often went out for lunch or a drink with Mike Geary to talk about my future. There were lots of option to ponder, such as professional football, professional wrestling, the Olympics, etc. Regardless, I was ready to make history my senior year in mat wrestling at OU. Everyone in the community and on campus was pulling for me.

I wrestled some interesting heavyweights that year. I pinned Gary Albright of the University of Nebraska quite easily. Ironically, Gary would become a professional wrestler and my partner in Japan. He was also a great friend. Likewise, I wrestled Dan Severn from Arizona State University. When I wrestled Dan, he was known as the "Pinning Artist," because he pinned everyone he wrestled.

> MIKE GEARY: ONE AFTERNOON, DOC AND I WERE HAVING A BEER AT AN ADULT ENTERTAINMENT ESTABLISHMENT NEAR CAMPUS. EVERYONE IN THE PLACE KNEW AND LIKED DOC. DOC AND I WERE SIMPLY CHITCHATTING AND MINDING OUR OWN BUSINESS. ALL OF A SUDDEN, A COUPLE OF FRATERNITY GUYS STARTED MAKING SMART TALK, "YOU JOCKS THINK YOU ARE SO TOUGH." I'M SURE IT WAS THE BEER TALKING.
>
> DOC HOWEVER, ONE TO NEVER TAKE CRAP FROM ANYONE, GOT UP FROM HIS STOOL AND HEADED TO THOSE PRETTY-BOYS. YOU COULD IMMEDIATELY SEE THAT THEY WISHED TIME COULD BE REVERSED. DOC SIMPLY GRABBED ONE OF THE GUYS AROUND THE SHIRT COLLAR AND JACKED HIM OFF THE BARSTOOL. HE LITERALLY HELD HIM TWO FEET OFF THE GROUND. I WASN'T GOING TO LET DOC BEAT HIM OR THE OTHERS UP OR ANYTHING LIKE THAT. I KNEW DOC JUST WANTED TO TEACH THEM A LESSON. AFTER MAKING HIS POINT, HE PITILESSLY LET THE FRAT BOY DOWN. THEY ALL SCATTERED.
>
> WITHIN MINUTES, WE HEARD THE POLICE SIRENS. I HEARD, "DOC, COME IN HERE." IT WAS THE STRIPPERS MOTIONING DOC TO GO AND HIDE IN THEIR DRESSING ROOMS. THE COPS CAME IN AND SEARCHED THE PLACE FOR DOC, AND OF COURSE THEY DIDN'T GO INTO THE DRESSING ROOM WHERE THERE WERE NAKED LADIES. EVERYBODY LOVED DOC.

Dan was good, but not good enough to beat Dr. Death. After I pinned Dan, I quipped to all, "So much for the Pinning Artist." Dan is a great person who went on to wrestle in the WWE. He still competes in Ultimate Fighting and mixed martial arts.

And then there was the "Bedlam Series" between the University of Oklahoma and Oklahoma State University. While the football and basketball Bedlam games stand today as the marquee events in the series, the term "Bedlam" has its roots based in the rivalry between our schools' prestigious wrestling programs. My final battle in this series was in Stillwater, and the crowd was hotter than I could ever recall.

We were down by a few points, and I needed eight or more in my match for us to have a chance at victory. As I was wrestling my opponent, David Hille, who I outweighed by some 70 pounds, it was obvious he had no intention of wrestling. As I was tossing Hille around, all of a sudden he head-butted me and then bit me on the arm. I was bleeding. I couldn't believe the referee didn't disqualify Hille. I pleaded my case, but the ref pretty much blew me off. He simply tapped Hille on the head and told him to stop. Hille smugly said, "Okay."

I didn't like the way the referee had handled the situation. So it was now payback time. As soon as I locked back up with this chump, I cross-faced him and about took his head off. Hille complained, and the ref told me to stop. I sarcastically said, "Okay." The fans were going nuts, and the atmosphere was very similar to a professional wrestling match. Despite Hille's dirty tactics, I still desperately wanted to win the match for our team. I tried to get the referee to calm Hille down during the match. But Hille continued butting me, holding onto my arms and backing to the edge of the mat. The referee finally made a decision to call a double disqualification with only 11 seconds left in our heavyweight match.

The Oklahoma State fans started running to the floor, and things quickly got out of control. The police had to escort me out of the arena. In the end, they beat us 20-17. The loss hurt, but the fact that I kicked the crap out of my opponent gave me some comfort.

Later that week, coach Stan Abel received a package in the mail. It was from an Oklahoma State fan. In the package was feces and a note attached which read, "Dr. Death is the shits!"

During two wrestling seasons, I had always come up short against Indiana State University's Bruce R. Baumgartner. As a senior, this was my last chance to beat Bruce. Unfortunately, once again, I lost to Bruce in the NCAA finals by a score of 4-3.

I don't want to take anything away from Bruce, because he was an outstanding mat wrestler, but he was beatable. I wholeheartedly believe that if I had exclusively trained year-round for wrestling as he did, I would have beaten him. I was training six months for football and six months for wrestling. The average wrestler probably had 80 matches under his belt compared to my 30 by the time the regular season ended. So, by the time the NCAA finals came around, I was just starting to get warmed up.

When my amateur wrestling career came to a close, it was a very sad day. Though I had my senior year in football left, wrestling was still in my blood. Unlike major sports, such as football, basketball, and baseball, which have professional and developmental leagues, once your amateur wrestling career is over, it's over. I ended my wrestling career at OU leaving behind a plethora of wrestling awards, such as:

- Best Overall Record: 1976, '77, '78
- Most Takedowns: 1977-78
- Most Pins: 1977-78
- Most Outstanding Wrestler: 1976, '77, '78
- Four-Time All-American: 1979-82
- Three-Time Big Eight Champion: 1980-82
- The fourth fastest pin time in OU history as I defeated Perr Kaufmann of Oklahoma State in 20 seconds in a 1981 match
- Jimmy White Award: 1981-82
- Member of the 1981 Big Eight Championship team

I vowed to enjoy my last year at the University of Oklahoma. With the start of the 1982 football season, I had now spent five years in Norman. It was a great time, and I enjoyed every moment. Yet I had to keep in perspective why I was in college in the first place: to become a professional football player.

Though my junior year was the worst season in Coach Switzer's eight years as head coach, I was excited about my senior season. We were a young team and still rebuilding. My good friend, Kelly Phelps, regained the starting quarterback position, so all was good in my book. Everyone in Norman was excited about this year because Coach Switzer managed to land the top high school prospect in the country, running back Marcus Dupree. At 6-foot-2 and weighing nearly 225 pounds, Marcus was fast and strong and gave us hope in an inexperienced backfield.

Marcus Dupree was a stud of a football player. Unlike Billy Sims, however, Marcus didn't like to practice. He was extremely fast, and come game day, Marcus was on. But during practice, you would never get the most out of him. He had a poor work ethic, and I believe that his lazy approach caused his knees to be unprepared for season-long contact.

I tried to help Marcus become an outstanding running back his freshman year. He didn't start until halfway into the season, but once he did, I took him under my wing and blew people out of the way so he could rack up the yardage. I used to tell Marcus, "You follow me brother, and whichever way I go and take out the defensive player, you go the other way."

Marcus messed up his knees and soon quit the team his junior season. He tried to walk on at Southern Mississippi, but NCCA rules required him to sit out a year. He eventually quit college football altogether. He tried to make it in the pros, but had an unsuccessful professional football career with both the USFL (Breakers) and NFL (Buccaneers and Rams).

We started out the 1982 season on a bad note. We were ranked ninth in the nation but got whipped at home 41-27 by the unranked West Virginia Mountaineers. It was the first time since 1965 that we lost a home opener and the first time since 1968 that we started the season 0-1. It was embarrassing, and I felt so bad for Coach Switzer, the fans, the alumni, and the university.

We did win the following week in Lexington, only to lose once again at home to USC. With a 1-2 record, I marveled at Coach Switzer's leadership. Coach never quit and made sure that neither did any of his players. We made some adjustments during the week and then went into Ames, beating Iowa State, 13-3. We then ran off seven straight wins, including a whipping of the 13th-ranked Texas Longhorns, 28-22. We controlled the clock and ran for nearly 400 yards against our archrivals.

After the victory over Texas, I remember standing in the middle of the Cotton Bowl as OU fans ran everywhere. It was such an emotional time for my teammates and me to celebrate with our fans. For the past five years, the Red River Classic had been part of my life. From the ringing of those darn cowbells to the great atmosphere, I was so happy to end my collegiate career with a defeat against the 'Horns.

> KELLY MITCHELL: DOC WAS AN AWESOME FOOTBALL PLAYER. THOUGH HE HAS A HEART OF GOLD, HE WAS DOWNRIGHT INTIMIDATING ON THE FIELD. HE WAS MEAN AND WOULD RUN YOU RIGHT OVER.

We finished the season with an 8-3 record and ranked No. 12 in the nation. We accepted an invitation to play the No. 11-ranked Arizona State University in the Fiesta Bowl. It would be the first-ever meeting between our two programs.

The Sun Devils were good and they apparently had a great defensive line and run defense. I was all fired up about this. The other linemen and I were going to make sure Marcus Dupree would have open lanes to run through. Come game day, our mission was accomplished, as we ripped apart that stellar defense and rushed for over 400 yards. Unfortunately, because of turnovers, we lost the game 32-21.

When my college athletic career came to an end, the reaction was mixed. I was sad because it was time to leave

> KEITH MEADOR (SOONERSTATS.COM): I HAVE SO MANY MEMORIES ABOUT STEVE. BUT IF I COULD HAVE MELDED ALL OF THEM TOGETHER INTO A SINGLE MEMORY, IT WOULD BE THAT HE WAS THE PRECURSOR TO "THE BOZ," BRIAN BOSWORTH. STEVE WAS A LOT MORE LIKEABLE.

Norman and all my friends and family. Yes, Oklahoma University is family. Once a Sooner, always a Sooner. I was especially going to miss Coach Switzer and Abel. They taught me accountability, responsibility, respect, and how to be man. They were like fathers to me, and I love them dearly.

On the other hand, I was happy, because now I could become a professional football player. I played my best football my senior season, and many experts thought that I had a chance to get drafted. With both the upcoming NFL and USFL draft, I felt like there was a good chance that some team would select me.

In the end, I was a two-time Big Eight Champion in football, a two-time Big Eight Champion in wrestling, and a four-time letterman in football and wrestling. I earned three Orange Bowl and one Sun Bowl ring, received one Fiesta Bowl watch, and received two awards as the person who made the greatest contribution to the OU wrestling team.

I trained extra hard after the football season and attended many workout sessions for the pros. During the USFL draft, I was selected by the New Jersey Generals. My childhood dream of becoming a professional football player had come true. My family was ecstatic, and I know my Mom and Dad were proud of me.

I signed a two-year, $50,000 "no-cut" contract with the Generals. They gave me a $20,000 signing bonus and I was on top of the world. The first thing I did with that bonus money was buy some new clothes. For five years, my wardrobe had consisted of mainly sweats, T-shirts, ball caps, and tennis shoes. I also purchased a car, as well as a gold bracelet that I still have to this day.

I was excited to be at training camp. Donald Trump was the owner, and he was very cordial and professional with the players. The head coach was Chuck Fairbanks. George Wheeler was the defensive line coach. Though I was an offensive guard in college, the Generals drafted me to play defensive nose tackle. During spring training, I thought they were going to teach me how to play my new position. I assumed they would at least help me make the transition. But the coaches were no Coach Switzer. I am not sure if it was their choice of beverages or their lack of interest, but they did minimal, at best.

The focus of training and our team was bar none the signing of running back Herschel Walker. The day of his lucrative and unprecedented signing, Herschel flew in with Donald Trump, landing Trump's helicopter in the middle of the practice field. Thirty thousand people must have been in attendance.

Herschel was an excellent football player and a nice person. He is a Christian and conducts himself in a very appropriate and professional manner. Though we were on opposite sides of the ball, we still managed to share a few prime rib dinners together.

When training camp concluded, I took temporary residence at the local Sheraton Hotel near Giants Stadium. I really liked the Sheraton, especially the restaurant and pool, but at close to $1,500 a week, I knew that I had better make other living arrangements. A few weeks later, I purchased my first home in the suburbs.

Once the season started, I was miserable. The depression began to set in during training camp. My entire life I played football because it was fun. It was now a job. I would watch game film, study the playbook, meet with the coaches, practice, train, eat, and sleep. Combine that with the ineptitude of Coaches Fairbanks and Wheeler, I was beginning to lose interest in professional football.

One day at practice, Coach Fairbanks stopped all the activity because he didn't like the way things were going. He called everyone over to the sidelines, including all the coaches. After a brief "intoxicating" rant, Coach Fairbanks started running practice and calling plays that the offense didn't even know. It was so funny, but also embarrassing. We now knew why the team performed so terribly.

It was a very tough first year. I was disciplined a few times for playing too rough. It was also difficult for me to make the transition from offense to defense without adequate coaching and guidance. I was soon cut. Along with the entire defensive line, I was released with three games to go in the season. We were horrible as a unit and the third-worst defensive team in the league, giving up a whopping 437 points.

I was shocked when they called me into the office, telling me to bring my playbook. I laughed. I thought that there was no way they could cut me because of the "no-cut" clause in my contract. But Coach Fairbanks simply told me that I wasn't getting the job done.

After I cleaned out my locker and blew up at the coaches on the way out, I went to my home in the country to relax. Because of my contract, I knew it would only be a day before I would be reinstated. To my dismay, this wasn't the case. I telephoned my agent and lawyer. Neither one would return my call. They were nowhere to be found. I was being blown off.

So what did I do? I went to the one person who was always there to help me no matter what: Dad! I called him and explained the entire situation. I told my dad what they were doing to me wasn't right and that they were still obligated to the terms of my contract. As always, Dad turned negatives into positives and calmed me down. He then calmly stated, "Steven, don't worry. I will take care of it."

Well, a few days later, I got a call from the Generals' front office. They paid me for the remainder of my contract and, for some reason, placed me on the injured reserve roster. They also gave me extra money to pay for another year of school at the University of Oklahoma. I guess my dad sure enough took care of it, huh?

I sold my house, packed everything up, and headed back to Lakewood. Since I had a few months before the fall semester started, I stayed a few weeks with my brother, Jerry, in San Diego. While in San Diego, I called Dan Reeves. Dan Reeves was the coach of the Denver Gold in the USFL. I asked him if there was a place for me on their roster, but Coach said that the unit was set for the year. We cordially chatted about other things, and he told me to check back with him before the start of training camp the next season.

As I relaxed in San Diego, I considered my future. With some money in the bank from my USFL contract, I knew that everything would temporarily be okay. I also spoke with Coach Switzer and some other friends at OU. I was excited to head back to Norman to complete my undergraduate education. The one thing I did know was that no matter what, I wouldn't give up or quit. To remind myself, I started humming the Oklahoma Boomer Sooner fight song:

Boomer Sooner, Boomer Sooner,
Boomer Sooner, Boomer Sooner,
Boomer Sooner, Boomer Sooner,
Boomer Sooner, OK-U!
Oklahoma, Oklahoma,
Oklahoma, Oklahoma,
Oklahoma, Oklahoma,
Oklahoma, OK-U!

I'm a Sooner born,
And a Sooner bred,
And when I die
I'll be Sooner dead!

Rah, Oklahoma! Rah, Oklahoma!
Rah, Oklahoma! OK-U!

EIGHT

PRO WRESTLING

When I was a senior in college, professional wrestling found me. In 1981, after I was defeated in the NCAA wrestling finals by Bruce Baumgartner, Bill Watts approached me about becoming a professional wrestler with his Mid-South promotion.

Dating back to both their Putnam City High School and University of Oklahoma days, Coach Abel and Bill Watts were close friends. One day, Coach Abel called Bill Watts and told him that he thought I would make an excellent professional wrestler. Bill Watts asked, "Is he tough?"

Coach Abel, who coached more than 50 All-Americans and had 13 national wrestling titles, said, "Bill, he is the toughest I have ever seen."

With one more year of football eligibility remaining at OU, I was unsure about his request. The Mid-South wrestling promotion was very popular in Oklahoma, and I used to enjoy watching it on TV. I would often tease everyone about becoming a professional wrestler one day. My goal at the time, however, was to have the best football year of my life so I could be drafted into the pros.

I decided to meet with Bill Watts, and I liked him from the start. He was friendly, straightforward, and had that look in his eye, as if he knew I had something beneficial to bring to his promotion. I had a national reputation and sensed Bill knew I was marketable. Watts said, "Kid, give it a shot."

At this point, academics weren't my highest priority and I needed some money. I said, "Okay, I'll give it a shot."

> BILL WATTS: DOC HAD GREAT ATHLETIC ABILITY AND GREAT POTENTIAL. I KNEW HE HAD THE NECESSARY SKILLS TO CONTRIBUTE TO THE WRESTLING BUSINESS.

I didn't tell anyone that I was training to become a professional wrestler. The only person who knew about it was Coach Abel—not my dad, mom, brothers, or even Coach Switzer. I was my own man and didn't feel that anyone needed to know my business. Later, I would have to tell my friend, Mike Geary, because he would take me to Bill's place.

I have known Mike since my days at OU. He was an air traffic controller and we met through former Los Angeles Rams linebacker, Mike Reilly. Even to this day, Mike Geary is one of my best friends. He has been by my side throughout my football and professional wrestling careers. We look after each other like brothers. He uplifts me, and I do the same for him. Mike is currently fighting cancer and I know that he will beat it.

Bill arranged for me to train at his house in Bixby, Oklahoma. Since I didn't have a car, Mike drove me from Norman to Bixby. When we arrived, I thought I was in a compound. There were huge fences and a bunch of mean-looking German Shepherd dogs everywhere. As Mike drove off, I wasn't feeling too comfortable with my surroundings.

> MIKE GEARY: DOC WOULD NEVER BACK DOWN FROM A CHALLENGE. I KNEW HE WANTED TO WRESTLE AND SAW IT AS A WAY TO MAKE SOME MONEY. BUT AS WE GOT CLOSER TO WATTS' HOME, I SENSED THE INTEREST WAS WANING.
>
> KEEP IN MIND, YOU HAVE THIS KID IN HIS EARLY 20S HEADING TO TRAIN AND STAY WITH BILL WATTS. BILL WAS HIMSELF ONE GRUFF AND INTIMIDATING GUY. HE WAS VERY BIG AND BURLY AND HAD A VERY AGGRESSIVE PERSONALITY. GRANTED THAT DOC WAS TO ME THE BADDEST GUY IN THE WORLD, BUT WE ARE TALKING ABOUT BILL WATTS, PROFESSIONAL WRESTLING, AND DRIVING TO A PLACE THAT WAS IN THE MIDDLE OF NOWHERE.
>
> AS I DROVE OVER WHAT SEEMED LIKE A MOAT, I WAS LOOKING FOR THE DARN DRAWBRIDGE TO OPEN AND CLOSE BEHIND US. I WAS MYSELF INTIMIDATED JUST BY HIS FACILITY. I PARKED THE CAR AT THE FRONT GATE AND DROPPED DOC OFF. AS I WAS LEAVING, DOC HAD A LOOK ON HIS FACE LIKE HE WAS GOING TO CRY. BUT HE DIDN'T. IT TURNED OUT TO BE A GREAT EXPERIENCE.

Bill greeted me and invited me into his home. Though he was tough, he treated me like a member of the family. He let me stay in his private cabana and provided me with three meals a day, and then some. I was advised that training would begin in the morning. So the rest of the day, Bill and I chatted and immediately bonded. Even though his German Shepherds never stopped barking, Bill's hospitality and friendliness calmed my nerves.

The next morning, I met my wrestling trainers, Billy Star and the TURK (Ali Baba). The three of us joined Bill Watts in his garage to start training. Bill had just built the garage, and you could still smell the fresh paint on the walls. There was no ring, just some amateur wrestling mats on top of the concrete floor.

> BILL WATTS: WHILE STEVE WAS AT OU, I GOT TO KNOW DOC'S FATHER, JERRY. WE BECAME GOOD FRIENDS. BECAUSE OF MY RELATIONSHIP WITH HIS DAD, I GOT TO KNOW DOC AND TREATED HIM LIKE A MEMBER OF MY FAMILY. I TREATED HIM WITH A LOT OF CARE AND RESPECT.

Billy Star and the TURK were average-looking guys and much smaller than I. Along with Bill Watts, the TURK was the main trainer, and he knew his stuff. I listened attentively to their direction and lessons. They started out my training with some cardiovascular work and stretching. I was then walked through some basic wrestling mat moves, which I quickly picked up.

Seeing that I caught on quite quickly, the TURK decided to teach me how to do a headlock. To demonstrate, he snatched me into this wrestling hold. The TURK then showed me how to run the ropes, even though there were none. The edge of the mats served as the ropes for demonstration purposes. I watched Billy and the TURK run the invisible ropes. I then watched as they shoulder-tackled each other coming off the ropes and then bumped (fell) to the mat.

Then it was my turn. I ran the invisible ropes. I took a shoulder tackle and bumped to the mat. When I landed, not only did I get the wind knocked out of me, but I felt a sharp pain in my back from the impact of the concrete floor. I got up, asking myself, "What in the world am I doing here?"

There I was, a consensus All-America football player preparing for the best year of my life. With hopes of being drafted by the NFL, why would I risk an injury and mess up everything I had worked so hard to achieve? I thought to myself it was time to find other summer job opportunities.

But you know what? I got up. And I got up again. And then I started to catch on and bump correctly. It wasn't that bad. I really started to enjoy the physical contact.

Once again, the TURK put me in a headlock. I was told to push him off into the invisible rope. We did it slowly the first time. We did it again and the TURK said, "This time, a little quicker." I pushed the TURK so hard that he hit the wall! Let me rephrase: I shoved him right into Bill Watts' brand new, freshly painted garage wall!

As you could imagine, Bill Watts was furious. He immediately stopped the training and told everyone to pack their bags. Bill said to me, "That is all the training here. You are going to Shreveport to train in a wrestling ring." I gathered my stuff and followed everyone to Shreveport. Bill asked me to drive his Mercedes. He had just sold his car to the Junkyard Dog and needed someone to drive it to him. I had no problem accommodating the request.

Once in Shreveport, we pulled into the local Boys Club, where Bill did his Mid-South TV tapings. It must have been 120 degrees in that place. But the TURK got me right in the ring and we continued training. I was definitely overdressed, in my basic amateur wrestling attire: singlet, sweats, plastics, and tennis shoes. By the end of the day, I was sweating so much from the heat that I trained in nothing but my underwear!

Let me categorically state that wrestling training was extremely difficult. Because of my background and excellent condition, I quickly grasped the basic wrestling moves. However, running the ropes was another story.

The TURK showed me how to properly run the ropes with real ropes. When it was my turn, I hit the ropes with full force. I couldn't believe the impact it had on my ribs. Every time I hit the ropes, it hurt even more. I was in some serious pain. And I was getting mad.

No one in attendance could believe how hard I hit the ropes. It seemed like I was trying to break them. And I was. I was mad that I had to train in the first place, not to mention that I had to do it in such a hot and humid building.

A few weeks passed as I learned other professional wrestling moves, such as a suplex, backdrop, and body slam. I really started to like the sport. I learned about safety and how to protect my opponent. Bill Watts taught me about the many aspects of the professional wrestling industry, but respect for the business and safety was paramount. To make it in the business you had to respect the business and the people in it. I listened to every word that came out of Bill's mouth. I valued what Bill said and I appreciated his commitment to the sport and his effort to go at it 110 percent.

I probably trained for about six weeks. Bill knew I could handle the basics of the mat, and the TURK and Billy taught me power moves and high spots. Bill knew that I had to get under the lights to truly learn. He knew that he had a great talent and by then, I was very much interested in the professional wrestling industry.

For the rest of the summer, I wrestled a few matches while paying my dues. I watched and listened to the veterans of the sport. I made some new friends and began to really enjoy the business. I also earned some spending money.

I left Shreveport in mid-summer. It was time for summer football practice back at OU. I literally went from wrestling a match Friday night to the football field Saturday morning. Though I had really taken an interest in professional wrestling, I was committed to playing left guard for Barry Switzer.

> BUDDY LANDELL: I MET STEVE WHEN HE WAS STILL AT OU. WE REALLY TOOK A LIKING TO EACH OTHER AND BECAME FRIENDS. I WRESTLED STEVE IN HIS FIRST PROFESSIONAL WRESTLING MATCH. THE ONE THING THAT STOOD OUT WAS THAT STEVE WAS SUPER STRONG. I REMEMBER TAKING A SHOULDER BLOCK FROM HIM AND IT FELT LIKE I WAS HIT BY A CAR.

Early in summer practice, word leaked out that I had

become a professional wrestler. My parents found out and they were okay with it. Plus, because Coach Switzer knew that I wasn't going to be wrestling anymore, or at least during the football season, he couldn't be upset with me. He used to tell reporters that he liked the idea of having a professional wrestler on his team.

During training camp, reporters from the entire county covered the Oklahoma football program. But they were also there to see me. A preseason All-America football player and a professional wrestler, I was the main event. I received a tremendous amount of attention—and I liked it.

It was at this time that I started to protect the wrestling business. Granted, I was "green," but I still remembered what Bill Watts and the others had taught me. Reporters asked me if wrestling was fake and other superficial things. I protected the business like I was a seasoned veteran.

One time before football practice, a reporter asked me if wrestling was fake. With a look of incomprehension, I pulled up my shirt revealing the bruises to my ribs and said, "Let me show you something. Count them!" The reporter counted 42 bruises on the side of my ribs. I continued, "You call this fake?"

Although we lost to Arizona State in the Fiesta Bowl, I knew that I had had a good enough senior year to be drafted. I didn't care about academics my final semester and yearned to get back into the ring. As I waited for the spring football draft, I went back to work for Bill Watts. Standing 6-foot-2 and weighing a natural 290 pounds at 23 years old, I started my first major professional wrestling angle with Bob Roop.

I had fallen in love with the business. From the wrestling moves to the physical conduct to the roar of the fans, I felt at home in the wrestling ring. As a heel, I loved to hear people "boo" me. The feeling that I had in the wrestling ring is unexplainable. Only those in the business can truly understand the emotion.

Subsequent to being drafted, my wrestling career was once again put on hold. But after being cut from the New Jersey Generals in the summer of 1984, I again contacted Bill Watts. Bill and I had kept in contact throughout my tenure in New Jersey. From my brother Jerry's house in San Diego, I asked, "Bill, can I come to work?"

Bill said, "I'll tell you what, kid. You have to promise me that you will NEVER go back into professional football again."

Hesitant, I told Bill, "Okay, I'll call you right back."

It was now decision-making time. My entire life had been committed to becoming a professional football player. Though I was cut from New Jersey, a part of me believed I could still play at the professional level.

After a few days of contemplation, I called Bill Watts. "Bill, I made up my mind, and I want to be a professional wrestler full time. I am done playing football."

Bill said, "Okay, kid. Hop on the next plane to New Orleans and I will meet you there." So I did.

I didn't sign any long-term contract. I didn't have a car or a place to stay. I had no health insurance and wasn't guaranteed anything. The only thing I had was Bill's word. He said that if I listened to him, he would take care of me. I respected and trusted him, and that was good enough for me. I became a full-time wrestler with the Mid-South wrestling promotion.

Bill had started the Mid-South wrestling promotion in 1979. He is viewed as one of the best promoters in the business. Because of his leadership and vision, people packed the arenas. They also watched us on TV, where our television shows garnered high ratings. We sold out every arena.

> JERRY WILLIAMS: AFTER STEVE WAS CUT AND LET GO FROM THE NJ GENERALS, HE CAME TO MY HOUSE TO VISIT. STEVE WAS DEVASTATED, BUT I TOLD HIM IF HE KEPT TRYING, HE WOULD MAKE IT TO EITHER THE USFL OR NFL. AFTER HOURS OF DISCUSSION AND TOGETHER EXAMINING THE PROS AND CONS OF WRESTLING, AS WELL AS THE MARKETABILITY OF "DR. DEATH" IN PROFESSIONAL WRESTLING, I SUPPORTED STEVE'S DECISION TO GO INTO WRESTLING FULL TIME. I ENCOURAGED STEVE SHORTLY AFTER THAT TO CREATE AN IMAGE THAT PEOPLE COULD RELATE TO, GOOD OR EVIL. HE DID MORE THAN THAT! STEVE LEARNED VERY QUICKLY ABOUT HOW TO CREATE A MARKETABLE IMAGE. STEVE'S DECISION TO QUIT FOOTBALL AND GET INTO WRESTLING WAS THE CORRECT ONE!

Mid-South had the best wrestlers who knew how to work the crowd. We had guys whose personas distorted the lines between good and evil. Unlike other promotions, which portrayed their talents as cartoon characters and conducted tacky interviews, Mid-South Wrestling was for real.

I think people really liked Mid-South because of our focus on energetic matches. With the creative mind of Bill Watts and also, later, Bill Dundee, every match was a main event. Everything we did in the ring made sense. The talent worked very hard to provide the fans with a match they would never forget. And we did it every day of the week.

> BILL WATTS: DOC FIT RIGHT IN WITH MID-SOUTH WRESTLING. I HAD THE BEST WORKERS AND TOUGHEST GUYS IN THE BUSINESS WORKING FOR ME. DOC WAS INDEED BOTH TOUGH AND RUGGED. HE WAS ALSO EXTREMELY TALENTED WITH LEGITIMATE ATHLETIC CREDENTIALS. I NEVER CONSIDERED DOC TO HAVE GREAT TECHNIQUE AND AT FIRST HE WASN'T A GREAT WORKER. BUT WHAT HE HAD WAS MORE SIGNIFICANT: A FORCE OF WILL AND A HEART. HE WOULD GO ALL OUT AND JUST DESTROY PEOPLE. HE GOT OVER IT BECAUSE OF HIS PERSONALITY AND BECAUSE HE WAS A FORCE.

The Mid-South territory hit all the big towns in the region, such as Shreveport, Jackson, Oklahoma City, Tulsa, Baton Rouge, and New Orleans. We also hit the small towns, like Lake Charles, Monroe, Houma, and Lafayette. At 23 years old, I loved every town. New Orleans was probably my favorite because of the French Quarter and Bourbon Street. I was fascinated by the hotels, restaurants, shops, historic homes, museums, attractions, and of course, the bars and clubs.

Since I wasn't driving, I didn't mind some of the long rides. The roads of Louisiana and Mississippi weren't the best, but I was young and full of energy. No matter where we were, we had to be in Shreveport on Wednesdays for our television tapings. At times I would catch a ride with Sylvester Ritter, the Junkyard Dog, after our Baton Rouge show. We would leave the venue around 1 a.m. and make the five-hour drive back to Shreveport in time for the 8 a.m. tapings.

Junkyard Dog was an excellent human being. He wasn't the greatest technical wrestler, but Bill always put him with workers who could make him look good. Without a shadow of doubt, he was the best on the microphone. Junkyard Dog got on the stick and talked to the fans in such a way that they believed every word coming from his mouth. More importantly, they came to the arena in droves to support him. Everyone loved the Junkyard Dog, especially the African-American fans in our territory.

I learned a lot from Junkyard Dog. He coached me in working on the microphone. He told me about the importance of psychology in the ring. He was a great teacher. When he died a few years back in an automobile accident, I was blown away.

At the time I was Bill Watts' protégé. Bill served as my mentor and looked out for me. But I was never given anything in the business. I started in the territory making anywhere from $15 to $25 a match. I always got paid with a business check. As an

RICKY MORTON: DURING A TAG MATCH BETWEEN RICKY AND ME [ROCK-N-ROLL EXPRESS] AGAINST DOC AND HERCULES HERNANDEZ IN HOUMA [LOUISIANA], I TOLD DOC BEFORE OUR MATCH TO WATCH THE FANS IN THIS TOWN. THEY ARE WILD AND CRAZY CAJUNS. IN ONLY A WAY DOC COULD RESPOND, HE SAID, "SCREW THEM."

WELL, HALFWAY THROUGH OUR MATCH, I'M SELLING BIG-TIME. DOC QUICKLY COMES OVER TO ME AND YELLS AT ME TO "GET UP AND MAKE A COMEBACK!" I LOOK ACROSS THE RING AND SEE ABOUT 30 RABID CAJUNS IN THE RING. DOC, IS FIGHTING THEM ONE BY ONE, AND ALSO TENDING TO OUR MATCH IN THE RING. IT WAS TOTAL PANDEMONIUM.

THE MATCH WAS CALLED A DISQUALIFICATION AND THE REF AND I HEADED BACK TO THE DRESSING ROOM. DOC, WHO IS THE STRONGEST AND TOUGHEST WRESTLER I HAVE EVER MET, WAS FIGHTING THE FANS AS HE HEADED BACK TO THE DRESSING ROOM. DOC MADE IT TO THE DRESSING ROOM, BUT LO AND BEHOLD THE DOOR WAS LOCKED. DOC COULDN'T GET IN!

WITH WHAT SEEMED LIKE MINIMAL EFFORT, DOC KICKED THE HEAVY STEEL DOOR DOWN, RIPPING IT RIGHT OF THE HINGES. IT WAS UNREAL. DOC GRABBED HIS STUFF AND WITH THE HELP OF THE POLICE AND SECURITY, LEFT THE ARENA UNSCRATCHED. THERE MUST HAVE BEEN 50 BEATEN COON-ASS CAJUNS LYING ON THE GROUND.

> BUDDY LANDELL: BILL WATTS LOVED STEVE WILLIAMS. THAT WAS HIS MAN. BILL IS A GREAT MAN AND ONE OF THE BEST PROMOTERS IN THE BUSINESS.

independent contractor, I was responsible for all my taxes and deductions. The amount of money received was based on the attendance from the gate. I always looked forward to wrestling in the New Orleans Superdome, where I was always guaranteed a nice payday—at least $150 for the night.

Bill Watts often exchanged talent with other promotions. I appreciated it when he sent me to work for Houston promoter Paul Boesch. Bill and Paul formed an alliance to feature Mid-South talent on the cards at the Sam Houston Coliseum. I wrestled guys like Gino Hernandez and Chris Adams. I really liked Houston and it paid well, sometimes $500 a night.

NINE

STORIES FROM MID-SOUTH

I was in the ring with some of the greatest athletes in the world. As the days and weeks went on, I learned and listened to the sport's veterans. I wanted to be the best. After mastering the actual wrestling part, I learned about strategy, psychology, and the ability to tell a story in the ring. I was a student learning from my wrestling professors, such as Ted DiBiase, Terry Taylor, Bob Sweetan, Barry Darsow, Buddy Landell, Jim Duggan, Ernie Ladd, Mike Sharpe, King Kong Bundy, and of course, Bill Watts.

> TED DIBIASE: I took Doc under my wing. We traveled together and worked as a tag-team. We even fought each other, and he is not afraid of anything. He is a great friend and we had and continue to have great times together.
>
> Doc is naturally strong. I don't think he ever realized how strong he really was. For example, one time I was wrestling against Steve in Lafayette [Louisiana]. I had Doc in the corner and told him that I wanted him to reverse me when I threw him into the turnbuckle, then dropped down into [his] football tackle stance. Well, Doc took me literally and instead of him dropping down into a stance where I would do a backdrop, he hit me with that three-point stand football tackle and knocked me clear across the ring into the far turnbuckle! I will never forget that move. I don't think he knew his own strength.

Ribbing was part of the business. Some were honestly pranks, whereas others were downright disgusting. The British Bulldogs were the mean ribbers. I didn't believe in mean ribbing, such as pissing and pooping in wrestlers' beds, like the Bulldogs did to this poor, drunk wrestler in Japan. When I first started out in the business, I was taught that my wrestling gear, boots, and pads for the show were packed in my bag. I didn't have the money to buy boots. Fortunately, Bill Watts gave me a pair of his fancy boots. My mentor looked out for me, and I took care of those boots.

Anyway, I always kept my stuff neatly packed and organized. On a trip to Baton Rouge, Louisiana, I shared a room with Billy Star. He had real long hair, and was a jobber in the business. He was a great guy and always made me laugh.

Unfortunately, when I got into my bag to get my boots for the show in the locker room, I couldn't find them. I was furious and started asking around. I went unglued. I thought somebody had stolen my boots. Nobody knew what had happened to them. I was cursing up a storm. I had to wrestle in my tennis shoes—and they weren't too comfortable.

When I got back to the hotel after the matches, my boots were stuck underneath my bed. Yep, Billy Star gave me my first rib in the business.

I played it off, acting like everything was fine. But revenge was on my mind. I guess you could say I put on my poker face and would get payback real soon. The next day, I went to the local WalMart and purchased a tube of Nair hair remover. I put it in Billy Star's hair conditioner. Remember, Bill had long hair. It took a few washes, but little by little, Billy's hair started turning a different color and eventually began to fall out. This was my rib of the business. I pulled many funny ribs throughout my career, such as super-gluing someone's shoes to the floor. But I never did or condoned mean ribs.

I remember one of my earlier matches against the Rock-n-Roll Express. Bill Watts invited the entire OU wrestling team to watch Ted DiBiase and me take on these pretty boys in Oklahoma City, Oklahoma. The entire team showed up, and they all had complimentary ringside seats.

As I beat the tar out of Ricky Morton, a fan favorite, I could hear the wrestling team chanting, "OU, OU, OU." Their chants were firing me up. With each chant, I hit Ricky harder and harder.

Ricky had enough and shouted to the wrestling team, "Stop saying OU, OU!"

Ricky's partner, Robert Gibson was even shouting to the crowd, "Stop saying OU, OU!"

The female fans were also getting mad at me because I was pounding the tar out of their pretty boys. I said nasty things to those women and then followed up with a cheap shot on Ricky Morton or Robert Gibson. These two guys had such a female fan following. After my matches with them, I often had to watch my back leaving the arena, because these ladies literally tried to hurt me.

The first person in Mid-South that I really got to know was Mike Sharpe. You could probably say that Mike mentored me throughout my first full year in Mid-South. Mike is a straight-up, classy guy. He is very personable and easy to talk to. Since I didn't own a car, I shared in the expense and rode with Mike from town to town. We were always the first ones to the arena and the last ones to leave.

He taught me about financial responsibility. He

RICKY MORTON: DOC IS A GREAT GUY, AND I REMEMBER WHEN HE FIRST GOT IN THE BUSINESS. HE WAS HUGE AND STRONG AS A BULL. AT A MATCH IN OKLAHOMA CITY BETWEEN TED DIBIASE AND DOC AGAINST ROBERT AND ME, THERE MUST HAVE BEEN 10,000 FANS IN THE BUILDING. WE WERE THE FACES AND DOC AND TED WERE THE HEELS. BOTH MEN ARE GREAT WORKERS, AND EVEN THOUGH THEY WERE MUCH LARGER THAN WE WERE, ESPECIALLY DOC, THEY WERE DOING THEIR JOB TO GET US OVER.

WELL, UNBEKNOWNST TO ME, DOC INVITED THE ENTIRE OU WRESTLING TEAM TO THE EVENT. THROUGHOUT THE MATCH, THESE GUYS WERE CHANTING AND SCREAMING, "OU, OU, OU!" IT WAS DEAFENING.

NEAR THE END OF THE MATCH, THE CHANTS ARE GETTING LOUDER. ALL OF A SUDDEN, THERE WAS A LOOK IN DOC'S EYES THAT HE WAS GOING TO SNAP ME IN HALF. HE SEEMED LIKE HE WAS IN A TRANCE. I WAS SCARED OUT OF MY MIND AND STARTED RUNNING AROUND THE RING AND DOING CARTWHEELS TO GET AWAY FROM DOC. I KEPT SAYING, "DOC, IT'S ME! PLEASE DON'T KILL ME!"

IN THE END, DOC WAS THE TRUE PROFESSIONAL, AND I PINNED HIM.

> MIKE GEARY: EVERY TIME DOC CAME TO OKLAHOMA, THE BOYS AND I WOULD GO TO HIS MATCHES. THOUGH DOC WAS A HEEL AT THE TIME, WE WOULD STILL CHANT FOR DOC. AFTER ONE MATCH IN TULSA AGAINST THE ROCK-N-ROLL EXPRESS, THESE FEMALE FANS WERE LIVID AT DOC FOR HIS TREATMENT OF BOTH THE EXPRESS AND THEM. HE WOULD SAY MANY BAD THINGS TO GET THE CROWD GOING.
>
> WE ALL FELL OUT OF OUR CHAIRS WHEN DOC TOLD THIS 300-PLUS-POUND LADY WHO WAS NAGGING HIM, "HEY LADY, DO YOU KNOW YOU ARE REALLY FAT?" THIS DIDN'T SET TO WELL WITH THE CROWD NOR THE DROVES OF DIE-HARD ROCK-N-ROLL EXPRESS FANS.
>
> WHEN THE MATCH EVENING CONCLUDING, THERE WERE ABOUT FIVE TO SIX YOUNG LADIES WAITING OUTSIDE THE ARENA TO JUMP DOC. SO WE PUT DOC IN THE TRUNK OF OUR CAR AND HE ESCAPED ANOTHER DAY TO DO FUTURE DAMAGE TO OTHER FAN FAVORITES.

told me to keep all my receipts that were business-related so I could write them off at the end of the year. I watched my spending and saved as much as I could. Mike genuinely looked out for me.

He also taught me about proper hygiene. Mike was a "clean freak." When we arrived at the arena, Mike would take a shower. After working some spots and preparing for the evening's matches, Mike would take another shower. Once his match concluded, Mike would take another shower. And when we arrived at the hotel, he would take what seemed like a three-hour shower right before bed. He must have taken four to five showers a day!

I also got to know Hacksaw Jim Duggan really well. After a few months of feeling each other out, Jim and I became the best of friends—and still are, even to this day. I learned a lot from Jim, especially respect for the business. Jim was also a great athlete, and we used to workout together. We even became roommates in the territory. Though Jim couldn't cook a lick, we had a great time sharing his home in Louisiana.

Jim and I also got into our share of trouble. I will never forget that night in Louisiana at the Lighthouse nightclub. It was your typical metal, square-box building with too many people and too many drinks. Hercules

Ray Hernandez and I were minding our own business at the bar counter, when all of a sudden we saw Jim throwing ice our way. Unfortunately, it hit this young lady we were talking with. Boy, she got so mad at Hacksaw that she went after him with her drinking glass. Next thing you know, Hercules and I had to fight our way out of the bar. We were knocking people out left and right. Even when we got to the parking lot, these rowdy guys were jumping and kicking our car. We knew we couldn't lose, because if we lost a bar fight, Bill Watts would have fired us. I never lost a bar fight. But before we could leave the parking lot, the police arrived and I was issued a DUI. I still don't know why Jim thought we had thrown ice at him.

> BILL WATTS: DURING HIS FIRST YEAR, WE WANTED TO PUT SOMEONE WITH DOC WHO WAS STABLE. MIKE WAS THAT PERSON. MIKE WAS NEVER A BIG-NAME WRESTLER, BUT HE WAS VERY RELIABLE. HE WAS ALWAYS ON TIME TO THE BUILDING, NEVER COMPLAINED, IN CONDITION, AND WORKED HARD IN THE RING. WE KNEW MIKE WOULD BE A VERY GOOD, STABILIZING INFLUENCE ON DOC WHILE HE WAS GETTING STARTED IN THE BUSINESS.

I love my ex-wife Tammy. We met while I was wrestling for Bill Watts' Mid-South promotion. She was extremely attractive and had a cute smile. I saw her a few times at the matches and decided to use the Steve Williams charm to woo her. Well, actually, I spoke to one of her friends and told her to tell Tammy that I was interested and wanted to visit

> HACKSAW JIM DUGGAN: DOC IS ONE OF ONLY THREE ROOMMATES THAT I HAVE HAD IN MY PROFESSIONAL WRESTLING CAREER [TERRY GORDY AND GINO HERNANDEZ ARE THE OTHERS]. THOUGH WE WERE LIKE THE ODD COUPLE, DOC WAS THE PERFECT ROOMMATE. HE WAS VERY NEAT AND CLEAN, AND ABSOLUTELY A GREAT COOK. I WAS THE MESSY AND SLOPPY GUY. WE USED TO ALSO RUN AND TRAIN TOGETHER. IN FACT, WE USED TO DO A LOT OF RUNNING. ON LONG ROAD TRIPS SUCH AS TO HOUSTON OR TULSA, MY WIFE, DEBBIE, WOULD STOP THE CAR AND DROP DOC AND ME OFF ON THE SIDE OF THE ROAD. SHE WOULD THEN DRIVE A FEW MILES DOWN THE ROAD AND WAIT FOR US.

Hacksaw Jim Duggan: Doc is one of the most legit tough guys in the business. One night at the Lighthouse nightclub, often referred to as the "Fight House," I started to get pelted with ice. I looked in the direction where it was coming from, and I saw Doc and Hercules Hernandez at the bar. I figured it had to be them. So, I took a chunk of ice and threw it at Doc. I missed Doc and hit this girl right next to him.

Well, this young lady was pissed off and she started coming at me with her glass in her hand. She telegraphed it like she was going to throw it at me. As she got closer, she threw the glass and I easily side-stepped it. Well, now she was really mad and started throwing punches at me. I managed to keep her away, but one of her friends came toward me and tried to take a shot. I decked this guy and knocked him clear across the room—right next to Doc and Hercules. This guy looked up at Hercules, who was a heel, and made a face like, "Let's get Hercules." Hercules simply knocked the guy completely out. All of a sudden, everybody in the place started attacking Doc and Hercules. Like a scene out of a John Wayne western movie, the band stopped playing, the lights came on, and the place was in total chaos.

Doc and Hercules had two completely different ways of throwing punches. Hercules threw these large windmill punches, where Doc was like a robot, throwing short, devastating jabs. Both of them were cleaning house, knocking people everywhere. There were bodies dropping all over the place. Since I was in a feud with them, the crowd started chanting: "Duggan, Duggan, Duggan," in an effort to get me to fight these heels. But I knew better. As Doc and Hercules were punching their way out of the building, I quickly exited through the back door. On the way out, I ran into Terry Taylor, who unluckily happened to walk right into the melee only to get knocked out! Funny thing is that to this day, Doc swears that it wasn't them who threw the ice.

with her. After some small talk, she decided to go out with me.

After some time, we got married. Tammy already had one child, Stormy. I adopted her. We later had a son together, Wyndam. Due to our differences, after seven years of marriage, Tammy and I divorced. After some reconciliation, we married again, only to divorce for a second time after five years.

I will be the first to admit that the wrestling business takes a toll on a relationship. The traveling, stress, and wear and tear on the body is overwhelming. If I could turn back time, I am sure that both of us would have done things differently. Though Tammy and I are divorced, we share the two most important people in my life, Stormy and Wyndam.

> TAMMY BREWSTER: I FIRST MET STEVEN WHEN I USED TO ATTEND THE WRESTLING MATCHES AT THE BOYS CLUB AT THE LOUISIANA FAIR GROUNDS IN SHREVEPORT. I WAS A WRESTLING FAN AND ENJOYED GOING TO THE MATCHES. ONE TIME, MY FRIEND, BELINDA HERNANDEZ, TOLD ME THAT STEVEN WAS INTERESTED IN ME AND WANTED TO TALK TO ME. I WAS A TAD CONCERNED BECAUSE I BELIEVED WRESTLING AND DIDN'T LIKE STEVE BECAUSE HE WAS ALWAYS BEATING UP TERRY TAYLOR.
>
> AFTER I GOT TO KNOW STEVEN, I REALLY TOOK A LIKING TO HIM. HE WASN'T MEAN AT ALL. HE WAS SWEET AND GENTLE, LIKE A BIG OL' TEDDY BEAR.

I got in many bar fights throughout my Mid-South wrestling tenure. Many occurred at a bar called Cowboys (it has since changed its name to the Rockin' Rodeo). Since all the talent had to be in Shreveport on Wednesday morning for TV, the boys tried to get back from Jackson, Lake Charles, Lafayette, or wherever they were Tuesday evening to go to Cowboys. It was located next to the Sheraton hotel, where we all stayed. Everybody at the bar knew and treated us well.

One evening, I was there with Buddy Landell, Hercules, and my ex-wife, Tammy. I had just started dating her and was madly in love. I was out on the dance floor dancing and kissing her all over. Out of nowhere, five police officers came up to me. They tapped me on the shoulder. I turned around, saw them, and quipped, "What in the world did I do now?"

TAMMY BREWSTER: I have often been asked what it is like to be married to Steven 'Dr. Death' Williams. We had our good times and bad times. He took me places that I had never been to and probably would have never seen without him. We were going to Japan and Hawaii on a regular basis. He also bought me very nice things.

Steve's lifestyle also affected our relationship in a bad way. I used to tell people I felt like I was living with a rock-n-roll star. He wasn't around a lot, and a few times I accused him of fooling around with other women. At times, our relationship was very emotional and hurtful.

Though he may not have always been the best husband, he is a wonderful dad. He even adopted my daughter, Stormy. Steven is categorically an excellent father to both Wyndam and Stormy. He is also like a father to my other child, Levi.

A cop pointed to the other side of the room and said, "You guys got to get out of here."

I had been drinking Greyhounds (vodka and grapefruit juice), so I was feeling pretty good. I asked, "Why do I have to get out of here? The only thing I have been doing is dancing and having fun with my girlfriend!"

One of the cops knew me and said, "Well, some of your buddies over there are causing trouble. They are talking trash, and it looks like they are going to start a fight."

I should have known. Buddy Landell was running his mouth again. Buddy was another guy I got along with. Buddy was a great worker and, at one time, was the Mid-South Television Champion. Sporting dyed blonde hair, "Nature Boy" Buddy Landell, like me, loved to drink and party. And we had a grand time on the road.

BUDDY LANDELL: Steve was this big, tough guy. I was the young and brash instigator. We just took a liking to each other. We got along real well. But when it came to fighting, I would always start the fight and run. And Steve would have to finish it.

The problem with Buddy was that he often couldn't keep his mouth shut. He was the "mouth of the south" and always looking to pick a fight. I loved the guy, but when the fights started he was nowhere to be found. I was often left to do the heavy hitting, as well as spend nights in jail.

Anyway, I looked to the back to see Buddy and Hercules surrounded by every male patron in the bar. There was about to be a huge gang fight, literally 100 versus two. I knew the patrons wouldn't stand a chance 100 versus three, but I was in love and was having a great time with my girlfriend. The last thing on my mind was fighting. So with the police behind me, I rushed over and told Buddy and Hercules, "We need to get out of here."

As we left the bar, the cops escorted Buddy and Hercules, my soon-to-be wife, Tammy, and me out of the bar. As I passed through the front door, some guy popped me in the face from behind. Man, like a bull, I went chasing after this coward. As I got closer, all of a sudden a cop stepped in front of the now-fallen punk and me. It was "go" time.

With rage running through my veins, I pointed my finger at this police officer and said, "Kid, you must be a rookie cop." I was going to beat the living tar out of this guy and anyone else who got in my way. But as I turned to Tammy, who was screaming for me to stop, this rookie cop jumped on my back and tried to put the sleeper hold on me. He also wedged his knee into my lower back.

Out of instinct, the only thing I could do was drop down in a three-point stand and head for something that would get this cop off my back. The first thing I saw was the police paddy wagon. With the target locked in, I headed right to it. I was running as fast as I could, like a snorting bull. With the cop screaming for me to stop, I put on the brakes right before hitting the paddy wagon. The cop flew off and he hit the paddy wagon, which knocked him unconscious. Simultaneously, I felt these sharp pains to my lower back and legs. I turned around and saw about 20 cops beating me down. I was soon handcuffed and my ankles were chained.

I was thrown in the police car and taken downtown. Tammy later told me that, when they arrested me, she overheard the police dispatch. The police called the jail and told them to move everybody out of the big jail cell. They had just arrested the toughest SOB around and they were bringing him in. The dispatcher radioed back and asked, "Who is it?"

They said, "Dr. Death is coming to jail."

The dispatcher simply replied in a concerned tone, "Oh, my."

I spent the night in jail, and the next morning I had my hearing. Twenty cops must have been in attendance. It seemed that everyone gave a statement. The judge told me to stand. He asked, "What were you thinking?"

I said, "Nothing. I was there with my girlfriend, minding my own business. I tried to be a good guy and get my friends out of there before a fight broke out. The next thing I know is that I get hit in the face from behind. I was simply defending myself."

After a few back-and-forth comments, the judge took a short break. When he came back, the judge asked me to stand. He then told me to approach the bar. In a stereotypical manner of Louisiana justice, he said, "Mr. Williams, to terminate the charge of battery on an officer, the fine is $5,000. I can give you a break, but I have to work with these officers for the rest of my life." I had just started the business and $5,000 was a lot of money to me back then. I had no choice, so I accepted the judge's offer and paid the fine.

Another incident that occurred at Cowboys could have really damaged my reputation and life. Prior to dating Tammy, I met a very attractive young lady on the dance floor. We drank and danced all night. When the bar shut down, we both headed back to my place. A few hours later, I dropped her back off at the bar parking lot.

The next morning, I got a knock on my door. The cops asked me a few questions. The police then told me that the young lady who had spent the early morning hours with me said I had raped her! I was stunned. I pleaded my side, but the police arrested me and took me downtown.

I couldn't believe this allegation. I once again appeared before the court. I pleaded not guilty and was released on bond. A court date was set. It was unreal, and evil things started to run through my mind.

Fortunately, the young lady eventually dropped all charges. I later found out that she made up this charge of rape because she felt I had disrespected her. She wanted to get all cozy and serious. In one short evening, she had somehow developed some feelings toward me. I simply used her and then dropped her back off at her vehicle without even getting her phone number or saying good night. I would be a whole lot more careful in the future.

The cops weren't always against me. One time, after partying all night long at Cowboys, Tammy and I jumped in my brand-new car to go back to the hotel. As I was backing up, I accidentally hit a parked semi truck. I shattered my front window and did major damage to the truck. I was pissed. But I was so drunk that I just left the car there and we walked back to my room at the Sheraton.

While at the hotel, I heard a knock on the door. Buck naked and still drunk, I opened the door. Three police officers were standing there. They said, "Mr. Williams, we need to talk to you."

I said, "What about?"

They said, "Why don't you go put on some clothes and let's talk outside." So I did just that.

Once in the hallway, the cops said, "Some people say you backed up your car into a semi, smashing both your car and doing major damage to the truck. And then you just left. That is called a hit and run."

I acknowledged the error. Yet, the cops surprisingly said, "But since we know you, we are going to let you off this time. Just don't let it happen again."

I said, "Thank you, I really appreciate it."

The next morning I had to drive to Oklahoma City in my Pontiac without a front window.

After a little more than a year wrestling full time for Mid-South, tragedy struck. My father died. After wrestling in a tag match with Ted DiBiase in Orange, Texas, I received a note to immediately call my mother. It had been more than a year since I had seen my mom or anyone else in the family. We talked quite frequently over the phone, and she always wanted to know when I was going to come home.

When I called Mom, she sounded serious and said, "Come home, Steven, your father is sick."

Shaken, I said, "Mom, what is wrong?"

I heard sniffles and sensed tears as Mom replied, "Just come home." She then hung up.

I was traumatized and didn't know what to think. Mom had never before spoken to me in that manner. She also had never told me to come home. I knew something was seriously wrong. About 60 seconds later, the phone I had called from rang. Once again, it was Mom. I asked what was wrong, and she said, "Steven, your father is dead. He died of a heart attack. Come home."

I stood there in shock for what seemed like an eternity. I couldn't believe that my father had passed away. I started weeping like a baby. I had lost my best friend.

After gaining my composure, I told Bill Watts that my father had died and I needed to go home. Bill hugged me and gave his condolences. He was pretty good friends with my dad and seemed truly upset. But Bill said that he still needed me for a show the next night in Houston, Texas.

Ted DiBiase and I were to defend our tag-team titles against Hector and Chavo Guerrero at the sold-out Sam Houston Coliseum. I was hesitant. Bill understood, but said, "If you work tomorrow night's show in Houston, when the show is over I will fly you in a private jet to Denver." Out of respect for Bill and the business, I reluctantly agreed.

It was a very sad evening and I didn't sleep all night. The boys—my extended family—were all compassionate and understanding. They all went out of their way to express their condolences.

As one could imagine, I was in no mood to perform the following evening. But I did. It wasn't hard to have a great match when you were in the ring with three great workers. As soon as it was over, I grabbed my stuff and was taken to the airport. I flew on a private jet nonstop to Stapleton Airport in Denver. When I arrived, my family was waiting for me.

Together, we began the mourning process and made all the funeral arrangements. It was the worst time in my life.

A few days after the funeral, my father's body was taken to the crematorium. He had wanted his ashes spread over the Colorado Mountains. Per Dad's request, the entire family drove up into the mountains. We went to the same place Dad used to take us fishing. It was a cloudy day. After saying the Lord's Prayer, we took his ashes from the urn and spread them along the mountains. Almost simultaneously, the clouds moved away and the sun started shining. We all knew that God had opened a path for my father to enter heaven.

After a couple of weeks of mourning with my family, I went back to work. I continued to team with and learn from Ted DiBiase. Ted was a class act and took his craft seriously. He was charming, in good shape, and an accomplished professional.

When Bill Watts brought in Ted, he told me to watch how Ted conducted himself in and out of the ring. I did just that. Ted was a technician, and I learned from him. I watched all his matches.

> TED DIBIASE: DOC ONCE TOOK ME TO A FOOTBALL GAME. AFTERWARDS, WE HAD TO GET OUT OF THE AREA AS QUICKLY AS POSSIBLE BECAUSE WE HAD A MATCH THAT EVENING. TO OUR DISMAY, TRAFFIC WAS AT A COMPLETE STANDSTILL. AFTER PATIENTLY WAITING, DOC LOOKED OVER AT ME WITH THAT CHILDISH GRIN. OUT OF THE BLUE, DOC FLOORED HIS VAN AND HE TOOK OFF, GOING IN THE OPPOSITE DIRECTION. THE COP WAS BLOWING HIS WHISTLE, ASKING DOC TO STOP. BUT WHAT COULD THE OFFICER DO? THERE WERE WAY TOO MANY PEOPLE. IN SHORT, DOC GOT US TO THE SHOW ON TIME
>
> IN ANOTHER TRAFFIC-RELATED STORY, THIS ONE CLOWN WAS SPEEDING IN AND OUT OF TRAFFIC AND WOULDN'T LET DOC PASS. HE KEPT SCREAMING AND CUSSING AT DOC. FINALLY, DOC WAS ABLE TO PASS THE MAN. DOC LOOKED OVER AND SAID, "I'M GOING TO TEACH THIS GUY A LESSON." DOC PUT ON HIS BRAKES, AND WE BOTH GET OUT OF THE CAR. WHEN THIS GUY SAW THE SIZE OF DOC, HE ROLLED UP HIS WINDOW AND LOOKED—NO PUN INTENDED—SCARED TO DEATH. HE DIDN'T SAY A PEEP THE ENTIRE TIME DOC WAS YELLING UP A STORM. RIGHT BEFORE WE LEFT, DOC SLAMMED HIS ARMS DOWN ON THE ROOF AND LEFT THE SHAPE OF A BIRDBATH ON HIS CAR. THE GUY STILL DIDN'T SAY A WORD.

Dick Murdoch and I go toe-to-toe.

Standing alongside my older brother, Jeff (22).

After one of many fishing trips, my dad and I show off our freshly caught Colorado Trout.

Heading out in my van on a ski trip in the Colorado Mountains with friends Kelly Mitchell, Tracy Kramer, and Eddie Stikes.

Even as an Oklahoma Sooner, I did my best to be an intimidating force in the ring.

Performing before large crowds has never been an issue for me.

Being interviewed at the NCAA nationals with coach Stan Abel and assistant coach Jeff Humphries.

Wearing no. 76, I also played football for the Sooners under legendary coach Barry Switzer.

Celebrating with my brother, Jeff, after he caught his first touchdown pass against Colorado.

Standing on Owen Field with my good friend, Jim Ross.

I give Paul Orndoff a suplex.

Donned in red and white, I fiercely enter the ring.

Massahiro Chono holds on for dear life right before he gets the Oklahoma Stampede.

Mat wrestling with Nikoli Volkoff in Mid-South.

Posing with my tag-team partner, Terry Gordy. Together, we dominated the wrestling world in the early '90s.

After winning the Triple Crown Heavyweight Championship in Tokyo, I celebrate with Johnny Ace.

My daughter, Stormy, rocks my son, Wyndam, on his first rocking horse.

My mother, Dottie, is always there for me.

Together with Stormy, Wyndam, and my ex-wife, Tammy, I enjoy Christmastime in Maui, Hawaii.

Shortly after being diagnosed with throat cancer, I am prepped for surgery at M.D. Anderson.

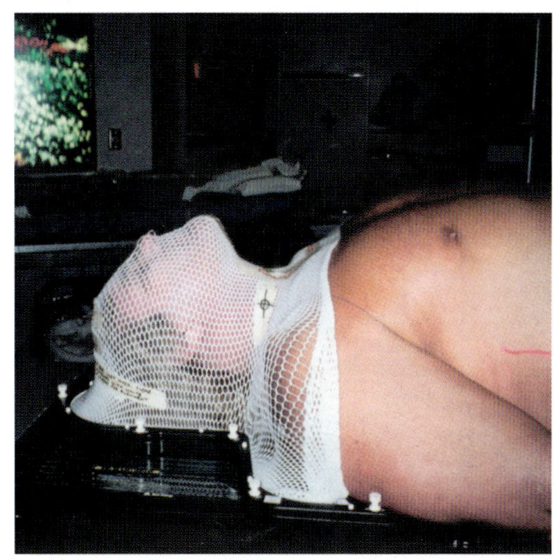

Unable to speak after my operation, I hold up a sign to show my frustration: "I can't stay here another day, it's killing me!"

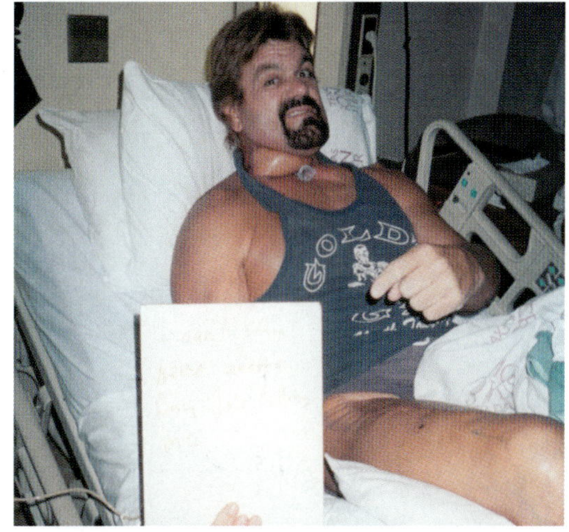

Stormy and her son, John Hudson, surprise me in recovery.

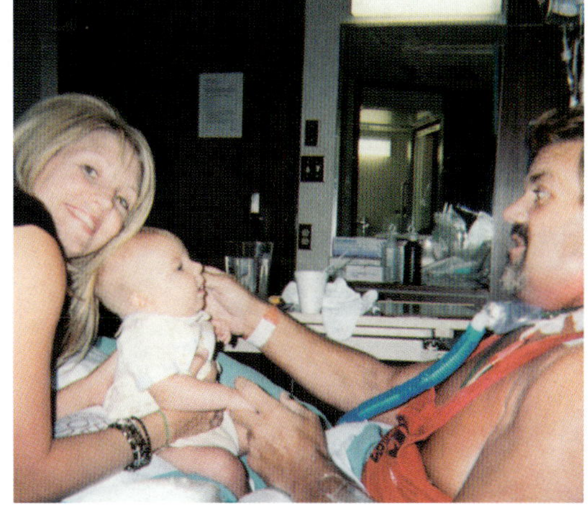

Standing with both Terry Funk and Jerry Lawler after we capture the MLW Six-Man tag belts.

Prior to a wrestling show, my son, Wyndam, and I let everyone know that the Buffalo wings are very hot at Six Flags in Buffalo, New York.

I now give my testimony to others in wrestling rings across the country.

Nobody could match up with Ted. When we teamed together, we were unstoppable.

Ted and I had many great times together. We both purchased a Nissan 300 ZX and sped down the roads like there was no tomorrow. We had great road trips in my van, and even though he is a Cornhusker fan, I still love him like my own flesh and blood. He taught me a tremendous amount in the business and has been a great influence on me in respect to Christianity.

Ted was probably the best technical wrestler I ever saw. But Andre the Giant was the biggest. I loved Andre. He was a great person and had a huge heart. He ate and drank more than any person I had ever seen. He was so big that my size 16 Big Eight championship ring barely fit over the nail of his pinky finger.

One evening, Andre and I teamed together against the Super Destroyer and John Studd. We were rocking and rolling in the ring. I tagged in Andre and, out of habit, lifted the second rope to let the legend in the ring. As I stuck my head down, Andre pushed his 500-plus pounds down and climbed over the top rope. The impact from his weight pushed that rope on my head and shoulder.

Then there was my match with Brad Armstrong. On June 5, 1985, Brad Armstrong and I met in Shreveport, Louisiana. Brad is a second-generation wrestler and great technical worker. Midway through our 20-minute scheduled match, I whipped him into the ropes for a clothesline. I hit him so hard that his elbow swung back and nailed me straight in the right eye. The impact forced me through the ropes, and I landed hard on the concrete floor. My eye was split open and my eyeball was totally exposed.

As Brad and the referee waited for my next move, I simply wiped the blood away. I shook my head up and down to acknowledge that I could continue. With blood gushing all over me, I climbed back in the ring and pinned Brad a few minutes later.

When we got to the back, Bill said that I had another match that evening. Ted DiBiase and I had to defend our belts. I said, "Oh my gosh.

Okay, Bill." The personnel in the back put some Vaseline around my eye and did their best to stop the bleeding. About one hour later, I went back out there, and Ted and I defeated the Fantastics to maintain our titles.

Later that night, I went to the local hospital and they sewed up my eye. The gash was so bad that it took 108 stitches! My eye was split wide open in four different places: two gaping cuts above the eyelid, one S-shaped slit under the eye, and a jagged cut in the corner of the eye. I had come within a quarter-inch of losing my right eye completely.

I spent half that night and the early morning hours in the hospital. The doctor suggested that I takc off at least three weeks, but there was no time to heed that advice. I got a few hours of sleep, drove to the next town, and wrestled that night with 108 fresh stitches over my eye. I was tough as nails and wasn't about to let the fans down.

TEN

THE UWF

I was making decent money working for Bill Watts. I earned enough to buy a home and own a few cars—and I loved my cars. I owned a van in which I would haul all the boys. After that, I bought the Nissan 300 ZX. I loved that car.

I started to hang out and team up with Ray "Hercules" Hernandez, and we became tag-team champions. Ray was a wonderful guy and had a great heart. He was a big guy with a rough and rugged look. He would fight anybody and never backed down from a challenge. Deep down, he was a big ol' Teddy Bear, but because of some problems in his personal life, he lived on the edge. He reminded me a lot of a walking time bomb.

I am not sure if it was the competition or alcohol, but Hercules and I butted heads

> TED DIBIASE: DOC AND I SPENT MANY MILES ON THE ROAD TOGETHER. I REMEMBER ONE JULY, DOC AND I WERE COMING HOME FROM A MATCH, DRIVING FROM MISSISSIPPI TO LITTLE ROCK [ARKANSAS]. IT WAS ONE OF THOSE HOT SUMMER NIGHTS. WE LET THE TOP OF MY 300 ZX DOWN AND ENJOYED THE AIR. WELL, I WAS DRIVING ABOUT 100 MPH AND DOC AND I WERE WAVING AT THE BOYS AS WE PASSED. WE GOT A MILE OR SO IN FRONT OF THEM AND NOTICED A FIREWORKS STAND. DOC AND I WENT IN TO PURCHASE A BUNDLE OF FIREWORKS. DOC AND I THEN GOT ABOUT HALF OF A MILE DOWN THE ROAD AND GOT INTO POSITION TO LIGHT ROMAN CANDLES AT THE BOYS AS THEY PASSED. IT WAS A BLAST AND WE REPEATED THIS ALL THE WAY TO LITTLE ROCK.

> MISSY HYATT: DR. DEATH, TED DIBIASE, AND I ALL BOUGHT THE NEW NISSAN 300 ZX TWIN TURBOS. IT WAS A WAY COOL CAR IN 1985. IT WAS THE FIRST CAR I BOUGHT BY MYSELF (MY DAD HAD TO CO-SIGN). I HAD IN MY HAND MY FIRST CONTRACT, AND AT THAT TIME I WAS MAKING THE SAME DOLLARS AS STING AND RICK STEINER—WOW, HOW THINGS CHANGE!

quite frequently. It seemed that a discussion would lead to an argument. The argument would transpire to pushing and shoving. And then the fists would start flying. We were like two big bulls. Often the environment and those close by suffered a lot more than either of us. The next morning we were buddies and went on like nothing ever happened.

Ray and I wrestled together and, after the matches, stopped at the bars on the way to the next town to party hard and slam down our favorite drinks, Salty Dogs. We would get up in the morning and work out for two hours, sweating out all the grapefruit juice and vodka. We played hard, but also worked out hard. Ray also taught me about steroids.

> RICKY MORTON: I RECALL ONE TIME THAT DOC AND HERCULES GOT IN A FIGHT. THOUGH IT WAS MAINLY CUSSING AND YELLING AS WELL AS THROWING THINGS, I WAS STUNNED TO SEE DOC TEAR OFF THE FRONT GLASS DOOR OF THE CLUB. THIS DOOR MUST HAVE WEIGHED 300 POUNDS AND DOC WAS CARRYING IT AROUND AND SWINGING IT LIKE A BASEBALL BAT.
>
> AFTER EVERYTHING CALMED DOWN, WE ARE ALL LEAVING TO HEAD TO THE HOTEL. I LOOKED OVER AND ASKED DOC IF HE WAS GOING TO BRING THE DOOR BACK INSIDE. DOC STILL HAD THIS 300-POUND DOOR IN IS HAND!

Ray was a very muscular guy. He worked a great strongman gimmick. Since I stayed with him on the road, I saw Ray take his shots. I didn't know much about steroids at that time; I was a natural 280-plus. Ray told me that those steroids could cut me up real good. A lot of guys in the business were using them, and the better you looked, the better chance you'd make more money.

One day I told Ray, "Let's go ahead and try it." I began to take Winstrol. I got on a cycle, and after a while, the steroid began to chisel my body.

Combined with my intense workouts, my body transformed. I then decided to also take Deca Durabolin, an anabolic steroid. Deca produces muscle growth and increases red blood cells, bone density, and appetite. After all the damage done to my joints, this steroid made me move a little better, which helped me out tremendously.

We would get the steroids on the black market. Lots of wrestlers were taking steroids, so it wasn't like you couldn't find them. To look good and advance in the business, steroids were a huge asset.

I had a great time with Lord Humungous. Jeff Van Kamp is a great guy and we rode up and down the road together. Jeff was very muscular and had an imposing stature. The only problem was that he had this babyface. To cover it up, they put him under a hood. It resembled the old-time hockey mask that Jason wore in the movie, *Friday the 13th*. He scared people in the arena.

Outside the arena was another story. When Jeff and I traveled together, he always wore his mask. As we drove down the road, it was hilarious to see people's faces. Likewise, when stopping at convenience stores to get a drink or gas up, I often had to tell the clerks, "Don't worry, he's a professional wrestler."

One time, I ribbed a cashier, telling him that there was a big, scary guy out front of the store in a hockey mask looking like he was going to rob the place. The clerk looked out the window at this giant of a man in a mask. The clerk about had a heart attack. I haven't see Jeff in a while, but I understand he is now a law enforcement officer in Pensacola, Florida.

After a year or so of riding with the boys, I decided to get my own vehicle. I purchased a $24,000 Chevrolet customized van. It was a double-decker with six captain chairs. It had a refrigerator for my beer and a couch in the back for any extracurricular activities. There was never a shortage of women available for our pleasure. After every match, women would be waiting for the boys in the back. We used to call them "arena rats."

I really liked that van. I drove all the boys in it. The veteran talent loved to ride with me and let me put the miles on my van. One night, after beating up fan-favorite Hacksaw Jim Duggan in Shreveport, I headed home to Alexandria, Louisiana. Most of the Mid-South talent lived in Alexandria. I went to the bar and had a few drinks. I then checked into the hotel for the night.

When I woke up in the morning, I headed to my van to meet some of the boys for breakfast. I couldn't believe my eyes. One entire side of my van was beaten up and broken into! Fans had followed me some two hours, all the way from Shreveport, to tear up my van for what I did to their fan favorite the night before! Mid-South wrestling was for real, and the people believed our storylines.

> MATT ROBERTS: DR. DEATH WAS A TREMENDOUS HEEL. HIS "LOADED FOREARM" PAD AND OU FOOTBALL HELMET CLAIMED MANY VICTORIES FOR THE COLLEGE ALL-AMERICAN. DR. DEATH WAS ALSO A STRONG FACE AND SINGLES PERFORMER. AS THE MID-SOUTH EVOLVED INTO THE UWF, DOC MADE THE TRANSITION FROM HEEL TO FACE AS SMOOTH AS ANYONE HAS IN THE BUSINESS.

Wrestling wasn't easy back in the Mid-South territory. We worked nine matches a week. We were constantly driving at night on poor roads in all types of weather. We lived in a different hotel in a new town every night. Often, I would sleep in my vehicle.

The driving conditions in the territory were horrible. There were two-lane roads everywhere, and people were very unconscious of other drivers. Ten minutes wouldn't pass before someone would have no problem cutting me off. You talk about road rage. I would get so mad. They used to call me the "Gatorade Kid." I used to drink so much of that energy drink that I should have purchased stock in the company. When drivers cut me off, I rolled my car window down and threw a Gatorade bottle, empty or full, at them.

In March 1986, Bill Watts took the regional Mid-South promotion national. He changed the name to the Universal Wrestling Federation (UWF). Bill was the brains behind this new federation and controlled it all.

Once we went nationwide, we started wrestling in larger venues and in larger cities, such as Chicago, Illinois, and Los Angeles, California. Due to this growth, Bill expanded the roster. He brought in some new guys and talent, including the Rock-n-Roll Express, the Midnight Express, Chris Adams, Black Bart, Skandor Akbar, and the beautiful Missy Hyatt. Bill would swap talent with Fritz Von Erich's World Class Championship Wrestling promotion.

> MARK GIVENS (GIVENS ENTERTAINMENT): GROWING UP IN SOUTH ARKANSAS IN THE EARLY TO MID-'80S, THERE WERE ONLY A FEW THINGS YOU COULD COUNT ON. ONE WAS THAT OUR FAMILY WAS GOING TO CHURCH EACH AND EVERY SUNDAY ... AND THE OTHER WAS THAT SATURDAY MORNINGS MEANT WATCHING MID-SOUTH WRESTLING. I WAS FASCINATED BY EVERYTHING ABOUT IT FROM THE WORD GO AND MY FAVORITES WERE ALWAYS THE HEELS: SKANDAR AKBAR, THE MIDNIGHT EXPRESS, AND DR. DEATH STEVE WILLIAMS. NOW GRANTED, HE WORKED AS BOTH A BABYFACE AND A HEEL, BUT I ALWAYS PREFERRED THE "BAD GUY" DOCTOR DEATH!

Bill added bookers such as Kenny Mantel, Grizzly Smith, Ernie Ladd, Terry Taylor, and Bill Dundee. Since Bill Dundee was the head booker, a lot of the Memphis-based talent came into the UWF.

Because of this popularity, Bill Watts also started a UWF wrestling camp. Guys who wanted to become wrestlers showed up to the arena before the matches. People paid a $200 tryout fee, per se. Bill would give me $100, and he would keep the other $100. I was the "trainer." I went out there and stretched these guys. I beat these folks down. Though I got paid, I hated doing it. It cut into my free time, so I took out my frustrations on those wanna-be wrestlers.

It was also around this time that I became a major babyface in the UWF. Because of my background, I had often rotated from a heel to a babyface. But a late-night drive with Rick Steiner down highway 13 to Beaumont, Texas, catapulted me to the biggest babyface in the federation.

After a huge event in Beaumont, Rick Steiner and I hopped into his car and headed to the next town. I was trying to sleep and Rick was doing his best to keep me awake. All of a sudden, Rick pushed my head so hard that I wanted to pop him right back. Rick said, "Look at this!" Still groggy, the only thing I could see was this huge ball of light down the road. I told Rick to leave me alone.

Shortly thereafter, Rick once again popped me on the head. I said, "You SOB! You do that again, and I'll kick your butt right here in front of everyone!" Though there was nobody out there, I had made my point. I did, however, see some lights heading up quickly from behind us. I thought they belonged to some of the boys trying to beat us home.

Rick slowed down and pointed to these two cars in flames. The fire was blowing at least 50 feet in the darkness. Rick pulled over. It was a major head-on collision and the worst car crash I had ever seen. We jumped out and decided to check on things. We saw a driver and two passengers in the inflamed vehicle. We needed to act fast if we wanted to save their lives.

About this time, the car that had been speeding behind us pulled up. It was actually a law enforcement officer. We motioned and screamed to the police officer, "Come on! Come on!" But he was so scared that he didn't even get out of his car. Rather, he got on the radio, screaming for the fire department and an ambulance.

With fire blazing everywhere, I noticed a driver and a passenger in the backseat of the other car. Rick and I ran over to get them out. We grabbed the guy out of the front seat. The neck of the person in back was wedged deep into the seat. Rick and I, our adrenaline flowing, used all our strength and ripped the door right off the car. We pulled him out. He was barely alive and his body was limp, like cooked spaghetti.

Rick and I rushed to the other car and pulled two passengers out. Their bodies were liquefied. They were dead. All of a sudden, we heard this moaning. The head-on collision had pushed the engine right into the backseat. We could barely see the moaning driver's body. After tearing off pieces of debris, we saw the driver. Almost half of his body was literally stuffed into the glove box.

We couldn't get to him because of the front seat. With all my might, I ripped that front seat right out, though some bolts may have been loosened because of the crash. I pulled him from the glove box area and was able to get him out of the burning car. Unfortunately, he was dead too.

Rick and I were truly shaken by the experience. We had driven up and down that road for years and had seen lots of accidents, but never one like this. The press also got wind of our heroics from the law enforcement officer and the lone survivor. It was all over the news. That real-life event transformed Rick and me into babyfaces. The people loved us.

A few weeks later we had a wrestling match in Fort Polk, Louisiana. Lo and behold, the sole survivor of the accident was there to see me. He was escorted to the back by security, and I immediately recognized his bruised body and scorched face. He extended his hand and said, "Thanks for saving my life. I would have probably died out there if it wasn't for you." In early 1987, due to the nationwide exposure of professional wrestling, the editors of *Pro Wrestling Illustrated (PWI)* decided to sponsor their first-ever tournament. Since the UWF had the best main-event quality wrestlers, PWI set up an agreement with Bill Watts to put on the first-ever PWI/UWF $50,000 Challenge Tournament.

For seven weeks, the best wrestlers in the UWF competed in different locations throughout the United States. It was a single-elimination, bracketed tournament. The matches would have a 30-minute time limit and a draw or double-disqualification would eliminate both wrestlers.

I entered the tournament feeling confident I'd win it all. The front runner was current UWF champion, Terry Gordy. Gordy proclaimed, "This is my federation. I have no intention of losing." Terry Taylor was coined as the dark horse to win it all. Taylor stated, "I will win the PWI/UWF tournament. I will prove to everybody the kind of wrestler Terry Taylor is."

Others in the tournament included Hacksaw Jim Duggan, Chris Adams, the One Man Gang, Jack Victory, Rick Steiner, Missing Link, John Tatum, Eddie Gilbert, Michael Hayes, Sting, Buddy Roberts, Savannah Jack, Bad Leroy Brown, and Chavo Guerrero.

After seven-plus grueling weeks, I defeated the One Man Gang in just under 22 minutes in Houston, Texas, to become the winner of the $50,000 *Pro Wrestling Illustrated*/UWF Challenge.

About this time, Bill Watts and Jim Crockett of the NWA/World Championship Wrestling signed an agreement. In an effort to go national and compete with the upstart World Wrestling Federation (WWF), they agreed that UWF and NWA/WCW wrestlers would be seen on the same cards. Bill lost both Ted DiBiase and Hacksaw Jim Duggan to the WWF. It was hoped that this move would counter any additional efforts by the WWF.

When Hacksaw Duggan left, we lost both a great talent and babyface. I was now elevated to the top tier of the UWF. Along with the One Man Gang, Terry Taylor, Big Bubba Rogers, and Terry Gordy, I packed out arenas throughout the United States. Bill then decided to give me a push to become the next UWF champion. And he wouldn't make it easy.

Big Bubba Rogers was now the UWF champion. The One Man Gang, Terry Gordy, and I fought in a number-one contenders match. The winner would face Bubba for the title. In front of a packed crowd in Tulsa, Oklahoma, I won the match.

Standing at a legitimate 6-foot-9 and weighing close to 460 pounds, the One Man Gang was an unbelievable athlete. At that time, I believe he was the best big-man worker in the business. The way he used to rock back and forth after a punch was unsurpassed. He personified the classic big man.

> MATT ROBERTS: ONE OF THE GREATEST MATCHES THAT I EVER WITNESSED WAS DOC'S BATTLE WITH THE ONE MAN GANG. DR. DEATH HAD JUST WON *PRO WRESTLING ILLUSTRATED*'S UWF TOURNAMENT OF CHAMPIONS. DOC DEFEATED THE OMG IN THE FINALS AND THIS WAS A REMATCH. BOTH WRESTLERS WERE YOUNG AND IN THEIR PRIME. GENERAL SKANDOR AKBAR WAS RINGSIDE AND DELIVERED A FEW SHOTS TO DOC WITH HIS INFAMOUS RIDING CROP. BOTH WRESTLERS WERE BLOODY AND THE MATCH GOT A HUGE POP. THE GANG CONNECTED ON HIS FINISHER—THE 747 BODY SPLASH. DR. DEATH KICKED OUT OF THE 747! NO ONE COULD BELIEVE THEIR EYES! A REJUVENATED DOC UNLOADED RIGHT HANDS TO THE GANG BEFORE PICKING UP THE NEARLY 500-POUND MEMBER OF DEVASTATION INCORPORATED AND "OKLAHOMA STAMPEDING" HIM TO THE CANVAS. DOC WINS ... AGAIN.

In April of 1987, at the "Superblast in the Superdome" in New

Orleans, Louisiana, I beat the One Man Gang by disqualification. Though he retained the title, I began my push toward capturing the UWF title. Dick Murdoch and Eddie Gilbert, however, had different plans.

In a ranking match between Eddie Gilbert and me in Tulsa, Oklahoma, I whipped "Hot Stuff" all over the ring. Out of the blue, Eddie signaled Dick Murdoch to interfere. Carrying a steel chair, Murdoch jumped in the ring and beat me down. The two of them proceeded to break my arm. I screamed in pain as Brad Armstrong, Barry Windham, and Tom Horner helped me to the back. Jim Ross, the best wrestling commentator ever in the history of the business, was the voice of the UWF. He put it over like no tomorrow.

Let me tell you how much I sold that injury and protected the business. I wore that cast for my wedding. I didn't even tell my wife that the cast was a "work." The tuxedo place had to cut the tux to fit it around my cast. I believed in our business and wanted everyone else to believe in it. This believability is something that is missing in the business today.

> Missy Hyatt: Jim Ross was our announcer. Since Dr. Death went to the University of Oklahoma and was a big-time football player there, which was also Jim's favorite team, Jim would go crazy during his matches and that made them even better.

Anyway, Eddie Gilbert and Dick Murdoch were proud of their devious act. Murdoch was from Texas, and he disliked me from the start. After the beatdown, he told the press that University of Oklahoma has low academic standards, and Texas' colleges were far more rigorous. He even had the audacity to crack on Barry Switzer's football program and all Sooner fans. Murdoch said, "The reason why they still run the Wishbone offense is because they can't count past two-snap counts. Switzer's got it painted on the field so they can line up without having to remember it."

Dick Murdoch was a tough guy. With his big belly and "Captain Redneck" attitude, he was a true heel. He took no prisoners and kicked you right in the teeth.

When I started in the business, I hung out with Dick. He always had a case of Rodeo Cold Beer in his truck. It didn't matter if it was a cold day or a hot day. It was always a good day with beer. Dick would say that he wasn't a beer drinker while chugging one down right after a match. I had to stay away from beer because it blew me up and packed on the pounds. Rather, I drank a vodka and grapefruit juice.

One night after a match in Shreveport, Dick said to me, "Come on, you young kid. You punk. Let's go to a real cowboy bar."

I said to myself, "Oh my gosh. Here we go." Even though I learned a lot about the business from him, Dick could also party with the best of them. We hopped in his Bronco and headed to Longview, Texas. It was about an hour drive, and Dick must have drunk a case of beer before we got there. We arrived at some honkytonk joint, and it seemed that everyone knew ol' Dicky. People were talking to me and I was having great time. All of a sudden, out of the corner of my eye, I saw a crowd. I looked over and, lo and behold, the main event was Dick Murdoch. But he wasn't fighting anybody. He was on all fours acting like a bull, bucking women up and down off him! It was hilarious!

Come closing time, Dick and I were both drunk. I stumbled out of the bar and laid in the backseat of the Bronco with my feet hanging out the back tailgate. When we got back to the Sheraton in Shreveport, my feet were so swollen I couldn't take my new cowboy boots off. I had to sleep with them on.

At any rate, in early June, I signed a contract to fight Bubba Rogers for the UWF title. In front of a hometown crowd in Oklahoma City on July 11, 1987, as part of the Great American Bash, I would get my shot. Bubba Rogers' manager, Skandor Akbar, said that I would only get "one chance at the belt." I only needed one shot. With a cast on my hand, I signed the contract.

Bubba Rogers was a big man. He must have stood 6-foot-6 and weighed about 325 pounds. He worked for every major promotion and, over his wrestling career, was both a heavyweight and tag-team champion. Bubba's real name is Ray Traylor. Ray was one of the nicest guys in the business.

Though we knew of each other during our UWF days, Ray and I didn't become good friends until we worked for All Japan. In one of my last tours of Japan for IWA in January 2004, I made sure that we booked Ray. He was a great talent and had a following in Japan. Unfortunately, later that year, Ray died of a heart attack at a young 42 years old.

To make sure I was ready, I went back to the University of Oklahoma to train. Under the guidance of Coach Switzer and OU football strength coach Pete Martinelli, I was put through a training program in Norman to prepare. Vignettes were shown every week building up to the championship match. Coach Switzer and Martinelli were supportive and troopers throughout the program. Barry Switzer had a blast. He loved pushing me for the match of my life. He is so close to me that we are like family.

JEREMY YOUNG: DOC BOOKED ME ON A TOUR IN JAPAN WITH THE IWA. I WAS IN AWE OF ALL THE WORKERS, ESPECIALLY BIG BUBBA. I REMEMBER AS A KID WATCHING HIM AS THE BODYGUARD FOR JIM CORNETTE AND LATER AS THE BIG BOSSMAN IN THE WWF. I KNEW HE WAS BIG, BUT IN PERSON, HE LOOKED LIKE A GIANT.

To make sure nothing would disrupt my one chance at the UWF title, I asked my good friend, Dusty Rhodes, to be with me ringside. Akbar had a history of interfering in matches to cause disqualifications. I couldn't win the title on a disqualification. Dusty accepted.

Akbar complained and the UWF decided to make a compromise. They ordered that both men be tied together with a bull-rope. Though Akbar protested about the stipulation, it was a done deal. Everything was now in place to ensure that I would have a clean match.

Prior to the match, Dusty and I went over everything. To say I was pumped up would be an understatement. When my music hit and I was introduced, the noise was deafening. Once the bell rang, we went all out. Though Bubba had a 100-pound advantage, I was determined. We were both bleeding profusely from headshots on the outside ringposts. Akbar tried to interfere, but Dusty kept him in check. After 30 grueling minutes, using all my might, I picked up Rogers for a body slam and walked him around the ring. The crowd was going nuts because they knew what was to follow. I delivered my patented "Oklahoma Stampede" power slam. I covered Bubba. In unison with the fans, the ref counted, "one, two, and three!" I became the new UWF champion. Jim Ross called the match, and as always, his energy and enthusiasm were unreal!

The postmatch celebration was unbelievable. Jim Ross, Shane Douglas, Brad Armstrong, Dusty, and others doused me with champagne. The celebration didn't last long, as talent from Bubba Rogers to Terry Gordy to Sting lined up for a shot at the new champ.

> JIM ROSS: THE NIGHT DOC WON THE TITLE, THE UWF LOCKER ROOM WAS MUCH LIKE BEING IN THE OKLAHOMA SOONERS LOCKER ROOM AFTER WINNING ANOTHER NATIONAL CHAMPIONSHIP IN FOOTBALL. DOC'S PEERS WERE HAPPY FOR HIM BECAUSE THEY RESPECTED DOC AND KNEW HE COULD REPRESENT THE UWF IN A BIG-TIME WAY. PLUS, THE MATCH WE ALL JUST WITNESSED WAS A CLASSIC. IT WAS QUITE THE CELEBRATION THAT LASTED WELL INTO THE EVENING.

A few months later, though we had already been exchanging talent for about a year, Bill Watts officially sold the UWF promotion to Jim Crockett Promotions.

And then there was the horse.

Frankie Brothers, one of the best trainers ever in the horse racing industry, named a horse "Dr. Death" after me. Throughout the 1980s, Brothers had been the leading trainer at Louisiana Downs. Frankie trained many horses, including Hansel, who finished 10th in the Kentucky Derby and followed up with victories in the Preakness and the Belmont Stakes. Hansel was also voted champion three-year-old male.

"Dr. Death" used to run at the fairgrounds in New Orleans. He was a beautiful, chestnut-colored horse and a very successful stallion. He had a skull and bones logo that read "Dr. Death." The patch was upside down and looked very intimidating on the race track.

Looking back, my tenure in Mid-South and UWF was unbelievable. Bill Watts ran a very professional organization. He believed in doing what was best for professional wrestling. To maintain this integrity, he had no problem fining workers. If a wrestler was late or used profanity, Bill would fine him. He ran a tight ship and an honest business. I believe he did what was in the best interests of both the company and industry.

Mid-South and UWF wrestling was a family-friendly environment. It was a place where a dad could bring his son without worrying about profanity or scantily dressed women soliciting a cheap pop. You saw the kids in the crowd and they had a ball.

Unlike today, all the boys looked out for each other. Nobody cared about the salary another worker was making. If you were short on money, you could always count on someone to help you out. All of us worked together and everything ran smoothly. Every one of us had a passion for the sport and worked our butts off to fill the seats every night. We were a fraternity and took care of each other.

> GERRI WOLLBERT: THE FANS JUST LOVED DR. DEATH THE HORSE. HE WAS A BIG, GOOD-LOOKING HORSE AND A CROWD PLEASER. HE WAS VERY FAST, AND EVERYONE LOVED THAT HORSE. WHEN DR. DEATH CAME OUT ON THE TRACK, THE FANS JUST LOVED HIM. IT WAS AWESOME.

ELEVEN

NWA/WCW

Jim Crockett's National Wrestling Alliance (NWA) promotion was very different than the UWF. To start, for the first time in my wrestling career, I was told by the promotion that I would receive a written contract and I would be guaranteed money for the duration of the contract. This was new to me, because under Bill Watts there were no contracts, nor were we promised money. With Bill, I was paid a check every two weeks based on attendance at the venues.

My wrestling career in the U.S. also began to change with the Crockett promotion—not for the better, but for the worse. In late 1986, Jim Crockett finalized the sale with Bill Watts. I was offered a six-figure, one-year contract. I never saw the contract and worked six months without one.

I wasn't the only UWF talent to be offered a contract with the Crockett promotion. Jim was getting some of the best wrestlers in the world, such as Sting, Bubba Rogers, the One Man Gang, Brad Armstrong, and Terry Taylor.

Soon thereafter, the plan was to have their two champions wrestle and unify the titles. This meant me, the UWF champion, versus the "Nature Boy" Ric Flair, the NWA champ. The match was scheduled to take place in Roanoke, Virginia.

I was very excited about this match. I had heard a lot of great things about Ric Flair. I saw some of his matches and thought he was a decent

Pressing my good friend and fellow throat-cancer survivor, Freebird, Buddy Roberts.

worker. It was also a smart business decision to unify the belts and garner fan interest. Whoever would win this unification bout, I thought, would bring in months of return matches throughout the country. This would mobilize fan interest, spearheading both the Crockett promotion and our careers.

While in the locker room, Ric and I didn't chat much. He looked very concerned. I was introduced to the ring first, and then the Nature Boy made his way out. A few minutes into the match, I hit Ric Flair so hard that he got scared. He started to panic, quickly got himself disqualified, and went home.

I couldn't believe it. Ric Flair, who had wrestled everyone from Bruno Sammartino to Harley Race to some of the toughest Japanese wrestlers in the world, was terrified of "Dr. Death" Steve Williams? The Nature Boy obviously didn't want any of Dr. Death.

In December of 1987, Jim Crockett retired the title. Rumors were circulating that he was selling the promotion. Due to its numerous territorial buyouts, the company was losing thousands of dollars. It also wasted a lot of money. Jim Crockett had his own private plane. The business had multiple administrative offices across various states and was constantly putting on costly parties. Often, the Rock-n-Roll Express and Four Horsemen would show up in separate limousines. One night in Charlotte, I vividly remember that almost every wrestler on the card had his own limousine! I thought to myself, "Bill Watts would never run a company in this manner."

During the six months that I worked with the Crockett promotion without a contract, I busted my butt for the company. I worked with some great talents, such as the Barbarian, Arn Anderson, Tully Blanchard, Barry Windham, and the Road Warriors. I wrestled nine matches a week. I worked 30 days on and four days off. I actually only had two days off, because I needed two days to travel to and from matches. I did this for three solid months. It wore me out. I was in and out of hotels. I ate on the run and worked out at a different fitness center every day. I worked literally 30 days nonstop.

About this time, the company started running the 1987 summer Great American Bashes. Though I still didn't have a contract, I was at least getting paid decently enough to purchase a home and provide for my family. I was involved with most wrestling cards and was quite over with the fans.

I knew it wasn't the most appropriate time to ask, but I was very concerned about my wrestling future. I was still wrestling without a written contract. I finally approached the company and I was told that it would be addressed after the conclusion of the Bashes. For the moment, I was relieved.

When the Bashes concluded, as promised, I sat down with the company brass. I was expecting to finally sign my six-figure contract when they decided to be more consistent with my pay: $100 a day!

I couldn't believe it. To say I was angry would be an understatement. I immediately went to the head booker, Dusty Rhodes. He told me that the promotion was about to file bankruptcy. At the moment money was tight, but Dusty said that things would work out.

Around this time, I was introduced to an unfortunate part of the business: cliques. To make it in the promotion or get a push, you had to be aligned with Dusty Rhodes, the Four Horsemen, or JJ Dillon. This "clique" thing didn't sit too well with me. I was never a clique guy. I never had to be.

Because I didn't attend their parties and suck up to them, the clique punished me. One time, I was told that it would be a good idea to show up at a party put on by JJ Dillon in the Carolinas. I wasn't interested in going to any party. I preferred to stay by myself. On my off time, I wanted to do my own thing. My independence and failure to play by their rules, however, started affecting my position and pay with the promotion. They literally started to break me.

Dusty Rhodes and JJ Dillon were the main guys behind this objective to make me into a team player. After promising me the win at the Bunkhouse Stampede in Nassau, New York, they changed the outcome. This seemed to be the pattern for the next few months. I was no longer getting the push. They had substantially cut my pay, and I sensed hostility in the locker room. Things were quickly going in reverse.

While at home during my four days off, I came back from a family outing to a fax. It was sent and signed by JJ Dillon and simply read that my services were "no longer needed." They had fired me.

I was enraged and immediately picked up the phone to call Dusty Rhodes. It took me a few days to get hold of him. They made me panic and sweat. The company knew that I had just gotten married and had a mortgage payment. I was just starting a life. When I finally got hold of Dusty Rhodes, he said, "Okay, Doc. Do I finally have your attention?"

I said, "Dusty, you got my attention. I have a brand-new house and bills to pay. And now you guys are screwing me! How can you fire me? What is the reason?"

Dusty simply said, "Well, you ain't going by the book! Do you want to play it our way or your way?" Realizing that they had me in a corner, I told Dusty that I would be a team player.

Since I was having problems with the Crockett promotion, I decided to accept some bookings in Japan. When I worked for Bill Watts in Mid-South, I had made some contacts in the Japanese wrestling market. I also knew Antonio Inoki.

Antonio Inoki is a professional wrestling icon and former owner of New Japan Wresting. He is also a brilliant man. Inoki was the first pro wrestler in the world to be elected as a legislator of a country. In 1989, he was elected to the House of Councillors of the National Diet of Japan.

I first met Inoki when he came to the states to wrestle for Fritz Von Erich's Texas-based World Class promotion. Fritz needed a stud wrestler to work over Inoki. Bill suggested me. I went to Dallas and had a great match with Inoki. And, of course, I had no problem putting him over. Later, Inoki and I spoke for a while and he told me that he really appreciated the great match. We also bonded over a meal and drinks. Inoki was the person who eventually spearheaded me to a career in the Japanese wrestling world.

Anyway, after a crazy and wild match against Dick Murdoch at the Great American Bash, I received a call from New Japan. They wanted to book me for a one-week tour. Because of all the problems with the Crockett promotion, I accepted their invitation. I told Dusty and left for Japan. It was unbelievable. I immediately connected with the Japanese culture, people, and workers. And I got another chance to wrestle Antonio Inoki.

I was the first person to ever knock out Antonio Inoki on live television. Midway through our match, I gave him a belly-to-belly suplex. He landed so hard that, when his head hit the canvas, he lost consciousness. The referee had to stop counting after two, because Inoki was out cold. The entire arena knew he was down for the count and they started booing.

I quickly improvised. In a seemingly vile manner, I put Inoki in my lap and started slapping him around. To maintain heat, I screamed and yelled at the crowd. Inoki eventually came to. We finished the match with him going over. I literally saved both Inoki and the match. Afterwards, Inoki was impressed with me both as a person and a worker. He asked me to stay an additional week. I agreed.

That evening, I telephoned Dusty. I told him that I really liked working for Inoki and his New Japan promotion. I liked it so much that I was going to resign from the Crockett promotion. Dusty was concerned, so we spoke for a long while. He was apologetic about his earlier threat of firing me. After a positive dialogue, Dusty convinced me not to resign. We did, however, come to the agreement that I would work for both companies.

Upon my return to the states, the rumor became a reality: the Crockett promotion had been sold. In 1988, Jim Crockett sold his wrestling assets to Ted Turner. Turner Broadcasting was now full fledged into professional wrestling. Turner later established a new company called World Championship Wrestling, Inc. (WCW).

Once in Atlanta, I had to meet with Jim Herd. Jim was the company's executive vice-president. I don't think Jim had too much professional

After Dick Murdoch broke my arm, I tried my hardest to return the favor.

wrestling experience, and many guys used to tease him because of his past employment with Pizza Hut. Still, I had to negotiate a contract with the guy. In the end, he offered me a decent, one-year guaranteed contract. I made sure that there was a provision in the contract allowing me to work in Japan. They agreed to the terms, and I accepted.

As part of WCW, I went from working in the main events to a middle-card worker. I became a heel and feuded with Barry Windham. I also had matches against Ronnie and Jimmy Garvin, Dick Murdoch, and the Road Warriors. Since they couldn't count on me playing by their rules or working for them on a continuous basis, the company needed a stud babyface. They were very fortunate to have Steve Borden, better known as STING.

STING was one of the Mid-South/UWF workers who came with me in the sale to the Crockett promotion. Because of the limited number of babyfaces, STING was one of the few guys in the locker room who had the ability to work main event matches on a nightly basis. WCW did what they could to give STING as much exposure as possible. During this time, he became the hottest babyface in the business, with the exception of Hulk Hogan.

STING was fortunate to be in the right place at the right time. And that is what the wrestling business is all about. He had a great body, a good gimmick, and worked very well in the ring. Also, he was over with the crowd.

I really like STING. He is a born-again Christian who has changed his life. STING is traveling the world and telling his testimony. He spreads the Word of God, telling people how great God is and how the Lord can change their lives. He currently wrestles for the TNA (Total Non-Stop Action) promotion.

George Scott and Kevin Sullivan came up with an idea. Though there were multiple WCW bookers over the years, George Scott is responsible for booking the Varsity Club.

In late 1997, Kevin Sullivan recruited Rick Steiner and Mike Rotunda. All three men were heels. Rick and Mike wore their letterman jackets to the ring. Both were outstanding college wresters and shooters. To add a twist to the angle, even though they were partners, Rotunda and Steiner would bicker with each other over which university was better, Syracuse or Michigan. When I returned from my commitments in Japan, I was added to the unit.

To build up my addition to the Varsity Club, Kevin Sullivan and Mike Rotunda "broke" Jimmy Garvin's leg. Rick Steiner, who was being pushed to turn face, didn't appreciate Mike's antics. He then quit the Varsity Club. To make up for the loss, Kevin Sullivan added another shooter: me. Kevin, Mike, and I would take the Varsity Club to an entirely new level of success. A few months later, Mike and I beat the Road Warriors to capture the WCW World Tag Team title.

Though we had a good thing going, the Varsity Club was suspended and disbanded not too long thereafter. I was stunned. This had a lot to do with George Scott being removed as the booker and Kevin Sullivan's attitude.

Unbeknownst to me, Jim Herd fired George Scott. George was a former wrestler and had a good head for the business. I liked and respected him. So did most of the wrestlers. Then why was he let go? To this day I am not sure.

The Varsity Club had the toughest shooters in the business. All of us were amateur wrestlers and/or had some athletic background. We were getting over big time with the crowd. But then there was the bizarre mindset of Kevin Sullivan.

There we were, coming to the ring in our letterman jackets. Instead of being a team player and coming out with a baseball cap, football shorts, a t-shirt that said "Coach," and blowing a whistle, Kevin wanted to do his devil gimmick. So he wore his devil-worshiping gear. It just didn't make sense. The Varsity Club should have lasted for years.

Before the Varsity Club's suspension, Dan Spivey had been added to the unit as well. Danny Spivey is a great friend; he has a heart of gold. We worked with and against each other in Japan and took care of each other on the road. He is also a great athlete. Standing nearly 6-foot-7 and weighing more than 300 pounds, Danny is one of the quickest men of his size to ever work in the squared circle. After the Varsity Club disbanded, Danny teamed with Sid Vicious to form The Skyscrapers tag-team. In the mid-1990s, he signed with the WWF and worked as a psycho character named "Waylon Mercy." Around that time, Danny suffered a back injury that eventually ended his wrestling career.

And then there is Mike Rotunda. We are great friends. I have known Mike since his amateur wrestling days, when I was at Oklahoma and he was at Syracuse. I enjoyed working with Mike. We had many great times together. He is a classy person, and I admire him and his family. His wife Stephanie, Blackjack Mulligan's daughter, is a wonderful woman. I really liked being around Mike and his family. In fact, when Wyndam was born, I named him after Mike's older son.

When Mike and I worked together in WCW, he used to bring his son, Wyndam, on the road. Wyndam was maybe seven or eight at the time. I even remember him running up and down the road with us. The three of us jogged in the humid summer in Southeast Georgia. He was a great kid. We had fun together and I loved Wyndam like my own son. He isn't little anymore. He now plays college football in California, stands about 6-foot-5, and weighs about 280 pounds.

Although I admired and respected Mike Rotunda, I didn't care for Kevin Sullivan. Kevin got his start in Florida Championship Wrestling. As mentioned, his gimmick was this devil-worshipping heel. He came to WCW as a worker and leader of the Varsity Club. Toward the end of the WCW's tenure, Sullivan was a member of the WCW booking committee. In 2000, he even made a brief television appearance with the reformed Varsity Club (Mike Rotunda and Rick Steiner). Kristina Laum was even part of this unit. Kristina, who was from Korea, went under the name of Leia Meow and played a cheerleader for the Varsity Club.

There was always something about Kevin Sullivan that bothered me. It seemed like he would shake your hand and then stab you in the back. He didn't want to be a team player. He cared more about dressing up as a devil-worshipper than doing what was best to advance the team.

I have known Rick Steiner ever since Bill Watts brought him into Mid-South. I like Rick, and we have had great times together. He was an amateur wrestling standout at the University of Michigan, placing fourth at an NCAA Championship competition. Rick is also a great tag-team worker. Scott and he were a very successful tag team both in the states and Japan.

In Mid-South, Rick and I used to work together to help him relax in the ring. Like me, he was a shooter and knew the basic wresting fundamentals. He just had to slow down. He was like the Energizer Bunny.

For years, Rick and I traveled up and down those awful Louisiana roads and exchanged many a conversation. We also experienced a lot together, including the rescue of those individuals from the car accident.

Rick is also a very smart guy. He's so intelligent that in 2005 he won a seat on the Cherokee school system's board of education in North Georgia. I really like Rick, and over the years I did what I could to help him in the business. I think Rick is both a terrific person and one of the better workers to ever put on a pair of wrestling trunks.

Barry Windham is another fantastic professional wrestler. He is also a great guy. Barry is the son of Blackjack Mulligan, but make no mistake, he never progressed in the business because his father. He can work face or heel. He can do technical wrestling or high spots. At 6-foot-4 and 270 pounds, Barry is a categorically complete wrestler.

I battled Barry many nights. I remember when he was the Western States Heritage Champion. During one of the Great American Bashes, Barry went up for a leap-frog. As he was about to jump over me, I decided to give him a forearm smash right to the nuts. It didn't matter how big he was, he went down. I then took over the match. Well, as you can imagine, the crowd was furious. They started booing me like I had never heard before. I was eventually disqualified. I am sure Barry still remembers that match.

I have a lot of respect for Barry. When I was the booker for IWA (International Wrestling Association of Japan), I even booked him to wrestle for the company. Unlike many American bookers, I always kept my word. While I worked in Japan, I learned about loyalty, honor, commitment, and respect from the greatest promoter/booker in the business, Giant Baba. I gave every worker, including Barry, everything that he was promised.

About this time, I was going through a divorce and my estranged wife was pregnant. I had been working like a maniac and running non-stop. One evening in Chicago, I got a phone call. I was told that my ex had gone into labor prematurely and there was a chance that my child wouldn't survive. I was scared to death. I told Jim Herd and the company about this emergency and asked to take a few days off. They refused. I was told, "Nothing personal, but business is business." I was furious.

Despite what the company had just told me, after my match, I decided to do what was best for my family. That night, I purchased a ticket to leave for Shreveport early the next morning. I spent the night in the airport.

When I got to the hospital, I was introduced to my son, Wyndam Carlton Williams, in an incubator. He weighed 2 pounds, 11 ounces and was no bigger than my hand. My little boy was a miracle baby. My ex and I spent every day in the hospital praying for Wyndam. I called Jim Herd, told him the situation, and said that I would be staying there for a while. He made some comments, but I tuned everything out. The only thing I cared about was my baby boy.

It was a tough couple of weeks. Every day I went to the hospital to see Wyndam. We monitored the baby's progress. We fed, talked, and took care of him the best we could. By the grace of God, Wyndam made it!

Wyndam was named after Mike Rotunda's son and my father, whose real name was Carlton. It is quite ironic that the initials of my son's name are "WCW!"

TWELVE

WCW CONTINUED

Michael Hegstrand stood 6-foot-3 and weighed nearly 280 pounds. He had a chiseled body and was as strong as a bull. He was one-half of arguably the most successful tag team in the history of American pro wrestling, the Road Warriors. Mike was better known as "Hawk."

Hawk and I didn't start out as friends. In fact, we almost tore each other's heads off. At a card in Chicago, Mike Rotunda and I were tagging against some team. During the course of the match, I decided to military press one of the guys. I used to do this move quite often. Rotunda and I eventually won the match.

When we got to the locker room, both Animal and Hawk were pissed off at me because I pressed the guy. Hawk got in my face and said, "Hey man, that is our deal. Nobody does that but the Road Warriors."

I replied, "Who said so?"

We were now about chest to chest. Hawk said, "Me say it!"

All eyes in the locker room were now on us. I said, "I don't care! I don't believe that! Nobody has a move that is patented. People have been doing my football tackle and stomping their feet like me for years, and I don't get mad at them. What is important is whatever makes me and the company money."

Hawk angrily said, "Oh, really?!"

Well, at that point, Hawk and I were ready to go outside and settle this like real men. We both had talked enough. In the words of Bill Watts, it was time to "hook it up!" Before anything could happen, though, we were separated. Hawk and I were given a modern-day time out and sent into separate rooms to cool off.

We eventually calmed down and came to the realization that it would be a heck of a fight. And somebody would lose. Funny thing is, just like in a family fight, shortly thereafter we mutually respected each other. We became close friends.

Like Hercules and Hacksaw, Hawk and I became roommates on the road. We also worked out hard together and did steroids. It seemed like Hawk filled the void that Hercules had left.

At any rate, when we were apart, I exercised alone. No matter what city I was in, I always found time to work out on a regular basis. Even to this day, the gym plays a major part of my life. I superset everything I do. This has been my routine for more that 25 years: chest on Monday, biceps and triceps on Tuesday, my back on Wednesday, shoulders on Thursday, and on Friday, I work every part of my body, but with less weight.

For my daily cardio, I use the Stairmaster. I don't work out my legs as much as I used to. When I was younger, my legs got so large it became uncomfortable. My thighs were so big that it was hard to put on a pair of pants. They would also rub up against each other, which led to blisters, chafing, and heat rash. Talk about some pain. I must have gone through a container of cornstarch every two days.

When I was 40 years old, I met Earvin "Magic" Johnson at World Gym in Maui, Hawaii. I lived about two miles from Magic's house on the beach. Prior to this time, I only saw Magic in passing. But it was in the gym that he fascinated me.

Magic is probably the greatest point guard in the history of professional basketball. He played on five NBA national championship teams with the Lakers and one NCAA national championship team, Michigan State. In 2002, Magic was elected to the Naismith Memorial Basketball Hall of Fame.

Although he didn't work out nonstop, Magic was in the gym for two hours a day. I loved to watch him. It was unbelievable. One day, I was so overwhelmed with Magic's workout that I decided to talk to him. I went up to him and said, "You are amazing. You are first class in my book. I see you in here for two hours every day. What is your secret?" Looking up at him, I shook his hand and Magic smiled as only he can. Before he could speak, I added, "and I notice you don't work out the whole time."

Magic said, "You're right. I spend one hour talking to my fans and another hour working out."

I took the words to heart. They showed me just how much the fans meant to him. Magic, being the big international superstar that he was, still found time in his daily life for his fans. How incredible. From that point on, I decided to model my workout after Magic Johnson.

The fans have given me, like Magic, everything. Though I worked for what I earned, if it weren't for the fans, there would be no wrestling venues. If the fans didn't attend the shows, there would be no pay-days. Wrestling is and should always be for the fans!

Anyway, Hawk and I lived together on the road. He had a heart of gold and was a very compassionate and understanding person. Hawk was a top star and got paid very well for his talent. On the other hand, the company wasn't paying me well at all. Hawk knew about this inequity, so, out of the kindness of his heart, he gave me money if I was short or in a bind. He treated me like a younger brother.

With my divorce, the birth of my premature baby, my life on the road, and my miserable contract, life became very difficult and stressful. Hawk was also going through a divorce. Though we looked larger than life on television and in the arena, we were emotionally and physically hurting. Life became very tough for both of us.

About this time, to escape our pain and troubles, Hawk introduced me to cocaine. I became addicted. I was still doing steroids, popping painkillers, drinking, and smoking marijuana. I was a drug addict.

For some reason, I thought these cravings would solve my problems and keep me alive. And I wasn't alone. There were many guys in the business who had to deal with the same issues. The company was running us hard. We were working nine matches a week, one on Saturday and two on Sundays. Hawk and I were like machines and felt invincible. Cocaine kept us going.

I was also chasing Benjamin Franklin. My life was all about getting as much money as possible. I sent some money home to my family. Some went in the bank. The rest went to my vices. I was living in the devil's den. My body was in pain from getting pounded every night. I was shooting in Japan and dealing with head games and stress in the states. I was also trying to keep my family together. I needed an outlet.

I am embarrassed today about my past addiction, but would never erase the wonderful memories and times that Hawk and I shared. Like me, Hawk became a born-again Christian and changed his life. Unfortunately, Hawk passed away in October of 2003 at the young age of 46.

It was during my period in NWA Wrestling that I got busted—two out of the three times in my career—for drugs. The first time it happened at the Detroit airport. They found a plethora of cocaine, pills, pot, and steroids in my luggage. Though they were simply for my own personal use, the authorities thought I was planning to sell the drugs in Japan. They confiscated everything, and I spent a night in jail.

With the help of a lawyer friend recommended by the Road Warriors, I was let go. But upon my return from Japan, federal agents were waiting for me in California. They showed up in the locker room and mistakenly grabbed Rip Morgan. They soon found me in Seattle, Washington. I had to pay a huge fine, received a one-year probation, and was sentenced to community service.

The second time, I was busted while working for All Japan. To cope with my divorce, I got high with some friends in Dallas prior to a tour in Japan. When I arrived at customs in Japan, they searched my wallet and found the roach of a joint. I had forgotten all about it.

I was immediately deported. Since I had embarrassed and disgraced the profession, Japan suspended me for one year. Fortunately, I met Giant Baba in California six months later. I deeply apologized for what I had done. Baba took care of me and brought me to All Japan after the one-year suspension expired.

The third and final time that I was arrested because of drugs was during my All Japan tenure. After my second divorce, I went to Mexico with some of my friends. We partied and had a grand time in Nuevo Laredo. As we headed back into the States, I was busted with illegally purchased prescription drugs. The incident was in all the newspapers, including the *USA Today*.

I spent all night in jail. Mexico's judicial system operates differently than that of the U.S. Through much negotiation and diplomacy, I was released after paying a major $10,000 fine.

At the end of my one-year contract with WCW, I decided to wrestle full time for New Japan. I stayed in Japan for many years until Bill Watts became the booker for WCW in 1992. Bill wanted Terry Gordy and me to work a program with the Steiner brothers. During this time, Terry and I were the hottest tag team in the world.

I never had any ambitions to go back to WCW. After my negative experiences with the promotion some five years earlier, returning to Atlanta wasn't on the top of my list. Plus, I was content in Japan. However, after talking to both Giant Baba and Bill Watts, I changed my mind. So did Terry. There weren't too many people I trusted in the business, but I undeniably trusted Bill.

More importantly, I valued Giant Baba. If Baba would have said no, Terry and I wouldn't have gone to WCW. But Baba thought it was a good idea to go. He saw it as an opportunity to help both our careers, as well as his company.

The deal that Terry and I were offered was very straightforward and rewarding. We were to work 100 days with WCW. We accepted.

I'm sorry to say that, due to family and personal problems, Terry couldn't finish out the contract. He managed to only complete 50 days. Because of politics, I only completed 75 days. Once again, WCW gave me the financial shaft. I had a signed contract for 100 days, but it wasn't fulfilled. The second-largest wrestling company in the world couldn't get me 100 days of bookings.

Wrestling is a cutthroat business. The only promoter/booker I could trust was Bill Watts. When the WCW didn't fulfill my contract or give me my guaranteed money, I got very mad at Bill. I also felt betrayed. I couldn't believe that my mentor would do this to me.

Then again, I didn't know how bad the situation was at WCW. Even Bill himself had been dodging politics to remain the booker. Bill was eventually released from the company. I never got my money. Bill and I have since rekindled our relationship, and I value him like a member of my own family.

Prior to Terry leaving, he and I had a great run in WCW. Upon our arrival in Atlanta, we immediately targeted the Steiner brothers. The American fans were consumed with them. In an interview to build up this feud, I said, "You know, before we came back to the States, all we ever heard was Rick and Scott this and Rick and Scott that. Terry and I couldn't go a day without somebody throwing those clowns' names into our faces. We will soon take care of the Steiners!"

The fans were thirsty for this unprecedented battle of elite tag teams. Our first match was a 30-minute draw at Beach Blast. It was a good match and there were lots of power moves. We were incrementally building up the angle between us, and the fans were becoming more and more interested. We kept telling them that we liked Japan better than the United States. They responded by telling us to go back to Japan.

Soon enough, we did the unthinkable by many—but not for us. We beat the Steiner brothers. Then, at the WCW's monthly Clash of the Champions (XIX), Terry and I beat and eliminated Rick and Scott in the second round. It was bittersweet, and the fans seemed stunned. It was only a matter of time until we became champions.

About this time, I had a run-in with one of Bill's agents, Ole Anderson. Ole was considered one tough cookie, but I was never intimidated by anybody in the business. Prior to a house show, I showed up early, as usual. While the agents checked everyone in, out of the blue, Ole Anderson came over to me. I guess he had heard about my reputation and wanted to set some parameters. He said, "Let me tell you something, son. If you take me down or hit me, I'll fire you. My name is Ole Anderson."

Not wanting to make any waves, I said, "Hold on. Let me introduce myself to you. My name is "Dr. Death" Steve Williams. You don't ever have to worry about me hitting you or taking you down unless you cross me." I reached out to shake his hand, and Ole wouldn't shake it.

A few weeks later, we beat the Steiner brothers to capture the WCW tag-team championship titles. It was a classic match in front of a packed house and an international television audience. As Scott was about to do a belly-to-belly suplex on Terry, I clipped Scott's legs from behind. Scott dropped, and Terry landed right on top of him. The referee counted, "One, two, and three!" Terry and I were the new champions.

We were now hated more by the fans than ever before. To show our superiority and to insult the fans further, Terry and I beat Barry Windham and Dustin Rhodes in the final round of the NWA tag-team tournament. We were getting over big-time. No two wrestlers in the world could stop us. And then Terry left the company for personal reasons.

After Terry left, I was holding two belts alone. I had to drop the tag-team straps. On September 21, 1992, Barry Windham and Dustin Rhodes became the new WCW tag-team champions. Guess who my special partner was for the evening? None other than the "other" Steve Williams: "Stunning" Steve Austin. Later, in the WWF/WWE, he went by the name Stone Cold Steve Austin.

To build up the match, Bill Watts explained to the crowd that Terry Gordy was injured or sick and couldn't work. Bill said that I could have another partner. I either chose or was given Stunning Steve Williams. We had a great match against Barry Windham and Dustin Rhodes. But in the end, Stunning Steve was pinned, and we lost the titles. Soon thereafter, I left WCW for good.

Steve Austin is an incredible person and great friend. We wrestled well as a tag team and got along outside the ring. Though early in his career he worked mainly as a tag-team wrestler with either Larry Zybysko or Brian Pillman, he worked very hard in the ring to become one of the best workers ever in the business.

I have the utmost respect for Steve. I will always have a special place in my heart for him. When I was suffering from throat cancer, Steve found time in his busy schedule to call and check on me. I will never forget that.

After my 75 days with WCW, I went back to Japan. I didn't want to have anything else to do with an American wrestling promotion. I was tired of the lies and shortcomings. In the states, a certified and signed contract didn't mean anything. It seemed like American wrestling contracts were meant to be broken.

Contrast this unethical approach to my dealings in Japan. The only thing I was given there was a handshake. And guess what? They fulfilled their word every time. They wired my money to the bank before the tour was even over!

I did a short run back with WCW in 2000. After my WWE experience, I appeared on their premier Monday-night program, *NITRO* with Ed Ferrara, who played the character mocking my good friend, Jim Ross. From my perspective, the skit was never intended to insult or degrade Jim. I never said a word in the skit and simply did what I had to do to make a living for my family. I was paid to wrestle a few more matches.

I recall wrestling Vampiro, who I would later book in Japan, and the members of the music band, Misfits. In one match, I remember throwing the lead singer of the band right into a steel cage and busting him wide open.

After refusing to put over the WALL, I wasn't offered a contract and went back to All Japan. I told Terry Taylor that there was no way that I would put over a green guy who had only been in the business three months. No way! Unfortunately, he passed away at the young age of 37.

In retrospect, my experiences with WCW are mixed. When I was with Mid-South and UWF, Bill Watts looked out for and took care of me. When the company was sold, I no longer had the luxury of being the promoter's protégée. I was just another worker on the totem poll. Like others, I didn't fit into the clique nor wanted to be part of it. Thus, I wasn't treated properly. Nor would I get that push to be in the main events.

On the road, there was no special treatment. Everyone was for himself, and the company cared nothing about you or your personal life. No one cared if you were hurting or in pain. Unlike in some businesses today, there were no counselors to help you with your personal life and problems. The only thing the company cared about was you being at that arena, ready to perform.

But I wouldn't trade this time and the memories for anything. The experiences and people, as well as the places I visited, will forever be etched in my mind. I made great friends and, though some may have forgotten about me, I will never forget any of them. The fans were great. Some even met me at the airport to take me to the arena.

But it was time to move on across the Pacific.

THIRTEEN

KONICHIWA, JAPAN

Antonio Inoki beat me on Christmas Day in Dallas, Texas, at Christmas Star Wars 1985. Though he won the match, we developed a tremendous relationship that has lasted a lifetime. It was one of the best Christmas presents I ever received.

From 1986 through 1990, I wrestled in both the United States and for New Japan Pro Wrestling. New Japan is a major professional wrestling federation founded by Antonio Inoki. Between my WCW stints, I had eight tours for New Japan.

I was also paid quite well to work in Japan. Having befriended Inoki, I was promised that I would be on every tour. I wrestled in Japan every other month. I really enjoyed both living and working in Japan.

Unlike working for various promoters in the United States, Antonio Inoki treated me with dignity and respect. Solely on his word, I spent four-plus great years learning my craft and gaining respect from the Japanese wrestlers and fans. I didn't have a contract. It wasn't needed. The only thing I had was his handshake and his word. He never let me down. Not once!

A typical tour had me leaving Shreveport and flying to Chicago. I changed planes and then either flew non-stop to Tokyo or changed planes in Honolulu, Los Angeles, or San Francisco. It was a good 14-hour flight. Fortunately, Inoki respected me enough to often fly me in business class. Believe me, I learned how to sleep on an airplane.

Upon my arrival, some handlers met and escorted me to my residence. I usually stayed in a small, 10-by-10 room that had the basics—a bed, desk, television, and small bathroom. Inoki took care of all the accommodations.

I always stayed up the first night to try to regain my faculties. I had dinner with the boys and did my best to get adjusted to the new time zone. I traveled from venue to venue by bullet train. I then got on the bus and was transported from town to town.

Unlike today, where babyfaces and heels share a dressing room, I was never in the same dressing room as the Japanese wrestlers. It was about respect for the business. Unless you were a major face from the United States, like Hulk Hogan or Kerry Von Erich, Americans, including me, wrestled as heels in Japan.

The Japanese promoters ran their companies like professional businesses. There was no nonsense, and workers showed up at the building three hours before bell time. The first half of the show was for the younger guys. After intermission, the shoot matches began.

I sincerely adore Japan. From the people to the scenic beauty to the food, I have nothing but the utmost love and respect for Japan and its population. When traveling by bus or rail to various cities to wrestle, I was in awe of its natural beauty. Some parts of Japan, especially the mountain regions, remind me a lot of Colorado.

I always enjoyed the springtime. This is when the cherry blossoms would be in full bloom. The cherry blossom, or sakura, is the unofficial national flower of Japan. The entire population would celebrate this time with all kinds of activities and festivals. I would get into it every year.

Japanese food is out of this world. As a person who loves to eat, I savored every opportunity to go to different restaurants. Some of my favorite dishes and entrees include sashimi, sushi, ramen noodle soup, onigiri, natto, and yakitori. I also devoured anything teriyaki. You name it: chicken, beef, fish, squid, or octopus. It is all so good. My beverages of choice included green tea and asahi (beer). And who doesn't love sake!

Many don't associate good fruit with Japan, but they have an excellent array of fruit products. I loved the Fuji apple. It is juicy and sweet as candy. Some of my other favorites include kaki (persimmons), mikan (Japanese tangerines), and nashi (Japanese pears).

Though the food and scenery in Japan are incredible, I think the most important reasons I love Japan are because of its culture and people. The population is very respectful and they treat people with sincerity and respect. They value their traditions and conduct themselves in a manner that is benevolent and magnanimous. Strangers welcomed me into their homes and treated me like family. It gave me a feeling of comfort and joy and is something I will always cherish and continue to appreciate each visit to Japan.

Though the pay was very good wrestling in Japan, like in the United States, I was required to pay for my own insurance and taxes. When I returned to the United States, I was taxed again. Because of this, I had to learn how to save money while on the road.

Food was expensive. I learned from my first tour that paying eight dollars for a cup of coffee wasn't too fiscally responsible. So I used to bring my own food from the States into Japan. Every trip, my bags were backed with tuna, protein and granola bars, shakes, coffee, and other items.

Vader is a big man, standing about 6-foot-6 and weighing about 450 pounds. He was a two-time Triple Crown World Heavyweight Champion with All Japan Pro Wrestling. He and I also became one-time Unified Tag-Team champions.

At any rate, about a week before Vader was to start an angle with Masa Saito, I had a match against the former Olympic wrestler. Mr. Saito is extremely tough and we were both very stiff toward each other. Our match started getting out of hand. We were literally beating the crud out of each other.

During the match, I blew out my knee. I was hurting. Mr. Saito went to work on it. Sensing I was injured, the Americans in the back ran to the ring to help me out. I knew for sure they were coming to protect me. This is what American wrestlers have always done. We look out for each other. And then Vader came out of the locker room.

Vader was the biggest guy around. When I saw him coming, I thought he was going to help me out. To my chagrin, Vader started beating up the Japanese wrestlers outside the ring. He never came into the ring to help. He was trying to make a name for himself at the expense of Dr. Death. Mr. Saito and the other Japanese wrestlers were taking pop shots at me and were doing damage to my legs. Like all matches, this was a shoot! Finally, the younger guys, like Johnny Smith, Owen Hart, and Chris Benoit, all protected me and cleared the ring.

Though my knee was swollen and I was in pain when I got back to the locker room, I was angry and went looking for Vader. I saw the exhausted and beet-red-faced Vader sitting in the corner. I went up to him, stuck my finger right in his eye, and said, "Who the hell do you think you are? I thought you were coming out to the ring to protect me. They were shooting on me and trying me. The only thing you did was try to make a name for yourself beating up Antonio Inoki and other Japanese workers off of my doggone match."

Vader replied, "I wasn't trying to make a name for myself."

I cut him off and said, "Buddy, if you think you are so #@$@ bad, then get up on this lily pad if you feel jumpy. Come get some of Dr. Death Steve Williams!"

As all the boys in the locker room were watching to see what was going to happen next, I continued, "I don't care how big you are. I am not afraid of you. I will fight you right here."

Fortunately for him, nothing happened. When the smoke cleared, I was still standing on my own two feet and he was still sitting down. By the time we got on the bus to head back to the hotel, Vader came up to me and apologized. He said, "I am sorry, Doc. I didn't mean to take anything away from your match."

Still angry I said, "Kid, go sit in the back of the bus!"

Johnny Mantel was the first person to show me the ropes in Japan. He took good care of me and introduced me to many great Japanese people in the wrestling business. Though Johnny never made it big in the States, he was a very good worker.

I had great times with Owen Hart and Chris Benoit in Japan. I enjoyed their company, and Owen would often make me laugh. We had many great evening meals together. Two other guys who stand out are my good friends Brad Rheingans and Johnny Smith.

It was an honor to have associated with Johnny Smith. I loved to hang out with Johnny and listen to him tell stories in his British accent. Johnny was an excellent wrestler, and I learned from him every chance I could. We ate a lot of barbecue and drank a lot of spirits. Like me, Johnny had a great outlook on life and trained like there was no tomorrow.

Brad Rheingans is another classy guy. Brad was a NCAA champion for his school, North Dakota State University. He even wrestled in the 1976 Summer Olympics, where he placed fourth. Even though he qualified for the 1980 Olympics, he didn't compete due to the U.S. boycott.

Though never a huge professional wrestling star in the United States, he has unbridled mat-wrestling abilities. On many occasions we wrestled as partners. He is tough as steel. Unfortunately, his professional wrestling career was cut short due to two major reconstructive knee surgeries. They literally cut both of his legs off at the knee. After fully recovering, he became a trainer for New Japan.

In July of 2007, Brad will introduce me into the prestigious Glen Brand Wrestling Hall of Fame of Iowa. Located in Waterloo, it awards only those persons who have managed to attain great achievements in wrestling. It is truly an honor to receive such recognition.

The Japanese wrestling scene is very different from that of the United States. First of all, every night is a shoot. I loved it. It made me strong as nails and I had no problem beating people up. For me, it wasn't a big adjustment. It reminded me a lot of my Mid-South days where everything was always stiff.

The Americans who wrestled in Japan mainly worked as heels. Unlike today where workers discuss their matches and moves, there was no communication in Japan. They didn't speak English, so you couldn't understand them anyway. They were also very tough. I was tested every night. The Japanese wrestlers wanted to test my stamina and toughness.

The Japanese wrestling fans are quite different. Like American fans, they are very energetic and passionate about the sport. But the Japanese show it differently. They have unmatched respect for the business. The fans treat it as a true professional sport.

It takes some time to get used to this respect. As a wrestler with a strongman gimmick, I did a lot of power moves. In the U.S., the fans would holler and scream after watching these moves. Not in Japan. Displaying class and respect, the Japanese fans simply clapped in approval. They also threw streamers in the ring. The fans were so into the matches.

> JEREMY YOUNG: THE JAPANESE FANS ARE AMAZING. THEY HAVE RESPECT FOR THE BUSINESS. WHEN DOC TOOK ME TO JAPAN, I WAS STUNNED BY THEIR REACTIONS. THERE IS NO UNNECESSARY HOLLERING OR SCREAMING. IT REMINDS ME OF A BOXING MATCH. THEY VIEW PROFESSIONAL WRESTLING AS A SPORT AND NOT ENTERTAINMENT.

I remember wrestling in the Sumo Hall (Ryogoku Kokugikan). The fans in attendance didn't sit on folding chairs or in the bleachers, but on pillows. If they thought the match was good, they filled the ring with their square pillows. After my match, the ring was packed with pillows. It was an unbelievable display of respect.

It took me many years to get over with the fans. I had to work very hard in and out of the ring to earn their respect. And I did work hard. I learned their culture and values. I befriended many people and attained sponsors who treated me like family. I did what I had to do to earn their respect and, in turn, I was and still am very much admired in Japan.

I always stayed in character. I remember going town to town either by bus or train. I was always the last one to leave. With my Halliburton in hand, I exited with a swagger. When fans tried to get close to me and snap photos, I swung my Halliburton at them, knocking their cameras out of their hands. Some would even break. The fans loved it and it even got me over more as a heel.

I watched many American wrestlers come to Japan and not enjoy their stay. They became upset when there was no silverware at a restaurant or when things were different from the States. In return, the fans wouldn't accept their talent. I guess the saying is true: to get respect, you have to earn it. Many Americans didn't give it nor earn it.

Over the years, I have had the privilege to wrestle with some of the greatest Japanese workers in the history of the business. There are so many stellar guys I want to tip my hat to. Each wrestler had a unique style and approach. But there was one thing that all of them had in common: respect for the business. I keep repeating this theme because they do.

One of my first opponents in Japan was the Black Cat. The Black Cat was both strong and could mat wrestle. I worked a strongman gimmick, and we complemented each other in the ring. He was very quick, and we put on many good matches. Whereas some matches today last only five minutes, most of mine lasted 20 minutes at the least.

Cards in Japan were organized in a manner that was fan-friendly. The first half of the card included stacked matches between the young guys and up-and-comers. They spiced in a comedy match for the kids prior to intermission. Afterward, the main event talent would perform.

Early on in New Japan, I wrestled Tatsumi Fujinami on many occasions. Tatsumi was a very sound ring technician and we worked great together. He is famous for two moves that are etched in the annals of professional wrestling: the Dragon Sleeper and the Dragon Suplex.

Another wrestler who stands out is Mitsuo Yoshida. He is better known by his wrestling name, Riki Choshu. For some time, he was not only one of the company's top stars, but also one of the most prominent workers in Japan. I had many tough matches with Riki. We wrestled one time at the Sumo Palace, and he gave me a clothesline that rang my bell.

Shinya Hashimoto is a huge man, almost sumo size. But he wasn't a sumo wrester. He, Masahiro Chono, and Keiji Mutoh were the original "Three Musketeers," dominating the promotion for some two decades. He was a very good worker, and we had many great matches together.

While with New Japan, a Russian gets a suplex while referee Peter Takashi looks on.

Yoshiaki Yatsu is another Olympic wrestler turned professional. Like Brad Rheingans, he competed in the 1976 Summer Olympic Games for Japan but didn't wrestle in the 1980 Summer Olympic Games because of the boycott. Yoshiaki also competed for a while in the WWF.

I really liked Yoshiaki. We had some good matches together. During one of our encounters in Kokugikan Hall, the two of us were going at it like there was no tomorrow. Standing 6-foot-1 and weighing close to 270 pounds, I gave him a side suplex to end the match. Unfortunately I also broke three of his ribs.

Every night was a fight in Japan. The Japanese wrestlers didn't want to lose in their homeland and neither did I or any of the other Americans. Yoshiaki Fujiwara was one of those guys who hated to lose and loved to fight. A former Muay Thai kickboxer, Fujiwara was one tough cookie.

During one of our early matches, we were going at it. We were beating the tar out of each other. All of a sudden, he threw me into the ropes.

When I came off them, he head-butted me right in the sternum. The low blow knocked the wind right out of me. To say it hurt would be an understatement. He sensed I was in pain and went for the kill. But his slight hesitation as he admired the blow gave me enough time to recover. He had awakened the "raging bull" inside of me.

Fujiwara reached down to pick me up and I grabbed his arm. I brought him down with a series of blows and put him in a Boston Crab. I sat back on him as hard as I could. He tried to reach for the ropes to get out, but he couldn't. I wasn't going to let him. I was trying to break him in half. The referee even told me to lighten up, but I didn't. I was angry and was going to teach this guy a lesson for the cheap shot. After I won the match, we gained each other's respect. We soon became good friends.

Mr. Saito is another great talent I worked with in New Japan. He was an international star and even worked in the AWA and WWF. I had many great matches with him. He was short, stocky, and very well trained. He was awfully strong and worked hard in the ring. I appreciated his friendship and guidance. Unfortunately, toward the end of his career, Saito got into an incident with the law. For the transgression, he was sentenced to two years in prison.

Some other Japanese talents I befriended during this time and worked with are Animal Hamaguchi, Masahiro Chono, Sanshiro Takagi, Masanori Saito, Keiichi Yamada, Jushin Liger, Kenjitakand, and Wakamutshui. These men are tremendous workers and are wrestling legends in both Japan and abroad.

In all my years of working in Japan, I got along with everyone except one person: Peter Takashi. Because his father was killed in WWII, Peter seemed to hold a grudge toward all the American wrestlers. Since most Americans didn't speak Japanese, we relied on the handlers that the company provided.

Peter spoke good English and was a referee for New Japan. He was also supposed to treat us well and help the Americans get adjusted. Peter treated everyone like crap.

During one of my early tours in Japan, we were way out in the country. Everyone got off the bus to get something to eat. In the restaurant, nobody knew what to order. Peter, who was supposed to help us, didn't make an effort to do anything.

Disgusted with his attitude, I went up to Peter's table. Of course, Peter was eating while everyone else was still trying to order. I shouted to Peter, "Fuck you! I can't believe the way you treat us. You don't even help us out to get something to eat!"

Angry, I stormed out of the restaurant and headed back to the bus. I was so aggravated that I was ready to unload all my bags and head back to the Tokyo airport. Unfortunately, we were in the middle of nowhere. I thought, "Who in their right mind would even pick me up?" So, like a little kid, I got back on the bus and pouted.

A few minutes later, Peter came onto the bus. He got in my face and said, "Nobody says 'fuck you' to me!"

I replied, "Fuck you!"

Peter repeated his earlier statement, as did I. It was just the two of us. For a referee, Peter was pretty stout. Still, I could have squashed him like a bug.

Out of respect for Antonio Inoki and the other workers, I decided to just move away from Peter. To my chagrin, Peter put his leg out in front of me, trying to prevent me from moving. He repeated, "Nobody in all my years has said 'fuck you' to me!"

I replied, "Fuck you! You don't help us out at all. Not even to help us get something to eat. If you were in our country, we would help you. I suggest you get out of my way or I will beat the shit out of you."

Peter moved and I went up to the front seat. About this time, the rest of the boys got back on the bus and we headed to the arena.

Throughout my tenure in Japan, we never said we were sorry to each other. We have held this grudge all these years.

FOURTEEN

WRESTLING OVERSEAS

During the 1980s and 1990s, New Japan and All Japan were the hottest wrestling companies in Japan—some even say in the world. Equivalent to the WCW vs. WWF battles in the States, both Japanese promotions packed out arenas throughout Nippon.

I really enjoyed my stay with New Japan. My four-plus years with Antonio Inoki were the best. But I wanted to do more, and so did Terry Gordy. Both of us came up with the idea of wrestling as a tag team. Unlike other teams, Terry and I were big men who came to the ring with energy and enthusiasm. We hit the ring with power and ran the ropes to intimidate our opponents. Our team wasn't going to be "just a tag team," but the greatest tag team ever assembled. We pitched the idea around, and in 1990, my friend and reporter, Toshi, arranged a meeting for us to meet with Shohei "Giant" Baba.

Giant Baba was the owner and promoter of All Japan. Standing nearly 6-foot-9, Baba himself was a great wrestler and athlete. Before entering professional wrestling, he played professional baseball as a pitcher for the Tokyo Giants.

As for wrestling, Baba was a three-time NWA heavyweight champion, beating Jack Brisco once and Harley Race twice—two of the greatest wrestlers in the history of the sport.

Baba's stable of wrestlers were second to none with stars such as Stan Hansen, Dan Spivey, Akira Taue, Genichiro Tenryu, Jumbo

My first tour of Japan, with New Japan in Tokyo.

Tsuruta, Kenta Kobashi, Keiji Mutoh, Satoshi Kojima, and Mitsuharu Misawa.

Terry and I immediately bonded with Baba and his wife, Motoko, who we simply called "Mrs. Baba." Giant Baba was the most respectful and classiest person I have ever met. For a giant man, he conducted himself in a manner that I had never experienced before. So did Mrs. Baba.

I want to go on record stating that Giant Baba was the best promoter I have ever worked for. Though Inoki is a close second, Baba treated me (and Gordy) like a son. His word was good as gold. Baba never betrayed me. Never. He and his wife would do anything to help me in and out of the ring.

I loved Baba like my own father. He loaned me money, helped me through personal problems, and stood by me through thick and thin. Even when I was experiencing depression and suffering from my drug addictions, Baba was always there for me. He even co-signed on a loan when Terry was trying to start a tanning saloon.

When he passed away from cancer in 1998, it was one of the saddest days in my life. It was also a sad day for the professional wrestling industry in Japan. Without Giant Baba, honor and loyalty went down the drain. So did respect. I miss Giant Baba.

Terry and I told Baba of our tag-team desires and he liked the idea. The rest is history. For the next four years, Terry and I dominated the tag-team wrestling world. We were known as the "Miracle Violence Combination." Nobody could touch us.

On March 6, 1990, Terry and I defeated Stan Hansen and Genichiro Tenryu for the All Japan tag-team straps. We would go on to capture those esteemed belts on three other occasions, as well as win the Real World Tag Team Tournament in Tokyo on December 6, 1991.

It should also be noted that during this time I accomplished what no other wrestler has ever done in the history of the business. During 1990, I wrestled simultaneously for both Inoki's New Japan Pro Wrestling and Baba's All Japan Pro Wrestling.

This feat would be the equivalent to Hulk Hogan's working for WCW and WWF at the same time. It was and is still a feat that will never be duplicated. Not only were they impressed with my talent, but more importantly, they appreciated my respect for them and the wrestling business.

In 1988, we were "Welcomed to the Jungle." In Tokyo, Terry and I partied with Guns N' Roses for four nights straight. In 1988, Guns N' Roses was the hottest band on the planet. They are also big wrestling fans. Through some connections, Terry and I headed to the hotel to meet Axl Rose (lead singer), Slash (lead guitar), and Rob Gardner (drummer). It was the afternoon of the first night of their concert.

As we waited in the lobby, some of the handlers and set-up guys began talking trash about wrestling. They sized themselves up to us and said that wrestling was fake and rigged. I went up to one of the bigger guys and told him that I would show him how fake it really was. I picked him up and pressed him. I then drop him straight to the ground and he lay there in pain while his friends ran to assist him. I guess he figured out quickly that you can't fake gravity.

Axl and Rob greeted us with respect and we chit chatted. They were honored to meet us, and vice versa. We were escorted to the VIP rooms. The spread was out of this world: liquor, beer, lobster, steak, cheeses, breads, fruits, etc. And then there were girls. Every one of them was "a perfect 10." Terry and I, along with Terry's cousin, Ray, drank and ate so much that it was near embarrassing.

Later that evening, I attended the greatest music concert of my life. Axl and the band's energy were unreal. Axl must have run 10 miles up and down the stage that evening. Afterward, we partied in the wee hours of the morning.

The next evening, we went right to the VIP room. This time, we also brought Tommy Rogers of the Fantastics. Tommy is a great guy, but I will never forget the look of the Guns N' Roses handlers after they saw Tommy eat 12 lobsters! Combine that with all the beer Terry was drinking and my own glutton, we were told in a gentle way to take it easy.

WHILE WORKING IN JAPAN, TERRY GORDY AND I WON COUNTLESS TAG-TEAM TOURNAMENTS.

The next two evenings were out of this world. Though most of the Japanese people can't speak English, they sure knew the words to every Guns N' Roses song. We had a great time, and I want to thank Axl, Slash, Rob, and the other members of the band for their hospitality and memories. The picture of us hanging in my office will always be cherished.

Throughout my stay and travels in Japan, I met many celebrities. I always managed to exchange conversation and get a photo-op with each star. Some include Magic Johnson, George Kennedy, and Chuck Norris (actors), as well as Muhammad Ali. I also met Sean Penn. I noticed him to my left as I was flying home first class from a tour in Japan. Throughout the early part of the flight, we stared back and forth at each other. I was marking out big-time. I loved his acting in *Fast Times at Ridgemont High, Bad Boys,* and *Casualties of War.* Sean pretty much blew off some of the boys and me. He drank quite a bit and I saw him take some pills. He seemed a tad nervous. All of a sudden, he was sound asleep and surprisingly slept the rest of the flight.

> Ricky Morton: Flying home with Doc from a tour in Japan, we saw Sean Penn. At the time, Sean was a big-time movie star. All of us wanted to meet him and get some pictures. Well, Sean was an asshole. He wouldn't acknowledge or talk to us. Doc said to me, "Don't worry, we will see him again."
>
> Sure enough, Doc was right. About three weeks later, we saw Sean. We were sitting at a restaurant eating. Sean looked lost. He was as nice as he could be. We ended up drinking and partying with Sean all night.

When we landed in the States, I was determined to get a picture with Sean. As he exited the plane and proceeded to the baggage terminal, I introduced myself. Sean was still groggy. He could barely walk. I literally had to hold a wobbly Sean Penn by my side as a picture was snapped. The poor guy was completely wiped out from the trip.

Not too long thereafter, I met up with Sean again. We were at the airport in Tokyo. Since Sean didn't speak Japanese, he seemed a little out of his element. Remembering a few of the boys and me, Sean came over to us at the restaurant in the airport. He was pretty cool and we hung out. He became our best friend. Also, this time, Sean was more than happy to pose with me for a photo.

Terry Gordy was my best friend. We were family, and I loved him like a brother. I first met Terry when he was in the UWF. A member of the Freebirds, Terry, at 6-foot-3 and nearly 290 pounds, had a rare combination of brute strength and quickness. I fought against him and tagged with him. We bled, cried, and laughed together. On July 16, 2001, at the young age of 40, Terry passed away from a heart attack. Though I couldn't attend the funeral because I was in Hawaii with my family, the services were held at the South Crest Chapel in Rossville, Tennessee. The interment followed at the Tennessee-Georgia Memorial Park.

I want people to remember Terry for his heart and not his demons. He did crack, popped pills, and loved his beer. But we all have demons. No one is perfect. Enough literature out there exploits both our past addictions.

What most people don't know is that Terry would go the extra mile for the business and fans. He respected the professional wrestling industry, and nobody worked harder in the ring. Terry was also a family man and a great father. He has a beautiful wife and family. I remember all the great times that we had together both in Japan and here at home in the States. He was funny and could make me laugh with his jokes. Before his passing, he accepted Christ as his Savior.

It was a joy for me in early 2006 when I had the opportunity to help his son, Ray. Ray is currently signed to a contract with the WWE and is wrestling with Deep South Wrestling in Atlanta. I spent a week in Atlanta for the WWE to help train and assist the developmental talent. I also saw Terry's wife. She is a great lady and I admire her empathy and strength.

As for Terry, I know I will see him again when we meet up in heaven. God bless my friend and brother in Christ, Terry Gordy!

In between my tours of Japan, I worked once again for a company called UWF (Universal Wrestling Federation). This wasn't Bill Watts' UWF. Rather, in 1990, this UWF was founded and run by Herb Abrams. I started working for Herb in 1991.

Herb was a dichotomy. Without a doubt, he was a heck of a nice guy. Herb was extremely funny and unequivocally treated me like a superstar. Herb flew me first class to all the events and had a limousine waiting for me at the airport. He put me up in the best hotels. But Herb was also a bullet train heading for a collision. He lived life to the fullest. Unfortunately, he lived on the wrong side of the track.

Herb loved to party, and he could party with the best. He loved his alcohol, marijuana, cocaine, and anything else you can think of. He also loved surrounding himself with beautiful women. I recall this one time in Las Vegas when Herb called me to his penthouse suite in one of those luxury hotels on the strip. Herb answered the door half-blitzed. In the room were five naked prostitutes with cocaine all over the place!

The UWF, however, was a legitimate company. Herb thought it could compete against the WWF and WCW. I am not sure where he got his money. Some say his parents. But he never short-changed me.

The UWF roster had the talent to compete with any wrestling brand in the world. He brought in the strongest, nastiest, and hardest-hitting wrestlers around, including Ken Patera, Bam Bam Bigelow, Johnny Ace, Paul Orndoff, the Warlord, me, and countless other superstars. Herb and the legendary Bruno Sammartino were the announcing team. Compared to Jim Ross and Jerry Lawler, Herb and Bruno were the classic example of what a good announcing team should not be.

In early 1991, I started feuding with Paul Orndoff. Paul was a major wrestling superstar in both the NWA and WWF. In 2005, he was inducted into the WWE Hall of Fame. Paul is a heck of an athlete. He was a star running back for the University of Tampa. He later played professional football for the Jacksonville Sharks in the World Football League (WFL). Paul is also an avid hunter, and was even showcased on a few *Outdoors* programs aired on ESPN.

Paul and I both entered the UWF as fan favorites. He is a great wrestler and one of the soundest technical workers I ever had the privilege to grapple. As a person who will do anything to help the business and pack the arena, I challenged Paul to a match. Though we were both fan favorites, I called Paul out: "I've always respected Paul. He reminds me a lot of myself. We both played college and pro football. We are both superstars in the industry. But I don't like him mouthing off in public about him being the best wrestler in the UWF. I am the star of this promotion. I was the UWF World Heavyweight champion in 1987, and if anyone is the star of this promotion, it is me!"

I continued one of the better promos of my career: "I don't take a back seat to anyone here in the UWF. So I challenge the loudmouth to a fair fight. To be the man, you have to go through me!"

Paul, who also wanted to see the UWF succeed, accepted my challenge. Our "fair" fight turned out to be a bloody encounter with tables and chairs. We continued to feud from Los Angeles to New York in an effort to make the UWF a top promotion.

Herb thought so much of me that I became the UWF's first and only World Heavyweight Champion. On June 9, 1991, at the Manatee Convention Center in Palmetto, Florida, I was scheduled to wrestle Bam Bam Bigelow for my championship.

Herb flew my wife, Tammy, and my then-six-year-old daughter, Stormy, down with me in first class. Herb took care of my family and me. He got us a limo, put us up in a nice hotel room on the beach, and gave us all top-rate accommodations.

I have always been impressed with Bam Bam Bigelow. He is a friend and a great ring worker. For a big guy, probably 6-foot-3 and close to 370 pounds, he is extremely versatile and quick. He had an intimidating look with these real tattoos shaped like flames on his head. God willing, he's still alive, because Bam Bam could party to the extreme.

During the match, I kept an eye on my wife and daughter sitting ringside. That was the first time Stormy had been to one of my matches. As the match progressed, Bam Bam hit me with something and busted me wide open. I was knocked outside the ring and landed near my daughter. She saw blood squirting out of her daddy's head and ran screaming toward the exit doors. I noticed Tammy following her.

Our match soon concluded. Both Bam Bam and I were bloody mess. In the end, I hit Bam Bam with the Oklahoma Stampede to retain my title. The celebration lasted into the night. And then, in a manner that only he could do it, Herb stiffed the building. I heard over the years he stiffed many workers.

The UWF's first and only national event aired on live TV was coined the *Blackjack Brawl*. In an effort to promote the *Brawl*, Herb told the media

STORMY MAXWELL: I REMEMBER BEING VERY SCARED AND RUNNING FROM MY SEAT TRYING TO LEAVE THE ARENA. I COULDN'T BELIEVE THAT MY DADDY WAS BLEEDING EVERYWHERE. I WAS SO OVERWHELMED AND WAS FREAKING OUT. MY MOM CALMED ME DOWN AND LATER, WHEN I SAW MY DAD, HE TOLD ME NOT TO BE AFRAID. WE EMBRACED AND I KNEW EVERYTHING WAS GOING TO BE OKAY.

that this event was light years ahead of any other in the history of professional wrestling. It was a state-of-the-art wrestling tournament.

Though the attendance was light, the card was a who's who of talent: Danny Spivey. B. Brian Blair, Cactus Jack, Jimmy Snuka, Sunny Beach, Tyler Mane, Jim Brunzell, and others.

There were 10 or 11 scheduled matches at the *Blackjack Brawl.* In the main event, I defended my belt against "Malicious" Sid Vicious. Sid and I had entered into a feud to build up for this match. I gave some great interviews and even tried to spin some things to get the UWF to the next level.

Sid Vicious is a decent guy and a good athlete. He is a legitimate 6-foot-7 and weighed close to 280 pounds at the time. He had an awesome physique and a sick Powerbomb for his finisher. He made some crazy facial expressions in the ring, and his look could be quite intimidating to the fans.

Sid started working in the business with my good friend Danny Spivey. In WCW, Danny and Sid formed a tag team known as The Skyscrapers. He became a decent singles wrestler as well, working for both WCW and WWF. Sid would later become a two-time WWF and WCW World Heavyweight Champion.

At a WCW pay-per-view in the early 2000s, Sid suffered a nasty leg fracture following his leap from the middle turnbuckle. It was more than a fracture. He broke his leg in half, with the fibula breaking through the skin! The injury was exploited by WCW and shown over and over again on TV. It was also all over the internet. Soon thereafter, Sid disappeared from the wrestling world.

Anyway, in an interview, I said, "My daughter saw Hulk Hogan on television the other day. He was boasting about him being the world champion. My daughter ran to me and said, 'Daddy, I thought you were the champion.' I gently explained to my daughter that there were top wrestlers in every wrestling company. But make no mistake about it, your daddy is the 'best wrestler of them all!'"

> MISSY HYATT: WHENEVER I HAVE BEEN ASKED "WHO THE TOUGHEST GUY IN THE BIZ IS FOR REAL," I HAVE ALWAYS SAID DR. DEATH AND "HAWK" OF THE ROAD WARRIORS. DR. DEATH IS REALLY COOL. HE WAS ALSO HERB ABRAMS' UWF CHAMPION. IN 1994, I WAS LUCKY TO WORK ON THIS HORRIBLE LIVE SPORTS CHANNEL SPECIAL. THE SHOW WAS THE FIRST EVENT IN THE ARENA AT THE LAS VEGAS MGM GRAND. A WEIRD THING WAS THAT ABRAMS SAID I COULD NOT WEAR PERFUME OR LIPSTICK AROUND HIM. TOO BAD HIS CHECK BOUNCED. SINCE I WAS NOT LISTED AS A "WRESTLER" FOR THE NEVADA SPORTS COMMISSION, I NEVER GOT MY PAY.

I got a good response from the interview. Herb tried to parlay the challenge to possibly tease the fans—to make them think that maybe another federation's champion might show up. Herb said to the media, "Dr. Death just told me that after he destroys Sid Vicious, he is going to challenge Hulk Hogan, Ric Flair, and Bret Hart to the Ultimate Championship Match to determine the greatest wrestler in the universe."

Broadcasting via Sports-Channel America at the MGM Grand in Las Vegas on September 23, 1994, I beat Sid Vicious to retain the World Heavyweight strap.

Herb Abrams never got the opportunity to see the UWF make it to the next level or the universe. Sorry to say, he died of a massive heart attack in middle age.

> MISSY HYATT: WHAT GOES AROUND COMES AROUND. ABRAMS DIED IN THE BACKSEAT OF AN NYPD COP CAR NAKED WITH COCAINE ALL OVER HIM. HE WAS ARRESTED AT HIS NYC OFFICE FOR MAKING TOO MUCH NOISE WITH HOOKERS. NOT SURE IF THEY HAD ON PERFUME OR LIPSTICK.

FIFTEEN

HOME SWEET HOME

Dick Beyer was one of Baba's best friends. Dick was better known as the Destroyer. Due to his battles with Freddie Blassie and Rikidozan, he is a legend in Japan. Along with Stan Hansen and Terry and Dory Funk, the Destroyer was one of the pioneers in Japanese wrestling.

Through my association with Baba, I got to know Dick. I have so much respect for him as both a person and worker. He helped out Baba by training many of the boys. I marveled at his amateur wrestling skills and was on the card for his retirement match in Japan. Even after retiring, he did a tremendous amount to bring amateur wrestlers from the States to Japan.

One time at an amateur wrestling banquet, the Destroyer was in attendance. I remember that he was dressed very nicely, wearing this remarkable tie with amateur wrestling designs. I had never seen a tie like that before and was impressed with it. Dick, who had much respect for me as well, said, "Steve Williams, this is a present from me to you." He took the tie right off his collar and handed it to me. Not too many people will give you the tie from around their neck.

One wrestler I truly admired in Japan and appreciate even to this day is none other than Stan Hansen. Stan is a man's man, and there isn't anyone tougher. At 6-foot-4 and 320 pounds, nobody told this Texan what to do. Stan initially wrestled in the World Wide Wrestling Federation in the late 1970s, where he claimed an international reputation. He gained this status by breaking Bruno Sammartino's neck.

The "story" was that Stan's powerful Lariat move caused this injury, but the truth is that a messed-up body slam did it. Still, the tale spread like wildfire, and Stan "Lariat" Hansen has been kicking butt and taking names for some 30 years. His battles with Mitsuharu Misawa for the Triple Crown in Japan are classics.

I had many great matches with him both in singles and tag-team competition. But, most importantly, I learned from Stan. Stan not only taught me how to be a better professional wrestler, but also about the Japanese culture. He introduced me to many people in the business and reminded me about respect. To this day, Stan is a great friend and we speak via phone and e-mail quite frequently. He has a beautiful Japanese wife and currently resides in Colorado.

Mitsuharu Misawa is very smart and an excellent technical wrestler. He now owns his own company, called NOAH. We fought in singles, tag-team, and even six-man matches. With his ring savvy and awesome spin kick, he can battle with the best.

Misawa has one heck of a forearm. He nailed me one time in the face, knocking me out. He is strong as a bull and could play linebacker for any NFL team. In Tokyo on July 28, 1994, I defeated Misawa to capture All Japan's Triple Crown Heavyweight Title.

Unfortunately, Misawa and I sort of had a falling out after Giant Baba passed away and I tried to help Baba's wife run the company. In mid-2000, after some disagreements with Mrs. Baba, Misawa split from All Japan.

Prior to his departure, Misawa was committed to finishing out his remaining matches. He was only booked for a few more shows. Taking advantage of this opportunity, I decided to stir things up. As a businessman, I have always tried to start my own angles in order to draw people to the arena.

I decided to make threatening comments about Misawa at the events and even to the papers. I bragged that I wanted to fight him and send him into retirement. During his matches, I stood outside the ring area and just watched Misawa. My look was cold and sincere. The people thought I was going to interfere and jump him. But that wasn't the case. I was trying to make a story and promote an angle.

This is what wrestling is supposed to be all about—doing things out of the ordinary to promote the business. Unlike today, in which writers tell you what to do in the ring, wrestling should be about the creativity of the individual. In my era, nobody knew in advance what was going to happen in the ring. It was tit for tat.

Well, I think these actions and efforts offended Misawa. He must have thought that the comments were personal and that I was going to hurt him. I was never going to hurt him. I respected Misawa. We had fought many matches together and battled like two warriors in the ring.

I want to go on record and say that I have always had the utmost appreciation for Misawa. I would never do anything to disrespect him. On no account would I ever downgrade him or his accomplishments. He is an idol. We respected each other in the ring.

Some newspapers blew the aforementioned incident out of proportion. They made me look like the bad guy. They put words in my mouth that apparently upset Misawa. I hope that everything will now be put to rest. Our lack of communication has gone on long enough. Now that the truth has been told, I hope to once again talk to my friend Misawa.

I liked wrestling Toshiaki Kawada. Though I respect him, we always had our differences in the ring. We beat the living crud out of each other. He was strong and could go toe-to-toe with anyone in the business. Every morning, I think of Kawada. He is the reason why I don't have any front teeth!

Toward the end of my run in Japan, some guys tried to steal moves that other wrestlers had made famous and/or perfected. Well, Kawada tried to take some of my moves, including the side suplex and back drop. There is only one "dangerous back drop driver" move, and Dr. Death, Steve Williams, created it!

Genichiro Tenryu is another tough worker that I tremendously respect. We feuded in both singles and tag-team matches. He has a scoop brainbuster and powerbomb that will rock your world.

Well, when he ventured from All Japan to start his own promotion, WAR (Wrestling And Romance), he had enough respect to contact me for his top foreign wrestler, or gaijin. During the courting process, Tenryu treated my family and me to a great stay at his home. I was in awe of this castle. The rooms were gigantic, and the master bedroom closet alone was as big as my double-car garage. We wined and dined at the finest restaurants and enjoyed Tenryu's hospitality.

All Japan was loaded with a roster of superstars who did a series of tours for the company. We packed 60,000 people at the Egg Dome in Tokyo on a regular basis, another 45,000 here, and another 30,000 there. All Japan was unreal. Some of the gaijin studs included Stan Hansen, Harley Race, Ric Flair, Johnny Ace, Gary Albright, Mil Mascaras, Dynamite Kid, Chris and Mark Youngblood, and the Road Warriors. The entire cadre of workers was unreal.

I really liked the Youngblood brothers. Chris and Mark were second-generation wrestlers. Their dad was Ricky Romero. Mark and Chris had an awesome Native American gimmick, the Renegade Warriors, and worked really hard in the ring. Though they weren't main eventers in Japan, the two always put on a match that excited the audience. Both guys were very dependable and had a great understanding of the business.

Young workers today could learn a lot from Chris and Mark. To be a success in the business, one doesn't have to be the main event. It takes the entire roster and slate of matches to bring the fans back. More wrestlers like the Youngbloods are needed in the business today.

After Terry Gordy went back to the States, I teamed with both Johnny Ace and Gary Albright. Johnny and I became tag-team champs in 1996, defeating Misawa and Jun Akiyama. More than a year later, Gary and I defeated Kenta Kobashi and Johnny Ace to become tag strap holders in All Japan for the sixth time.

The WWF and All Japan sometimes held joint shows together in Japan. During one combined tour, Terry was supposed to fight Hulk Hogan. But at the last minute, they replaced Terry with Stan Hansen. For the occasion, Terry Gordy brought his wife (Connie—a great lady) and I brought Tammy to Japan. Overall, we had a nice mini-vacation. At one point, though, our wives chewed us out. While at a local karaoke bar, Terry and I made fun of all the Japanese people. We were in character, but the ladies thought we were very insensitive.

Anyway, the next night we were at the Tokyo Dome. About 60,000 people were in attendance. Tammy was excited to be there. Fans were chanting her name as well as mine. As I watched the action from the back, I saw my wife in the monitor. Jake "the Snake" Roberts was wrestling somebody. After about 10 minutes, I happened to glance at the monitor again and noticed this beautiful lady in a red dress running and screaming. It was Tammy! Jake was chasing her with his boa constrictor, Damien!

Gary Albright was a big man. He stood about 6-foot-3 and weighed close to 360 pounds. I knew Gary from college when he wrestled at the University of Nebraska. I beat him in the Big Eight championship.

Before the start of the tournament, Gary and I were swimming at the hotel pool. We had fun throwing the little guys around. They always tried the heavyweights. Gary and I just tossed them around like rubber duckies and tried to drown them. During a down moment, Gary asked, "Doc, how do you become a professional wrestler?"

At that time, I was already training to be a wrestler in Mid-South. I said, "Gary, this is a tough business. You can do it, but if you don't make it in five years, quit."

Well, to his credit, Gary worked very hard to become a professional wrestler. I am not sure who trained him, but because he started wrestling in Stu Hart's Stampede Wrestling promotion, I assume the Hart family trained him. He did lots of shoot fighting and was quite successful.

After Terry Gordy faded out in Japan, Giant Baba asked Gary to come to All Japan. He soon became my partner. Let me tell you, Gary thought he was invincible. He lived life on the edge. I used to call him "Dr. Jekyll and Mr. Hyde."

I remember one "Dr. Jekyll and Mr. Hyde" moment as if it were yesterday. Gary was engaged to be married. The wedding was scheduled like a year in advance. So for almost a year, we had what seemed like a mini-

Chris Youngblood: My brother Mark and I made several tours for All Japan Pro Wrestling between 1987-1997. A particular incident that stands out in my mind was the time a group of guys from the roster went out on the town in Tokyo. The place was Roppongi, a Las Vegas-style strip of everything imaginable set in the heart of Tokyo. After a grueling match between Stan Hansen and Bobby Duncum Jr. at Korukuen Hall, Mark and Johnny Ace suggested a few of the boys go to the Hard Rock Café in Roppongi and maybe over to Pibbs Bar for some foosball.

So we all took off in taxis: Doc, Mark, Johnny, Ricky Santana, Richie Slinger, Johnny Smith, and me. We all ate well at the Rock and a few of us went to Pibbs and some left to go back to the Hotel Ginza. Doc, Mark, Richie, and I went bar hopping and noticed a bar with the face of a streamliner train as the entrance. We went inside. Road Warrior "Hawk" was inside and bought a round of "Hell Raiser Hellbounds," flaming shots you had to drink fast with a straw or they would melt.

After that, Mark and I disbanded and went to several nightclubs and karaoke bars. Then we made a huge circle on the strip back to Pibb; it was well past 4 a.m. Mark and I were trying to flag a taxi back to the Hotel Ginza and noticed Dr. Death was also looking for a taxi. So we ran across the streets between cars and motorcycles and met back with Doc.

We decided to share a taxi back to the hotel. Doc got in the passenger side as Mark and I got in back. The driver had a surprised look on his face when he realized who all he had in his taxi. We took off into some back street neighborhoods when Mark and I noticed Doc had a microphone in his hand.

Doc started belting out in his burly voice the words to "Volare," or one of those Rat Packer songs. With my window rolled down a little, I noticed the song was blaring off the buildings outside the taxi. The taxi had a speaker inside and outside of the taxi, so Doc turned up the volume and handed the microphone to us in the back. WOW! I grabbed the mic and started singing "Danka Schoen" like Ferris Bueller. Then Mark was pulling on the mic to get his song in.

The whole while the driver kept talking to us, but we didn't understand him a bit. Doc got the mic back and was crashing notes when the taxi came to a stop. That was one of the fastest trips back to the hotel, but it didn't look like the Ginza. It had frosted glass doors and bars on the window! Wait, this was a police station. Evidently the driver was telling us all along that it was unlawful to use the outside karaoke speaker after 12:00 a.m.!

So Doc and he were arguing, and I was freaking out that we were headed to the pokey. Doc, being the great negotiator he is, talked the driver into taking us —in silence—back to the Ginza. That was one of my favorite times of my life ... thanks, Doc, for the wonderful memories.

bachelor party in every town in Japan. But the main one was planned in Maui, where he was to be married.

When our tour concluded, Gary and I, along with about six of the boys, hopped on a plane to attend Gary's bachelor party and wedding. The night before we took off, Gary got blitzed on Dom Perignon in Osaka. We told him not to drink it. But he did.

While on the plane ride to the scheduled bachelor party at Duke's in Waikiki, Gary turned into a drunken fool. He kept saying, "I'm going home to see Mama. I don't want to get married." He embarrassed everyone. Johnny Smith, Jim Steele (Lacrosse, who made up the "Triangle of Power" faction with Gary and me in 1997), and the others told the stewardess to just leave him alone. Gary eventually passed out, and upon our arrival, he woke up like nothing had ever happened. The bachelor party was unforgettable, and Gary got married as scheduled.

Gary was one tough man. He wasn't too technically sound, but he knew how to do suplexes (German, belly-to-belly, and snap double underhook) and was strong enough to throw anyone all over the ring. When he got mad, it wasn't pretty. He had a temper and burned many a bridge in Japan.

I was always scared for him. I used to tell him to slow down. Gary would reply, "Yeah Doc, I am going to go as long as I can go." Gary was a diabetic and often did not take care of his condition. He loved to drink and partied way too much. In early 2000, Gary died in the ring of a heart attack. God rest his soul.

After leaving Japan for two years to work for the WWF and a short stint in WCW, I returned to All Japan in 2000. I was once again "back home." Since Baba had passed away, I decided to both wrestle and book for the International Wrestling Association of Japan (IWA).

I was in charge of bringing in workers and buying airplane tickets. It was a big responsibility, but I enjoyed the opportunity to help build a quality promotion in Japan. I brought in Ted DiBiase, Bubba Rogers, Mike Rotunda, Terry Taylor, Hacksaw Jim Duggan, and many other great talents.

In October of 2002, Johnny Smith, Mike Rotunda, and I beat Ryuji, Mitsuya Nagai, and Yoji Anjoh. It was a great match, and I had the opportunity to work with my two dear friends. But I was soon forced out of the IWA as a booker and talent because I made a mistake. I brought in this huge kid named Harper. He was nearly seven feet tall and had this Roman Gladiator gimmick. I thought he had a good look and asked him to come on over.

When working in Japan, you have to have a working visa. I can't recall if we didn't have enough time or what, but he didn't get the visa. So I clearly told him, "Keep quiet, and don't tell anyone you are coming to Japan to work. You are coming to Japan simply as a tourist."

Guess what? On the trip over, the kid started running his mouth, saying that he was a professional wrestler coming to Japan to wrestle. Upon arrival in Tokyo, customs nabbed him. He opened his mouth, spilled the beans, and was sent back to the States. Not only did I lose the company's airfare, but I also lost my job.

I was ready to slow down. It was time for me to spend more time with my family. My son had reached the age at which he needed a full-time dad. In 2003, I retired to spend more time with Wyndam and to follow through on a potential lead as a wrestling trainer/worker with the now-WWE (World Wrestling Entertainment).

Sayonara, Japan.

SIXTEEN

WWE/WWF

In early 1998, my good friend Jim Ross telephoned. At the time, I was living in Hawaii. My ex-wife and family were staying with me for about a month. Jim was working for the WWF. Over the years, the two of us communicated back and forth about a variety of issues, including the possibility of working for the WWF.

Jim spoke to my ex for about two hours. We then spoke, and he asked me if I wanted to come back to work in the United States. I was offered a $300,000 contract for two years. I was blown away. Combining this amount with the potential merchandise sales and other financial opportunities, I knew that I would have enough revenue to take care of my family for the rest of my life. The timing was right, so I accepted the offer.

I wasn't aware, however, that I had to do a tryout match. Being in the business for 20 years, I felt insulted. I had already signed a contract. But thinking of the financial security I would be able to provide for my family, I agreed to the match and wrestled Too Cold Scorpio.

After the successful tryout, I met and spoke with Vince McMahon and other executives within the company. The WWE/F's headquarters is a state-of-the-art facility. I was impressed by the professionalism and was treated with respect. I guess that had a lot to do with me being Jim's boy.

I listened to Jim Ross. He told me that I was going to have a six-month run against none other than Stone Cold Steve Austin. This opportunity meant more money, videos, merchandise, and who knows what else.

Stone Cold, besides being an excellent worker and great person, was the hottest name in the business. I felt I could work well with Stone Cold. I would be the big, bad heel, and him the babyface.

I was pretty much a loner during my tenure with the WWF. I protected myself. I was cordial to all the workers and never started any trouble. I didn't disrespect anybody, but I was focused on my primary objective: to do what I had to do to work a program with Stone Cold.

During my stay, I did my best to interact when necessary. Sable's former husband, Marc Mero, is a very nice guy, and we chatted on occasion. The same went for a few of the other guys, such as Steve Blackman, Too Cold Scorpio, Road Warrior Hawk, and the Godfather.

Due to his class and strength, I respected the Godfather. He is a very sophisticated person and super strong. I would say he was probably one of the toughest guys in the WWE. He had a good run with the company, using different gimmicks such as Papa Shango, The Goodfather, and the Godfather.

One day, I was eating lunch in the cafeteria. As I was tearing up a piece of meat, I heard this deep voice behind me say, "Hi, Doc." I turned to see who this guy was and what he wanted. To my dismay, it wasn't a guy. Rather, it was the finely chiseled Chyna. Chyna, of course, is a female wrestler dubbed "The Ninth Wonder of the World." She was an excellent worker and treated me with a tremendous amount of respect. Chyna went on to accomplish probably more in the ring than any other woman in the history of the wrestling business.

Before my feud with Stone Cold could begin, the WWF came up with the *Brawl for All* shoot tournament. I am not sure if this was the creation of Jim Ross, Bruce Pritchard, or Vince McMahon. Any way you looked at it, the brawl wasn't really a total shoot. All the combatants would have to wear boxing gloves. There were also rules. In a shoot, there usually aren't any rules, and if so, few at best—but not with the *Brawl for All.*

Each match consisted of three one-minute rounds. The wrestler who connected with the most punches per round scored five points. In addition, a clean takedown scored five points and a knockdown was worth 10.

A knockout ended the match. The matches were scored by ringside judges.

I wasn't too keen about having my hands tied up. From the football field to the wrestling mat to the bar room to the street, I always depended on my hands for success. Despite the concern, I entered the brawl.

It was an all-volunteer tournament, and many guys refused to enter because they could suffer serious injury. I recall Ken Shamrock backing out. Ultimate Fighter Dan "The Beast" Severn withdrew afterward because of his frustration at the rules and the idea of having to wear boxing gloves. Along with guys like Bradshaw, Steve Blackman, the Godfather, Savio Vega, Bart Gunn, and Bob Holly, I entered the tournament.

The brawl paid $10,000 per match and $100,000 to the winner. I asked Jim Ross and Bruce Pritchard what would happen if I hurt one of the entrants. I was told that it was a shoot, and every person knew the consequences.

I could sense, and was later told, that many people wanted to see Dr. Death get knocked down. I had come in with the reputation as the toughest man in the business. The boys wanted to see how bad Dr. Death really was in the ring. It was also a modified shoot, so everyone had an interest in the event.

Because of my name, I was favored to win the brawl. My first match was against Pierre Carl Ouellet. Pierre is a big man, standing about 6 foot and weighing close to 250 pounds. I had nothing personal against the guy, but I came out swinging like there was no tomorrow. I wasn't a boxer, and that was my strategy. I felt I was in good enough shape to implement this approach. I eventually wore Pierre out and advanced to the second round.

As I awaited my second-round opponent, the rules and format kept changing. The changes also benefited the boxer rather than the wrestler. I needed to get someone down. Once on the mat, I could tie him up like a pretzel. Well, by then, the rules stated that if you took someone down, you had to let them back up.

After defeating Pierre, I was supposed to fight Too Cold Scorpio. Unbeknownst to me, however, the Godfather and I had switched places.

I was now facing Bart Gunn. Unfortunately, and not by choice, I was knocked out in the second round of the tournament. Though I had a torn hamstring and torn butt muscle, I never gave up. With my hands down by my side, I got back up on my feet.

I must have seen the video a thousand times. I walked right into Bart Gunn's right and got knocked down. Bart Gunn made a name for himself and eventually was crowned the winner of the brawl, defeating Bradshaw in the championship by TKO.

Besides me, a number of other WWF talents got dinged in the brawl. Both Steve Blackman and Road Warrior Hawk had to take time off. Savio Vega aggravated an old arm injury and would never work for WWF again.

The tournament was considered a failure by many. In the end, they tried to parlay Bart's victory against a legitimate professional boxer. At *WrestleMania XV* in Philadelphia, Butterbean knocked out Bart Gunn 35 seconds into the first round. The brawl concept was soon scraped.

Though I was injured, I was determined to rehab my hamstring and get into the best shape of my career. I had a run with Stone Cold in the future, and I wanted to make sure Steve and I rocked the house.

Shortly thereafter, the WWF was about to debut its new weekly program, *SMACKDOWN*, on UPN. I was told that after rehab, I would appear on this program. I was in high spirits. I began rehabbing and pushing it like no tomorrow. Dory Funk Jr. was the head trainer for the WWF's Dojo. With his guidance and leadership, I made strides in the ring. I was sent down to Dr. Andrews in Birmingham to get cleared. It would soon be Stone Cold time.

I had a few matches prior to being called up. I will never forget the match I had against Bob Holly. During the contest, I gave Bob my patented side suplex. I guess it was too stiff for Bob, because he squealed like a pig and ran to Vince McMahon. Combine that with my throwing Bart Gunn off the stage onto tables at a live event, and it was soon the beginning of the end for Dr. Death in the WWF.

Shortly thereafter, someone in creative central came up with the idea to put me under a hood. Can you imagine Dr. Death wearing a mask? Why the mask? The writers couldn't figure out what to do with me. Jim Ross even went to bat for me, saying, "How can you cover up someone with the credentials of Steve 'Dr. Death' Williams after all he has done and accomplished?" But with Vince Russo and others in creative central trying to push JR out, it was only a matter of time before they buried me.

I also sensed that Vince McMahon was upset with me. Due to my performance in the brawl and my resulting injury, Vince looked at me as a used car. There went my run with Stone Cold.

I was later told to work for the Frontier Martial Arts Wrestling (FMW) promotion in Japan. During this time, the WWF and FMW exchanged talent and had some agreements with each other.

> MIKE GEARY: DOC SHOULD HAVE KNOWN BETTER THAN TO ENTER THIS EVENT. HE IS AS STRONG AS A BULL, BUT NEEDS HIS HANDS TO DO HIS DAMAGE. DOC KNOWS ALL THE WRESTLING MOVES AND COULD LITERALLY SNAP A PERSON INTO TWO. BUT HE NEEDS THE USE OF HIS HANDS.
>
> AS FOR BART, DOC HAD WHIPPED HIM ON NUMEROUS OCCASIONS WHEN THEY WRESTLED IN JAPAN. DOC TOSSED HIM AROUND LIKE A FEATHERWEIGHT. LIKE A HOLE IN ONE ON THE GOLF COURSE, HOWEVER, THIS TIME DOC GOT SUCKERED INTO A LUCKY PUNCH AND GOT KNOCKED DOWN. IT WAS SOMETHING THAT ONLY HAPPENS ONCE IN A LIFETIME.

I refused to go. There was no way that I was going to do that to Giant Baba. I was loyal to Baba and would never work for a rival promotion. When my two-year run with the WWF expired, I planned to return to All Japan. I wasn't going to do anything to disgrace or dishonor Baba.

The next thing I knew, the Federal Express truck delivered some papers to me. They simply stated: "Mr. Williams, you have breached your contract." In short, I was no longer entitled to my $300,000. I thought about taking the WWF to court, but it was economically unfeasible for me to hire lawyers at the time. See, I was already fighting another major personal legal battle.

JIM ROSS: THE *BRAWL FOR ALL* CONCEPT LOOKED GOOD ON PAPER, BUT WAS A DISASTER. VIRTUALLY EVERYONE THAT PARTICIPATED IN IT GOT HURT IN VARYING FORMS. IT WAS INTRIGUING BUT DANGEROUS. DOC LOSING WAS A SURPRISE BECAUSE OF HIS WRESTLING SKILLS AND STREET-FIGHTING ABILITIES. DOC WAS CERTAINLY ONE OF THE FAVORITES, AND IF HE HAD WON THE COMPETITION HANDILY, HE WOULD HAVE GOTTEN HIMSELF OVER TO THE MASSES THAT DID NOT KNOW HIM BECAUSE OF HIS YEARS IN JAPAN, OF WHICH MOST AMERICAN FANS KNEW NOTHING ABOUT.

DOC FINISHING A FIGHT WITH A TORN, OFF-THE-BONE QUADRICEP WAS THE STUFF OF LEGEND. ONE CAN ONLY IMAGINE THE PAIN HE WAS IN, BUT HE BECAME THE ONE-LEGGED MAN IN AN ASS-KICKING CONTEST.

In early 1998, I was slapped with a paternity lawsuit. This "Deadbeat Dad" case made national and international news. It was in the *USA Today* and other major media headlines. There I was, an international wrestling superstar, heading to the WWF for my biggest payout ever. But all of it was overshadowed by my being portrayed as an irresponsible father.

A few years back, a groupie came up to our hotel room in Tulsa, Oklahoma. Buzz Sawyer, John Norton, and I engaged in a youthful indiscretion which I am embarrassed by to this day. Seeing that I was going to be rolling in the dough with the WWF, the woman claimed that I was the father of her child.

In front of a packed courthouse with media galore, I had to unnecessarily subject my family to this untruth. I had to take two DNA tests; in front of everyone, they swabbed my mouth with these large Q-tips. The results unequivocally proved that I wasn't the father. Yet the humiliation to me and the shame to my family was indecent and offensive.

In the end, the case cost me slightly more than $100,000! Between lawyer fees, court costs, testing, travel, and other related expenses, all the money I had saved over the last few years was gone. Though I won the case and was vindicated, the lawyers were the only ones to benefit from the sham.

JIM ROSS: AUSTIN WAS SO HOT THAT VIRTUALLY ANYONE WHO HAD ANY ABILITIES AT ALL WOULD HAVE DRAWN BIG MONEY WITH HIM. IF DOC HAD BEEN ABLE TO COME THROUGH THE *BRAWL FOR ALL* AND WOULD HAVE BEEN GIVEN A MANAGER TO HELP HIM WITH HIS PROMOS, WITH DOC'S SKILLS IT WOULD HAVE BEEN A GOOD IN-RING PROGRAM. I THINK BOTH AUSTIN AND DOC WOULD HAVE HAD GOOD CHEMISTRY AND WOULD HAVE HAD A GOOD RUN.

THE QUAD INJURY REALLY SPELLED THE END OF DOC'S RUN IN THE WWE. DOC WAS CONSIDERED MY BOY AND WITH VINCE RUSSO LOOKING TO ASCEND TO MORE POWER AND USE ME AS A STEPPING STONE, DOC WAS CREATIVELY DOOMED AND FEW KNEW IT. IT WAS NOT MEANT TO BE. PERHAPS FIVE OR 10 YEARS EARLIER DOC COULD HAVE BEEN ON MAIN EVENTS, BUT NOT SO MUCH AT THE AGE HE CAME IN AND ESPECIALLY AFTER THE *BRAWL FOR ALL* FIASCO.

After my WWF debacle, I returned to All Japan. To make a dollar and try to repair my relationship with the WWF, I made a couple of appearances for the now-WWE in May of 2003. I wrestled Lance Storm twice, both of us scoring a victory apiece. I hoped the showing would secure me a position in some capacity, wrestler or trainer, with the company. Unfortunately, I didn't attain anything.

While still trying to catch on with the WWE, I had a three-month run with Major League Wrestling (MLW). This was a very progressive organization founded by Court Bauer. Court is a classy person, and I have a tremendous amount of respect for him. Court's promotion was about fighting and wrestling, not sports entertainment.

In September of 2003, as part of MLW's *WAR GAMES*, I worked an eight-man tag match. Teaming with Terry Funk, Sabu, and the Sandman, we made up the "Funkin Army." We whipped the Extreme Horsemen, led by Steve Corino.

In December 2003, I went with Ricky Nelson's promotion to China. I defeated Terry Taylor to win the NWA Mid-Atlantic Heavyweight title. Soon thereafter, I was diagnosed with throat cancer. My life would never be the same.

SEVENTEEN

GOODBYE, DR. DEATH

I have always believed in God. Growing up in Colorado, my parents took me to church. It had a relaxed atmosphere, and I always felt comfortable. The leaders and clergy were forthright, and I respected the church. I learned about prayer, Jesus, the Holy Spirit, and eternal life.

Throughout my high school, college, and early professional wrestling years, I didn't attend church on a regular basis but tried to live a proper life. My mother and father taught me the difference between right and wrong. Often, however, I would yield to the temptation of late-night parties and the young ladies. But I always believed in God.

I wasn't a bad or evil guy. I never deliberately hurt anyone and always opened my heart to those in need. Over the years, I have helped many members of my family, close friends, individuals in the wrestling business, and people in general.

> RICKY MORTON: I LOVE DOC AND BELIEVE HE IS A TRUE CREDIT TO THE WRESTLING BUSINESS. HE HAD DIRECTION AND A STRONG WORK ETHIC. THOUGH HE LOOKED LIKE A MONSTER, HE HAD A HEART OF A TEDDY BEAR—ESPECIALLY IF HE LIKED YOU.
>
> IN FACT, DOC WAS THE ONE WHO GOT ROBERT AND ME OUR JOBS WITH THE CROCKETT PROMOTION. IN A MATCH AGAINST TED AND DOC, THEY PUT US OVER AND SOLD FOR US BIG TIME. THANKS, DOC!

I will never forget the spring of 2006. I received a call from Johnny Ace of the WWE. He asked me if I was interested in being a special referee when they came to the old Mid-South cities–Monroe, Shreveport, Lafayette, and Baton Rouge. I overwhelmingly appreciated and without hesitation accepted the offer. After all I had been through, this gesture was a sign from the Lord that I was working my way back into the wrestling business.

The WWE wanted me to do some radio and television promotional work for the upcoming shows in both Monroe and Shreveport. The company treated me first class and even provided me with limousine service to and from Shreveport and Monroe.

While I was in Monroe, I met the mayor, Jamie Mayo. I also received an e-mail and phone call from a young lady who worked as a nurse at a local retirement home. She wanted me to come down and visit. Many seniors at the home were wrestling fans.

Throughout my entire wrestling career, I have never forgotten about the fans. I showed up with bells on and had a grand time. I remember one lady was 103 years old. I joked with her, saying that her aging secret needed to rub off on me. She laughed and I gave her a big hug.

I also met an 86-year-old man in a wheelchair. He was mimicking a wrestler and wanted to drop an elbow on me. I let him, and it made his day. We also hugged. I signed autographs and gave many fans wrestling paraphernalia. I did this for a couple of hours. I also gave Dr. Death T-shirts to 10 fans who I knew were going to attend the show in Monroe.

I was truly blessed to have the opportunity to visit these fans. With an 83-year-old mother, this experience hit close to home. I know God wanted me there to share with those people. To offer them hope and love. To show them unbridled compassion and understanding. Though many of the men and women were excited to see me, it was Steve Williams, Dr. Life, who was humored and privileged to visit with them.

I also remember working as Santa Claus. Not as part of a wrestling show, but during the holiday season at a mall. I first worked as Santa Claus during high school. I really love the Christmas season and needed some quick money for presents. So I went down to the local mall in Lakewood. They hired me on the spot. I got my Santa outfit, and since I was so big, I didn't even need a pillow. They gave me a bell, and I loved to ring it.

I had a great time. I would sit down in a chair as an elf brought children of all ages to me. The elf would get the children's' names beforehand. They would sit on my lap, and I would say, "Ho, Ho, Ho. Merry Christmas little Johnny (or Julie). What do you want for Christmas?"

It was so much fun to see the vast array of personalities. Some would be very excited to sit on Santa's lap. Others would cry like there were no tomorrow.

I must have worked about a week on the job when an incident occurred. A little boy, maybe two years old, sat on my lap. I was as jovial as could be and asked him what he wanted for Christmas. All of a sudden, I felt this wet sensation on my lap. And it was flowing down my leg. I don't know if he had just drunk a gallon of milk, but my lap and legs were soaking wet!

I called the elf over and told him that we were going on break. I went to the main office that hired me and turned in my Santa uniform. I quit on the spot. Talk about a "White Christmas!"

In my early 30s, I decided to once again play Santa Claus. After my ex and I divorced, there was a major void in my life. I wrestled and ran my Body Blaster's Gym in Bossier City. After work, I went home to an empty house. It was the Christmas season, and I became very depressed.

In an effort to alleviate the pain, I went down to the management office of Pierre Bossier Mall in Bossier City. I asked for a job as Santa Claus. They all knew me and hired me on the spot. I only asked that they wouldn't tell anyone it was me. They agreed.

I worked as Santa as much as I could until Christmas. I had a blast. The interaction with children and people temporarily helped me to deal with my pain. Also, nobody knew it was me. It was great. I even called my ex and told her to bring Wyndam down to the mall to see Santa. As Wyndam sat on my lap, crying, he had no clue that Santa was his daddy.

I donated all the money I made working as Santa. I took the roughly $500 down to Fred Lowery. Fred is the senior pastor of First Baptist

> TAMMY BREWSTER: I TOOK WYNDAM TO SEE SANTA. WYNDAM, THOUGH NOT FOR LONG, SAT ON SANTA'S LAP. I COULDN'T BELIEVE THAT HE DID NOT REALIZE IT WAS HIS DAD.

Church in Bossier City. I told him to give it to a family or children who didn't have anyone or anything for Christmas.

The wrestling business is tough, and I did the best that I could while on the road. But I was wild, crazy, and full of ambition. I wanted to be the best, and often took my eyes off what was Godly. The temptations, lifestyle, stress, and other youthful indiscretions often hindered my growth in the Lord.

This unfortunate time in my life reminds me of the last two paragraphs of the revered *Footprints in the Sand* narrative:

"LORD, you said that once I decided to follow you, you'd walk with me all the way. But I have noticed that during the most troublesome times in my life, there is only one set of footprints. I don't understand why when I needed you most you would leave me." The LORD replied: "My son, my precious child, I love you and I would never leave you. During your times of trial and suffering, when you see only one set of footprints, it was then that I carried you."

My faith in the Lord and my personal relationship with Jesus Christ began to change when I met my ex-wife. She was attending the Shreveport Community Church—an Assemblies of God denomination. Their motto was and is: "The best is yet to come."

I wasn't too familiar with this particular house of worship. Yet, trying to be a good husband while simultaneously trying to improve my relationship with God, I started to regularly attend her church. It was also at this time, in my early 30s, that I accepted Jesus Christ as my personal savior.

For God so loved the world that he gave his one and only Son, that whoever believes in him shall not perish but have eternal life. John 3:16

The members of the Assemblies of God church are very evangelical. The atmosphere is very exciting and dynamic. The people raise their hands while praying. They jump and run around the church, praising God. There is much singing and praising, as well as the speaking of tongues.

At first, this atmosphere was very different from what I had experienced in the past. I had attended Protestant churches a few times, but I had never seen such fundamentalism as this before. It wasn't that I was against it, but as you can imagine, it took some time to get used to.

Recently married with an adopted daughter, I attended the church with my family as often as I could during my time off. In between my Japanese tours and wrestling in the States, I tried my best to be a good parent, spouse, and to improve my relationship with God.

One time after a long tour, I reluctantly went to church in a foul mood. The devil was working awfully hard to break me. It was very hot in the church, and I was sweating profusely. It felt like I was in a sauna; I was miserable. I looked over to Tammy and snapped at her, "For crying out loud, don't they turn on the air conditioner in this place?"

With sweat dripping down my face, I got up and proceeded to the foyer. Trying to cool down, I went into the bathroom and dried up. I looked into the mirror and tried to compose myself. At that moment, I knew that the devil was working me.

I wasn't going to let Satan win. Unlike in the past, I knew what I did was wrong. Like all Christians, I knew that I wasn't perfect. We are only forgiven. I took deep breaths and immediately prayed for forgiveness, guidance, and patience. I could feel the presence of God. After a few minutes, I cooled down and went back to my seat. From there on out, everything went fine.

My ex was a very devout Christian, and she was a good role model for me, an infant in Christ. Though not yet a member, she always went to church while I was on the road. She could even speak in tongues. Her faith and commitment to Christ were unreal. I valued her interaction with the Lord, and I wanted to be just like her.

Unfortunately, my ex gave me a hard time. She nagged me about why I didn't raise my arms in church or do the other fundamentalist things she did, which included speaking in tongues.

Also, I never went up to the altar during altar call. I just sat there praying and asking God to guide and show me. After a while, I began to get used to the environment. To be honest, however, I still didn't understand this Assemblies of God religion.

I wasn't home that much because I was chasing that almighty dollar. I worked like there was no tomorrow to give my family everything I didn't have growing up: a big house, nice cars, braces for my adopted daughter's teeth, and anything else anyone in my family needed or wanted. God was once again carrying me.

While I was on the road, my ex decided to join the church with both her mother and Stormy. I was hurt by this effort, because we were a family. We had discussions about joining the church together, but because of my wrestling schedule, our plans kept getting postponed.

When I got home from an exhausting tour, she told me they had joined the church and wanted to know if I were going to. I was very upset. I really loved my ex but was saddened by her decision. As a couple, I thought we were a team. A team is supposed to do things together. Nonetheless, I was a family man who wanted to grow in Christ. So shortly thereafter, I also joined the church. I tried my best to make my family happy.

Unfortunately, though, my ex and I later divorced; this really hurt me. I had committed my life to Tammy and my family, and then they were gone. I was grief-stricken and anxious about how I would live. I felt angry, guilty, and depressed. Though saved, I was still running hard. To cope with my divorce and the demands of the wrestling business, I continued smoking, drinking, and doing steroids.

Yet, through faith, I worked through the trauma, trial, and tribulation. Unlike in the past, this time I found time to go to church. The more I attended, the more comfortable I became with the Assemblies of God. The pastor and its members always treated me in an exceptional manner.

I also started to educate myself on both the Pentecostal denomination and the Bible. I became more informed on church beliefs and doctrines. I studied the Bible and became more aware of the Holy Spirit, the power of prayer, supernatural healing, and speaking in tongues.

One day they had a calling to the altar. I walked to the front. This church has about 5,000 members, so it was packed to the max. Pastor

THE TWO TOUGHEST MEN ON THE PLANET FROM TWO DIFFERENT GENERATIONS, GENE KINISKI AND ME.

Denny Duron and his wife, Deanza (who today are also my neighbors), and others were laying hands on people and praying for them. As an athlete who has suffered numerous shoulder injuries, my shoulders are pretty much shot. So I had a hard time raising and stretching my arms out for a long period of time when praying to God.

Under the lights, it was hot and I was sweating. But unlike in the past, I was more concerned about prayer than sweat and pain. Hands were placed upon me and others prayed for me. They were trying to get the Holy Spirit inside of me, so I would become anointed and speak in tongues.

It didn't happen. I asked myself, "Why isn't this working?" Still in prayer, I tried to relax. I put my arms down and took a few deep breaths.

Pastor Duron said, "Okay, Dr. Life. You can do it." Since my salvation, I have been called "Dr. Life." Simultaneously, I thought, "God, let's try this one more time."

But it still didn't happen. I didn't speak in tongues. I became very angry and frustrated and acted in a very un-Christian manner. After church, I hopped in my car and sped off to visit friends in Dallas. Behind the wheel, I started to question the entire process. I wondered why they had laid hands on me to try to get me to speak in tongues. I was genuinely upset.

As I reflect, speaking in tongues is not something of man. Rather, it is a supernatural gift from God. As Apostle Paul so eloquently wrote in First Corinthians:

For he that speaketh in an unknown tongue speaketh not unto men, but unto God: for no man understandeth him; howbeit in the spirit he speaketh mysteries.

Nonetheless, as I proceeded down Interstate 20 to Dallas, I was determined not to go back to church. I wasn't denouncing my faith or salvation, but I simply wanted no part of the Assemblies of God.

I kept my word for a couple of weeks. But you know what? There was a void in my life. I felt empty inside. I enjoyed attending church. I was hurting from the divorce, but church made me feel better. All these people in the church genuinely loved me as a brother in Christ. Church also brought compassion and peace to my life. Deep down, I felt something unique about this place of worship.

As the weeks progressed, I attended a class at church taught by Pastor Johnny Booty. Pastor Booty is the father of current USC quarterback John David Booty. Pastor Booty is presently the athletic director at Calvary Baptist Academy in Shreveport.

The class was an introduction to the doctrines and beliefs of the Assemblies of God church. I enrolled and attended the four-weekend session. And I honestly got into it. I learned in depth what the Assemblies of God is all about: praising God, raising arms, speaking in tongues, etc.

During this time, I once again committed my life to Jesus Christ. Though I had accepted Christ earlier, I was backsliding. I was still smoking and drinking to cope with stress. I was shooting steroids to keep up in the wrestling business. I was chasing the dollar to provide my family with a good life and future. But I had forgotten about my relationship with God. Once again, the Lord was carrying me.

> TED DIBIASE: I STARTED SEEING A CHANGE IN DOC BEFORE THE CANCER. I DON'T KNOW IF I HAD AN INFLUENCE ON HIM BY SHARING MY STORY AND CHANGE, BUT I NOTICED THAT HE WAS GENUINELY CHANGING.
>
> AND THEN DOC HAD TO DEAL WITH CANCER. AS A MINISTER, I OFTEN TELL FOLKS THAT GOD WILL DO WHAT HE HAS TO DO TO GET YOUR ATTENTION. I WATCHED HIM GO THROUGH CANCER. NOT TOO MANY PEOPLE COULD HAVE HANDLED IT THE WAY DOC DID. HIS FAITH COULD HAVE WAVERED, BUT IT DIDN'T.
>
> I HAVE ALWAYS ADMIRED DOC AS BEING A TOUGH GUY AND GREAT ATHLETE. THOUGH HE IS FEARLESS AND TENACIOUS, DEEP DOWN HE IS A LOVEABLE PUPPY DOG.
>
> I THINK DOC IS BEING A CALLED TO THE MINISTRY. AS PART OF MY WRESTLING CRUSADES, I WANT DOC TO BE PART OF THIS BATTLE. HE HAS A POWERFUL TESTIMONY. BECAUSE OF HIS HUMILITY AND WHO HE IS, DOC CAN HELP REALIZE HOW GREAT GOD CAN BE WITH HIS UNBARRING FORGIVENESS.

And then it happened. In September of 2003, I was diagnosed with cancer. Many thought I would be dead within six months. Some gave me a year. I was scared. But deep down, I knew better. There was only one entity that had been by my side through both good and bad times. It was God.

For a lifetime, though the Lord was always carrying me, I no longer wanted to do things my way. Frank Sinatra was my hero, and like ol' Blue Eyes, I had always done things my way. In fact, I have a photo of my ex and me at a Sinatra concert in Las Vegas some years ago on New Year's.

Facing adversity like never before, I turned toward God. I quit smoking, drinking, and doing steroids. I surrendered my life completely to the Lord.

I continued to attend Bible study. One evening, I was feeling queasy because of the radiation treatment. The doctors literally had been cooking the tumor in my throat. The Bible study teacher, Delores Winder, along with her husband, Bill, and other close church members—Gary and Jamie Cislaghi, Harriette Johnson, Dennis Dunn, David Kreamer, "Doc" Bailey, Larry Crane, and James McKeal—started praying and laying hands on me.

All of a sudden, pieces of the tumor shot from my mouth and nose. Pieces of skin the size of my thumb flew everywhere. The power of God was at work.

I believe this experience was the turning point in my battle with cancer. I knew that God was going to heal me and that I was going to survive.

A lot of praying went on between the doctor visits, radiation, and chemotherapy. I started to ask God why I had gotten cancer. I thought that it might have been payback for all the bad things that I had done to people over the years. Maybe it was a way for me to settle down and get out of an industry that was ruining my life. I didn't know the answer, but I did know that God would decide the outcome.

> DELORES WINDER: WE MET STEVE WHEN HE WAS IN THE MIDST OF HIS BATTLE WITH CANCER. HE WAS A NEW CHRISTIAN AND SOLD OUT TO JESUS. HE JOINED OUR PRAYER GROUP AND NEVER ONCE TALKED OF DYING; HE KNEW THE LORD WOULD HEAL HIM. ALTHOUGH HIS BODY WAS IN DESTRUCTION, HIS SPIRIT WAS STRONG. HE OFTEN SAID, "DON'T EVER QUIT; TRUST THE LORD." TODAY WE THANK GOD HE IS HEALED AND THIS BOOK WILL BE A BLESSING TO MANY. GOD'S LOVE FLOWS THROUGH STEVE!

There were many days that I thought I wasn't going to make it. One time after I had had radiation and chemo, I was lying in my bedroom. I was all swelled up and couldn't breathe. I felt like I was suffocating. I got on my knees and prayed to God, "God, please don't let me die now. I have a son and a daughter to take care of. I have grandchildren to look after. Please spare my life. I will be a new man and a great father. One day I will be a great husband to somebody. I'll be a new person. In the name of Jesus, I ask this, Amen."

All of a sudden, I calmed. I started to breathe normally, but the relief didn't last long. Unexpectedly, I began sucking air. I thought I was going to die. But I somehow managed to once more pray, "God, please give me another chance. Please don't let me die now." Again, I started to calm.

Not knowing what would happen next, I quickly telephoned my ex. Instead of rushing over to help, she told me to go to the local hospital. I wasn't sure if that was the right decision. I thought, "What would the local hospital do about my situation?" So I calmly told my ex that I would talk to her later.

As I pondered my next move, I became breathless for the third time. Thinking three strikes and I would be out, I once again prayed for an opportunity. God spared me one more time.

Led by God, I jumped into my vehicle and finally decided to head to the emergency room. Barbara Grappe, my ex's mother-in-law, met me at the hospital. She is a great lady, and it was such a blessing to have someone like her there with me.

The doctors sprayed a steroid steam into my throat to open up my air passage. It was very painful and wasn't working. I was crying and screaming. I had to explain to them that I needed a special gel. This was the same gel used at M.D. Anderson. Once they located the gel, I took the bottle from the physician and emptied its entire contents into my throat, numbing everything.

The next day I went by myself to M.D. Anderson. Because the tumor had swelled up and blocked my air passage, they had to surgically make a stoma in my throat so I could breathe.

EIGHTEEN

HELLO, DR. LIFE

Right before my major surgery, I was lying in the hospital bed praying and preparing for the will of God. As with all major surgeries, a member of the clergy came by to pray with me. Along with my brother, Jeff, we engaged in deep prayer.

While praying, I felt the Holy Spirit working inside my body. The presence of God was unequivocally in the room. Because of this, I knew that everything was going to be fine and that the Lord would spare my life.

Sure enough, almost nine hours later, I had survived the operation. Barely conscious, I saw my brother Jeff. They wheeled me from the operating room to recovery. After some time, I was awake enough to see that they had cut my head from ear to ear. My head was swollen. I had a hole in my neck. I couldn't talk. As a person who made a living based on appearance, I was in total shock by the way I looked. I was also in serious pain. Next to God, morphine was my best friend.

At any rate, while convalescing, I kept my promises to God. I prayed and read the Bible. I also reflected on my past sins: drinking beer, smoking pot, snorting cocaine, popping pills, chasing women, etc. But now I had something a whole lot better: ENTERNAL LIFE THROUGH THE BLOOD OF JESUS CHRIST!

My clash with cancer was a test of my faith. While I battled this sickness, many people supported me. My pastor, Denny Duron, believed in me. He prayed for me. He hugged me and showed compassion and love.

I had a great church family who prayed and loved me. Many church members even organized a "Fast for Dr. Life." Can you imagine people fasting to help save Steve Williams? Though I had my extended church family, as well as my brothers and mother, praying for me, I felt that only God was by my side.

From the time of my radiation and chemotherapy to my major surgery, I read the Bible and prayed like never before. I love to pray, and even to this day believe in the power of prayer. I memorized and repeated prayers over and over again. I still say Psalms 23 every day:

The Lord is my shepherd; I shall not want. He maketh me to lie down in green pastures: He leadeth me beside the still waters. He restoreth my soul: He leadeth me in the paths of righteousness for His name's sake. Yea, though I walk through the valley of the shadow of death, I will fear no evil: for thou art with me; thy rod and thy staff they comfort me. Thou preparest a table before me in the presence of mine enemies: thou anointest my head with oil; my cup runneth over. Surely goodness and mercy shall follow me all the days of my life: and I will dwell in the house of the LORD forever.

I promised God that if He spared my life, I would read the entire Bible. I have never been a reader of books, and I even used to skim through the Bible. Not anymore. I have now read it cover to cover, and still read it on a daily basis.

I also started to tithe. I have worked very hard for my money and have been a penny-pincher my entire life. I rarely wasted money and saved everything for my family. But once I started reading the Bible, I learned the importance of tithing. I believe tithing is an acknowledgment that everything I have comes from God. As stated in Malachi 3:10:

Bring ye the whole tithe into the store-house, that there may be food in My house, and try Me now herewith, saith the LORD of hosts, if I will not open you the windows of heaven, and pour you out a blessing, that there shall be more than sufficiency.

Since my salvation, even while I was fighting cancer, I tithed $100 a week. Today, even though I am broke and literally live week to week, I give $50. I understand the importance of tithing and know that God will pro-

DENNY DURON: THE LIFE OF STEVE WILLIAMS READS LIKE A GREAT NOVEL. NOT ONLY IS STEVE A WORLD-FAMOUS WRESTLER, A FORMER ALL-AMERICAN FOOTBALL PLAYER, AND A WELL-KNOWN CELEBRITY, BUT HE IS ALSO A WONDERFUL FATHER, DEVOTED CHRISTIAN, AND COMMITTED MINISTER OF THE GOSPEL.

vide much, much more. He has already given back to me something that is priceless: my life and eternal life.

Every man according as he purposeth in his heart, so let him give; not grudgingly, or of necessity: for God loveth a cheerful giver. 2 Corinthians 9:7

Since my defeat of cancer, God had been so good to me. After my surgery, I weighed 206 pounds. My body looked wrinkled, and my skin looked like it was going to fall off of me. By the grace of God, two-plus years later, I now weigh 275 pounds. I am working out harder than ever before. God has given me my body back.

I no longer live for myself. I live for the Lord. Everything that I do is in God's hands. He spared my life and now I know the Lord wants me to share my testimony. Every day I strive to be a better Christian. I want to be a Centurion for the Lord. Come judgment day, I want to be the person who opens those pearly gates.

God has opened my eyes to make sure that I will never again neglect my family. I am categorically committed to Wyndam in every aspect of life. I will continue to witness to him, will be his role model, and will make sure he is a much better person than his father. The same goes for my beautiful daughter, Stormy, and my three lovely grandchildren.

God has reminded me that I never did things "my way." As much as I thought I did, I was wrong. God has given me everything: wonderful parents, the chance to graduate high school, great friends, a full-ride wrestling scholarship at OU, four-time All-American honors in wrestling, a stellar collegiate football career at OU under one of the greatest coaches in the history of the sport, Barry Switzer, the opportunity to wrestle in the U.S. Olympics, a professional football contract, international professional wrestling superstardom in every major company, a great church and wonderful pastor, and a great son, daughter, and family. GOD IS SO GREAT!

After my surgery, I wasn't sure how I was going to make a living. I have been a workaholic my entire life. I had respect for my profession and took it seriously. But now I am trying to figure out how to make a living. Like everyone else, I have bills to pay.

I know that God will provide, but I am only human. I am sure that he wants me to grow as a Christian, stay at home, and remain close to my son, Wyndam. Since I am divorced, his mother is not around. He needs his father to guide and take care of him and to give him love. He is everything to me.

Moreover, I have to remind myself that through faith and prayer, when one trusts in the Lord, things happen. I like to think that I am on vacation. I have a tough time accepting the fact that nobody wants to hire me. In all my years of professional wrestling, I have helped many people with bookings and opportunities. The fact that there isn't a place for me in the business is a hard pill to swallow. Then again, it must not be the Lord's will. If it is meant to be, God will make it happen. Only God knows what will happen next.

It seems that God has recently opened some doors. Ever since I turned 46 on May 14, 2006, my phone hasn't stopped ringing. I have already been in the ring 11 times, though it isn't steady work. Including a steel-cage match at the old ECW arena, I have wrestled, refereed, and have been interviewed. And with the help of my good friends, Johnny Ace and Jim Ross, I have also done some training, helping new talents learn the art of professional wrestling, for the WWE with both their Ohio Valley Wrestling (OVW) and Deep South Wrestling (DSW) developmental promotions.

I have also worked for the Christian Wrestling Federation (CWF). Because my focus is to win souls for Jesus Christ, I really enjoy working here and for other Christian organizations.

Unlike in traditional companies, after the wrestling show (which is less violent and more family-friendly), all the wrestlers come to the ring

Stormy Maxwell: Everyone always asks me, "What's it like having Dr. Death (now Dr. Life) for a dad?" I would always answer, "He is just a great big teddy bear!"

I can remember being six years old and sitting in a lawyer's office chair and across the desk sat of a man in a suit who asked me why did I want Mr. Williams to adopt me. I remember my response: "Because he is my daddy and I love him!"

There are a lot of memories from the past with Daddy, but my favorites are of him always just wanting to have fun and all the great shoulder rides. He always wanted to see me smile, and I can remember going through adolescence and him always picking at me. I was thinking he just wanted to give me a hard time, but now I know it was just to get a smile out of me. He always told me he would wear a purple Barney suit to my graduation. Thank God he didn't! When I went to college, Daddy told me to do my best, work hard, but most of all enjoy myself, because these were the best days of my life.

The first time I brought my husband Mitchell home when we were dating, he asked him if his palms were sweating when we called to tell him we were getting close to being there. Mitchell did not know what to think. I guess having Dr. Death as a father-in-law was a little too much to think about. Today, however, they love each other very much.

I can remember six years ago walking down the aisle for my daddy to give me away with tears in his eyes, and at the end of the aisle, thanks to great strength, he had to literally pick me up and put me at the top of the steps, as my tulle bottom dress was caught under me.

I also remember our fun father-daughter dance to "Brown-Eyed Girl." Just the other day I called him after I heard it to reminisce about that wonderful night. After my parents divorced the first time, there was a period that I did not spend a lot of time with him because of things that went on with my parents' relationship. But those things have been mended.

However, I do remember a lot of days of walking on eggshells, so to say, because drugs made him flip his lid at the drop of a hat.

Daddy has always been there for me. Be it a shoulder to cry on or uplifting words, he always is an encourager. He always says I love you and lets you know that you are in his thoughts and prayers through many beautiful cards throughout the years.

Daddy was there with movies, food, gifts, and love at the birth of his first grandchild, Alli Grace, and the same with his second, John Hudson. During this time, Daddy was diagnosed with throat cancer. I can remember being pregnant and meeting with the ear, nose, and throat physician and him giving us the devastating news. But we knew if anyone could fight this fight, it would be Daddy.

He did not get through it, however, without lots of prayers. There were many days we thought might be the last. Even though I could not always be there, Daddy knew I was only a phone call a way. During times of surgery and chemo the doctors would call and update me on a daily basis. We would always chat, and I would try to keep his spirits up during the long treatments. Even during the times when Daddy could not speak we still made a way to communicate, one for yes and two for no, but I could still see the tears of fear.

After surgery, that was the scariest moment seeing Daddy in such a bad state, but I was right there helping him in any way I could. I never thought I would be bathing my dad at such a young age; he had to swallow a lot of pride during this time. I know the Lord allowed him to go through that time for him to be the man he is today.

I always prayed and wished for a daddy who loved the Lord and now that is exactly what I have. Daddy has now been there for me in that same way I was there for him in the past. After a very fragile pregnancy and delivering at 26 weeks, I delivered the third grandchild who weighed two pounds and two ounces. After meningitis and a rollercoaster ride of other problems, we are overcoming these things. Through all of this, Daddy stood in prayer for Anne Claire.

Daddy and I always touch base every day and continue to be there for one another, whether to share praise reports or to uplift one another. As an adult I have not only a father who is a great man of God but the greatest friend ever.

Wyndam Williams: I love my dad so much. He is my best friend and means everything to me.

With this said, still, when it comes to my dad, there are amazing, sad, and miracle stories. I remember when I was little and we would go out to places just like anyone else would go—the grocery store, movies, shopping mall, out to eat, etc. No matter where or when we would go, people knew my father. They would always ask for pictures and autographs. My dad would always talk to them and treat them nicely.

Because of all this attention, I always thought I was Mr. Big Stuff. Everyone knew my dad, and he is Steve "Dr. Death" Williams.

There were also some great times when my parents were still together. We would go to Maui every summer. We would stay at Dad's condo. I remember Dad teaching me how to swim, surf and boogey board. It was a blast and I had so much fun!

Maybe the greatest trip I ever went on with my dad was when he took me to Japan. One summer while my dad was wrestling on a tour in Japan, we vacationed in between his matches. My dad was and still is a legend in Japan, so there were always pictures being taken of him and autographs being signed by Dad.

But the coolest part of this trip was that because of my dad's fame, I was getting famous. I remember all these little Japanese kids screaming my name and asking me for autographs. This was all so cool for a ten-year-old kid.

And then there are the sad times. Less than three years ago, my dad started the toughest "fight" of his life. He was diagnosed with throat cancer. For me, I never realized how much I loved my dad until he was dying. Because my mom and dad are divorced, the only persons that were there for my dad were me and my sister. Since my sister lived about an hour away, I was the ONLY person that saw my dad dying more than anybody else. I went through some of the most heartbreaking and powerful stuff you could imagine with my dad.

I can never forget when Dad couldn't talk. He had to write stuff down so I would know what he wanted me to do. What he wanted to say, as well as his thoughts and ideas. At times it got so frustrating—it was starting to bring the Dr. Death out of me.

It was also quite depressing when I would go down with Dad to M.D. Anderson in Houston (Texas). I had never seen anything sadder than the people and their families at that hospital. How they would sit and wait, cry and cry some more, hope and pray, that their loved one stricken with cancer would survive.

And I was also one of those families. I was there when my dad went through seven hours of chemotherapy and radiation, when his head got cut off three times, and when he "died" three times at the hospital.

I know that the only reason why my father is alive and well is because he reunited with the Lord of all Lords, Jesus Christ. ... Dad and I have always been Christians. However, what we experienced and went through together, it was clearly a miracle from God. We saw how powerful and how great God really is!

The greatest day of my life was less than a year ago when my dad was diagnosed and told that he was cancer-free.

I just thank God every day for keeping my dad alive! If there is anybody reading this book that is not right with God, then you should get to be best friends with the Lord. My dad and I did, and through the blood of Jesus Christ, He worked miracles in our life and kept my dad alive. Because of this, now you know how Dr. Death became Dr. Life!

and pray. I remember one stint where Wyndam and I spent four days in Buffalo, New York, at a Christian convention. The event was located inside the Six Flags theme park. Not only did I wrestle, but Wyndam and I had a great time riding all the rides.

After the matches, the preacher gave a sermon and asked people to give their life to Jesus. Sure enough, many people came to the ring for the altar call and accepted Christ as their Savior. It is so great to help bring people to the Lord!

Additionally, on January 19, 2007, I am once again organizing and will be part of the Fourth Annual KTBS TV Boat and Sport Show, held at the Convention Center in Shreveport, Louisiana. KTBS Channel 3 is sponsoring it. I started this event four years ago, and it has evolved into a great show. I hope to see some old acquaintances at the show, such as Tracy

Smothers, Leatherface, Skandor Akbar, and some of the other guys in TNA, as well as current friends Jeremy "Fire" Young, Scott Murdoch, Blake Wiggins, Johnny T, and a few others.

I get up every morning at five a.m. I then get a full breakfast of Bible study and worship. First I watch Pastor Joyce Meyer. She is one of the world's leading practical Bible teachers. I really like her because she speaks candidly and practically about her experiences, so that others, like me, can apply what she has learned to their lives.

After Pastor Meyer, I listen to Joel Osteen. I have been to Joel's church in Houston. I even sat right next to Joel, his wife, and Mrs. Dodi Osteen, who also had cancer. Throughout the rest of the day I pray, read my Bible, and do my best to follow the lead of my savior, Jesus Christ.

> JEREMY YOUNG: DOC HAS SO MUCH KNOWLEDGE AND PASSION FOR PROFESSIONAL WRESTLING. HE RESPECTS THE INDUSTRY AND STILL BELIEVES IN PROTECTING THE BUSINESS. HE IS ALSO AN EXCELLENT TRAINER. HE TAKES HIS TIME. HE WILL CORRECT YOU WHEN MESSING UP AND MAKE SURE YOU DO IT RIGHT. HE TEACHES ONE HOW TO TELL A STORY. HE IS A MASTER OF IN-RING PSYCHOLOGY. HE IS A TRUE TEACHER.
>
> I SOMETIMES WORRY ABOUT DOC GETTING BACK IN THE RING. I AM NOT PARTICULARLY WORRIED ABOUT HIM, BECAUSE I KNOW HE IS MORE THAN CAPABLE OF TAKING CARE OF HIMSELF. BUT IT IS THE GUYS HE WORKS AGAINST THAT CONCERN ME. ALL IT TAKES IS ONE MISSED SPOT, AND IT COULD LEAD TO A FATALITY.

I have had many callings in my life. I believe now that my calling is in the ministry. If it is God's will, then it will happen. Though I may have to talk for the rest of my life by sticking my thumb into a hole in my throat, it seems like the Lord is leading the way.

In early May of 2006, I had the privilege to give my testimony at my church in Shreveport. The presentation was a TV taping for the Trinity Broadcasting Network (TBN). Steve Borden (STING) also gave his testimony. We go way back. It is great that the Lord has both of us on the right track.

Likewise, from June 23–25 of 2006, I was invited to attend the *Trek Expo 2006* in Tulsa, Oklahoma. Besides signing autographs along with

After cancer surgery, Dr. Life is back, weighing only 225 pounds!

Chewbacca, Jonathan Frakes (Captain William Riker), Richard Kiel (JAWWWS), and others, I was asked to go to the local Boys Club to present my testimony. About 70 boys were in attendance. I helped bring about 50 of them to the Lord! Praise God!

I will never forget one little boy who attended the *Expo*. While I was signing autographs at the table, he seemed miserable. I watched him as he proceeded from table to table to get autographs or just to see what was happening. Each time our eyes met, I smiled to try to cheer him up.

When he finally made it to my table, I asked him if he would like an autographed photo. He said, "Yeah."

In a flippant manner, I responded, "Well, I will give you one if you turn that frown upside down." The young man started to smile.

After some small chitchat, I said, "I don't know what you have been through or what is going on in your life. But I'll tell you what, a smile on your face will make your face feel a whole lot better. It will also make others feel better."

I continued, "Son, are you a Christian?"

He said, "Yeah, I was." I said, "What do you mean, you were?" He just shrugged.

Sensing he needed a friend, I asked him if he had a Bible. The following response from this young boy is still etched in my mind. He said, "I did, but somebody stole it." I just wanted to cry with him and hold and hug him.

Before I could step up and buy him a Bible on the spot, somebody who was with him said, "I am going to buy you a Bible tomorrow."

I finished the conversation telling him to give his life up to Christ, because He would take him to places that he couldn't imagine. Before he left, I gave the boy a big thumbs-up. I watched him walk out. As he headed out the door, he looked at me, smiling ear-to-ear. He also gave me a big thumbs-up!

On September 16, 2006, I was invited to be part of Alicia's House Fourth Annual Celebrity Golf Outing, dinner, and silent auction in Crete, Illinois. Alicia's House was founded to honor the memory of Alicia Diaz, who passed away at the age of four on January 14, 2001. Alicia's House feeds hundreds of families each month. I was at this event with many celebrities, such as Scott Schwartz (Hollywood's Ultimate Bad Guy), Mike Pappas (a former Chicago Cub), the "Turd" (an entertainer), the Smiths (a gospel music group); and Juan Hernandez (the main guy who ran the event).

After the golf tournament, I went to talk to about 100 kids at a local karate class. Their ages ranged from nine to 15. I told them my story. Two

I relate my story to author Tom Caiazzo in December 2006, Atlanta, Georgia.

services were scheduled for the next morning and evening at a local Pentecostal church. I preached and gave my testimony at the first service, and shared the second service with my friend, pastor Ricky Smith.

Ricky Smith had the place fired up and I wasn't sure what I was going to speak about when he concluded. I didn't want to repeat my testimony, because many of the parishioners had attended the morning service with me. So I prayed, asking God to guide me. All of a sudden, my mouth started running about 30 to 40 miles an hour. My lips were moving and silent words started to flow from me. I was speaking in tongues through the power of God. Nobody heard this except me. It was incredible:

When the day of Pentecost came, they were all together in one place. Suddenly a sound like the blowing of a violent wind came from heaven and filled the whole house where they were sitting. They saw what seemed to be tongues of fire that separated and came to rest on each of them. All of them were filled with the Holy Spirit and began to speak in other tongues as the Spirit enabled them. (Acts 2:1-4).

God gave me the words to preach. For 30 minutes, I spoke from my heart through the guidance of the Holy Spirit. My message was about the need for people to spend more time with God. I preached that people spent too much time talking on their cell phones. It was time for people to put those phones down and instead communicate with God.

I wasted some 25 years beating, fighting, punching, and slapping people with my hands on a daily basis. It was time to put my hands together and pray to God.

At the end of my message, Pastor Randy Denn gathered everyone around to pray for those at the altar. Another pastor, who I did not know, prayed for me. He told me that he had a message from God. He said, "You will no longer be wrestling in the flesh, but wrestling to win people over to God."

Without a shadow of a doubt, the Lord is leading the way. I still love the wrestling business and want to get back involved in some capacity. I feel a calling to preach; but unlike in the past, I am not doing things my way. I am doing them the Lord's way. I am walking the straight and narrow and will follow the Lord's will. I am unequivocally a new person with a new mission in life: to serve the Lord.

> TAMMY BREWSTER: STEVEN HAS CHANGED A LOT. HE USED TO ACT LIKE A BULLY AND LOSE HIS TEMPER. NOT ANY MORE. THOUGH HE WAS SCARED AND NOT MAKING ANY MONEY, HE TRUSTS THE LORD. THROUGH CHRIST, HE FINALLY HAS PEACE IN HIS LIFE. HE IS SEEING THE BLESSINGS OF GOD. IT IS GREAT TO SEE HIM SHARE HIS TESTIMONY.
>
> STEVEN HAS GROWN TREMENDOUSLY IN THE LORD. I NEVER THOUGHT I WOULD SEE THE DAY THAT HE WOULD BE ATTENDING A CLASS TO BECOME A PREACHER. IT IS A TRUE TESTAMENT TO THE LORD.

In mid-November of 2006, Tom Caiazzo and I met in Atlanta to complete the particulars of this book. After an evening meal at the restaurant Cracker Barrel, a man recognized me. He introduced himself and we shook hands. He then asked for a picture. Before leaving, he said he had heard that I was sick, but looked great. I told him I was feeling great, and it was all because of the grace of God. He thanked me and said, "Take care, Dr. Death." I smiled and thanked him. Before we departed, however, I reminded him that I am no longer Dr. Death, but Dr. Life.

The wages of sin is death; but the gift of God is eternal life through Jesus Christ our Lord. Romans 6:23

EPILOGUE

In late October of 2006, I attended a men's weekend retreat sponsored by my church. I really didn't want to go, but after lots of prayer, I was moved by the Holy Spirit to attend. Pastor Duron started the retreat with prayer and a brief service. We then were broken into groups to talk about a variety of life issues and experiences.

The weekend was designed for us to face our truths and cleanse our hearts, and most of us did just that. I listened to about seven guys tell me about their lives and give their testimonies. Some were more in-depth and thorough than others. As you could imagine, people were nervous, and it took a while for everyone to open up. Then it was my turn. I told my testimony and shared my experiences. I felt like I was the pastor.

After the group sessions, I went back into the church with all the attendees. As I sat in the pew praying, I reflected on my life. I thought of my best friend in my life, Dad. I miss him so much. He was always there for me. He was everything to me. When I lost him, my life changed. If my dad was alive, I am sure that things would have been different. I burst into tears.

I also came to the painful realization that I had hurt many people over the years with my voice. I was verbally abusive to my family, ex, and others. As a tough guy, I talked in a hostile and mean manner. It was the way I spoke on the football field, amateur wrestling mat, the microphone, and in the ring. I took the Lord's name in vain and used profanity. To me, the F-word was an adjective.

Though it took a near-death experience to show me these shortcomings, I now speak to people in a calm and passive manner. I try to use appropriate words and listen a whole lot more before speaking. I only raise my voice when preaching the Word of God.

Some people can hear God and some people can't. But I hear the Lord. After years of doing things my way, I now do things for the Lord. As I continued to pray, I truly felt my calling to the ministry. Be it in a pulpit or the wrestling ring, the Lord wants me to give my testimony. He wants me to help bring people of all ages to Jesus so that they can have eternal life.

Toward the end of the evening, we all watched the video *The Passion of the Christ*. It was very heavy. During the scene in which they whipped Jesus, I started to cry. I was watching my Savior, Jesus, being beaten. It was sad to watch someone take that kind of beating. And he took it for you and me.

I thought, "What a gracious God. I have a 26-year-old daughter, a 14-year-old son, a wonderful mother, and siblings with great families. I love them very much and could never give my kids up. I have great friends in Mike Geary, Kelly Mitchell, Tom Caiazzo, Jeremy Young, Barry Switzer, Jim Ross, Jim Duggan, and Denny Duron. I don't think I could ever give up any of them for their sins. But God did. He gave up his only son, Jesus, for our sins. Amen!"

The Pastor then called our group to the front. He gave us a giant nail and told us that we were the ones who had nailed Jesus to the cross. When I grabbed that nail, I experienced the same feeling I had when my father passed away. I dropped right down to my knees and started praying.

Afterward, the entire group went outside and we had a bonfire. The pastor said, "It is now time for us to throw away all our problems, to get rid of our past and start anew." Though I didn't have a voice, I could hear everyone else cheering and rejoicing. But in my mind, I was screaming as loudly as I could. I was a new man. Rejuvenated and reenergized through the blood of Jesus.

After the retreat was over, I headed home. It was crystal clear that the Lord has a purpose for me. Though my biggest challenge is to bring adults to Jesus, I believe, by the grace of God, He will somehow give me the strength and wisdom to lead the way: *For by grace you have been saved through faith; and that not of yourselves, it is the gift of God, not as a result of works, that no one should boast.* [Ephesians 2:6, 7]

APPENDIX A

WORD ASSOCIATIONS AND TIDBITS

Below are brief descriptions of the many people I have met and places I have frequented over the years. I have included wrestlers, football players, and other personalities. They are in no specific order, but just as they came in my mind. Enjoy.

INDIVIDUALS

Vince McMahon: An energetic person who successfully changed professional wrestling to sports entertainment.

Barry Switzer: A wonderful friend, father figure, and person. The best coach I ever played for.

Billy Sims: A gentle man with a big heart and an overall fantastic person. He just opened a new barbecue restaurant, and the atmosphere and food are awesome.

Brian Bosworth: An average OU football player who unsuccessfully tried to be like JC Watts, Billy Sims, and me. His shooting off at the mouth often got the best of him, as he was a flop in the pros.

Bob Sapp: A fantastic person and bar none the best shoot fighter/PRIDE worker in the world today. Hands down!

Patriot: A rip-off worker. I have no clue how he sleeps at night after what he did to Giant Baba.

Muhammad Ali: Greatest boxer of all time and treated me like a pro. We hugged in the Superdome, and he is a big fan of professional wrestling.

Regis Philbin: The preeminent TV personality in the business. I watch Kelly and him every morning.

David Allan Coe: Outstanding singer who played a very important part in the wrestling business during the Great American Bashes. Greatest country singer I ever met.

Buddy Hackett: Funniest guy in the world. When Tammy and I were in Aspen, Buddy ran up to me and tried to drop an elbow on me. He knew me, but I had no idea who this short, fat guy was. We had a blast!

George Kennedy: A true man's man, a grand actor, and tough guy. Bad to the bone. When I met him in first class on Japan Airlines, he treated me with respect and vice versa. We took a liking to each other and we even took a picture together.

Jean-Claude Van Damme: The BEST martial arts actor around. He is very down to earth and humble. I met him at Japan Airlines lounge. He spoke very nicely about professional wrestling and I did the same about his movies, especially *Bloodsport.*

Rick and Scott Steiner: A fantastic tag team, but they could never beat Dr. Death and Bam Bam Gordy.

Bart Gunn: A better tough-man worker than wrestler. He has a good right and a better left hand. He will go down in the history as the only man ever to knock out Dr. Death.

Stone Cold Steve Austin: The greatest worker ever in the sports entertainment era and a true friend.

Kurt Angle: An Olympic champion who became a great shooter and professional wrestler. He has the chance to be one of the greatest of all time.

Shawn Michaels: HBK is the most flamboyant worker in the business today. I remember when he started out in the business. He has come a long way. He has also changed his life and is now living for the Lord.

Terry Funk: Excellent worker and hardcore fighter. He is a friend and still very much active in professional wrestling.

Harley Race: A good friend and the champ! He helped me a lot while I was in the business. He is still assisting me today. Unlike many, he is honest and has integrity.

Jim Crockett: Always trying to figure out how to be as good as Bill Watts. And he never could.

Ted DiBiase: A good friend, great worker, and the "Million Dollar Man." I learned so much from Ted throughout the years. He is one of the best technical wrestlers ever. Ted is a strong Christian who is bringing, and will continue to bring, many people to the Lord.

Mil Mascaras: The greatest Mexican wrestler ever. He is very popular all over the world. The Japanese people love him dearly.

Bob Roop: A very hard worker who operated with style in the ring. Tough as nails and could pin anyone at any time.

Black Bart: A good heel worker to help get over the babyfaces. He loved his chewing tobacco!

Steve and Shaun Simpson: They come from a great wrestling family and the girls used to pack the arenas to see them.

J.J. Dillon: The biggest butt-kisser in the business. Always had to either be part of a clique or form his own to protect himself.

Eric Bischoff: Categorically and unequivocally a wannabe promoter!

Mick Foley: Without any doubt, the greatest hardcore wrestler ever.

Gene Kiniski: In his era, the toughest man ever to step in the ring.

Jesse Ventura: A very charismatic wrestler, great color commentator, and excellent politician.

Mr. Wrestling II: A classy man. He protected the business to the fullest. He was the only guy I knew who wore a mask wherever he went. He is the greatest high-knee lifter ever in the sport of professional wrestling.

Ernie Ladd: The "Big Cat" is the most talented, pure athlete for his size that I ever had the privilege to know.

Bruiser Bob Sweetan: A very, very tough man. Back in the days when the biz was wrestling, he was involved in many brawls and knocked out lots of people.

Grappler: Len Denton was the best to work his gimmick by kicking the mat and loading up his boot. A serious worker who valued his craft.

Ric Rude: A good wrestler, great technician, and a personal friend. He would have been one of the best in the business. It was sad when he passed way. He left this world way too soon.

Randy Savage: The "Macho Man" was a very hard worker and put the "w" in wrestling. Enjoyed watching his work; he would give 110% every time. Also, "Snap into a Slim Jim!"

Tony Schiavone: Thought he was the "godfather" of all the commentators. WRONG! The "godfather" is JR, Jim Ross, the man he could never be.

Dick Slater: Great heel who went out there and proved he could work with anybody. He could make a broomstick look like a million bucks.

Dustin Rhodes: One of my great friends in the business. Worked hard, put it all on the mat, and when he became "Goldust," he took his talent to a higher level.

Larry Zybysko: Great technician with perfect microphone skills. Today's wrestlers can learn a lot from the approach, skills, and demeanor of Larry.

Vince Russo: Vinnie the Russo. A wannabe promoter. Tried to make a name for himself, but like other wannabes, fizzled right out of the business.

Kane: A great creature in the business who handles every angle put in front of him with professionalism and precision. He was Wyndam's favorite wrestler growing up.

Mark Henry: The true "King Kong" of professional wrestling. He is undoubtedly the strongest man in the world. I have never seen a thicker guy than him.

Sgt. Slaughter: A real man's man. He has a heart of gold, and when he tells you what is going to happen, it is the truth. You can bank on it.

Rey Mysterio Jr.: One of the greatest acrobatic wrestlers in the business. I have a lot of respect for him. I have never seen anybody do such high spots in the ring. He is the first guy of his size I have ever seen beat a huge wrestler like the Big Show.

Curt Henning: Nice guy and clearly "Mr. Perfect." He was probably one of the top 10 technicians in the business. Good friend who should still be alive today.

Roddy Piper: The "Rowdy" one is very entertaining and a great heel. He helped make the WWE what it is today.

Chris Benoit: Excellent wrestler and very close friend. Tough as nails and can work with any type of talent. I have known Chris since we worked together in New Japan.

Skandor Akbar: One of the greatest wrestling managers of all time. He was the manager of the "Rat Pack," and if you don't know the "Rat Pack," you don't know wrestling.

Abdullah the Butcher: Awesome big-man wrestler who could work the fans right out of their seats. Even today, he can still work and entertain people.

Buzz Sawyer: One of the best bumpers in the business. It was sad that drugs ended his life.

Jody Hamilton: The "Assassin" is a great promoter, wrestler, and heel. He has a son that is one of the best referees of all time, Nick Patrick.

Missing Link: In the 1980s, he had an awesome gimmick and was a very different type of creature in the wrestling business. He was a spooky kind of guy. To watch him work and run his head into the steel post outside the ring was unbelievable.

Dean and Joe Malenko: Great tag team and friends. We had a wonderful time in Japan wrestling matches and enjoying the Tokyo nightlife.

Rob Van Dam: An excellent martial arts wrestler in the business. He is one guy who isn't afraid to tell you he smokes pot. He was even on the cover of *High Times*.

Kamala: The "Ugandan Warrior" is a great big-man wrestler, and worked his gimmick to the "T." We had many great matches together that burned the house down.

Great Muta: A guy that I took care of when he was in the United States. I took him from town to town, showed him the ropes, and introduced him to influential people. Unfortunately, when he became the owner of All Japan Pro Wrestling, he killed Dr. Death, and thus killed AJPW.

Terry Taylor: One of my friends. We had many unbelievable matches against each other. I learned a lot from him. He could have been a great promoter. For some reason, however, even though I always scratched his back, he didn't scratch mine.

Jerry Lawler: A nice guy, good wrestler, and an even better color commentator. He works very well together with Jim Ross.

Maxx Payne: A guy who was always trying to figure out what he was going to be in the business.

Super Destroyer: One of the greatest and toughest wrestlers to ever wear a mask. I wrestled against him and Big John Studd. My partner was none other than Andre the Giant. We tore the house down in Oklahoma City.

Bret Hart: An excellent worker who is a very classy person. The "best there is, the best there was, and the best there ever will be!"

Owen Hart: Like his brother, a superb worker. He was a funny guy and we shared many great times in Japan together. He should still be alive today. May God rest his soul.

Nikita Koloff: His Russian gimmick was over when he turned face. He had a great clothesline. He has now turned his life over to God and is ministering in Africa.

Midnight Express: A very good tag team. Bobby Eaton and Dennis Condery were both excellent technical wrestlers. They put on many classic matches against the Rock-n-Roll Express. Their manager, Jim Cornette, complemented them well, and is also a decent guy.

Bruiser Brody: With Stan Hansen, he was part of the greatest tag team in Japan before Terry Gordy and me. Both men remind me a lot of us. As for Bruiser, God bless his soul. He should still be running hard in the business.

Stacy Keibler: The hottest legs in the wrestling business and a terrific dancer.

Tony St. Clair: One of the finest British workers in the history of the professional wrestling business.

Too Cold Scorpio: A very nice guy and was always a solid worker to help put over the heels.

Rip Rogers: See Too Cold Scorpio.

Missy Hyatt: The "first lady" of wrestling. A very beautiful woman and an excellent commentator, manager, and talent in the business.

Ricky Morton: One half of the Rock-n-Roll Express. A great tag-team worker, but an even better singles wrestler. We had great times in Mid-South and Japan.

GEOGRAPHY

Norman: Boomer Sooner!!!

Philadelphia: The best Italian food around. The cheesesteaks are great, but for real Italian food, check out Tre Scalini's on 11th Street.

Japan: This is my second home. Every city in Japan is awesome and the people treat you like family. I love their culture! The Tokyo nightlife is the best.

Maui: The beach, weather, and people are out of this world.

Seattle: Beautiful country, and of course, Starbucks.

Detroit: Great fans, but very cold! Try to catch a Pistons game in Auburn Hills.

Alaska: Scenic beauty and wonderful fishing. My son and I had a blast vacationing there a few years back.

Atlanta: Great city, home of Deep South Wrestling. Be sure to stop at Abdullah the Butcher's restaurant.

St. Louis: A very impressive Gateway Arch and home of my friend, Harley Race.

Orlando: Many attractions to visit including Disney World, Animal Kingdom, Sea World, and Epcot.

Dallas: The Metro-plex is Von Erich turf. It can get toasty in the summer. Be sure to eat at Fogo de Chão. Besides the tasty meat, the warm cheese bread, fried bananas, and seasoned mashed potatoes are out of this world.

San Diego: See Maui.

Shreveport: My home and the birthplace of Mid-South Wrestling. Some of the most passionate wrestling fans in the world!

Los Angeles: Exciting city with lots to do. The hotels, restaurants, and clubs are unreal. Also, keep your eyes open, you never know what celebrity you will run into.

Chicago: "The Windy City" with great deep-dish pizza. Try Giordano's on Rush Street.

Las Vegas: Lights and more lights. Great shows and all-you-can-eat buffets worth every penny. Stay at the MGM Grand or Tropicana.

Lafayette: The best Cajun food in the state of Louisiana. Every place is good, but check out the Blue Dog Café.

San Antonio: The River Walk is out of this world. For delicious great Mexican food overlooking the river, try the Casa Rio.

Savannah: Great history, and of course, check out River Street. One-Eyed Lizzies has the best grouper fingers. It is also the home of my pal, Tommy Nero.

Charlotte: Awesome wrestling town, very clean, lots of passionate wrestling fans, and the home of the "Nature Boy," Ric Flair.

Birmingham: Nested away in the Deep South, this is one vibrant, cosmopolitan city. It is a fun place with lots of shops, clubs, and restaurants–especially the barbecue. The wrestling fans are out of this world.

Memphis: Wonderful city with many die-hard wrestling fans. The food is unreal. Again, awesome barbecue. Be sure to try Pin-n-Whistle.

New York: The city that never sleeps. The shopping, people, food, and everything else are incredible. Try a slice of pizza from any restaurant, especially Una Pizza Napoletana.

Portland: Tucked away in the Pacific Northwest, it is one very beautiful city with very friendly people.

Houston: I have so many fond wrestling memories from this city. It is also the home of M.D. Anderson Cancer Center.

Florida Panhandle: Excellent beaches, great climate, and tasty seafood. Be sure to check out Pineapple Willy's on Panama City Beach.

Denver: This is where it all began for Steve Williams. With the Rocky Mountains, the city is so majestic. It is literally God's county.

APPENDIX B

WHAT OTHERS SAY ABOUT DR. DEATH

I hope you find the letters below as inspirational and touching as I have. If one of these letters helps make your day or life better, I have accomplished my objective. Never stop believing and never quit, because with God, all things are possible.

Doc:

I have never had the pleasure of watching "Dr. Death" wrestle, I have only heard about his amazing amateur and pro career. But his most brutal match never came inside of a pro wrestling ring or on an amateur wrestling mat. Despite his towering peaks of triumph, this man had to face the hellish troughs of despair while dueling with the real possibility of death, and an extremely agonizing one at that. I have something in common with Steve Williams. I was also looking the grim reaper square in the face before my life-saving liver transplant—it's not fun, take it from us. I had the honor of praying for the Doc during his hour of most need. Many folks were, including a lot of pro wrestlers. Personally, I believe what pulled the Doc through was the Doc. This man is a true testament to the power of the human will. God has put in all of us a measure of willpower. The man Steve Williams, in his most weakened and abandoned state, was able to bite the bullet and tap into that willpower. This is the sign of a true champion. No one will ever be able to understand the true hell this man had to endure. He truly is a remarkable human being and I count it an honor to be considered a friend.

Superstar Billy Graham

Steve:

Even though I am not a cancer patient, it has affected my life in many different ways. I've lost friends and family to that disease and it has changed the way I live. I don't hate much about life, but I do hate cancer and wish our medical professionals could do more to stop it. In relation to that, I've known you since 1986 and have seen you in many physically demanding roles. I have always thought of you as a strong, unstoppable human being, but since you've been able to beat this disease that has changed your life, I am even more aware of the strength and determination that you possess. I'm sure you're aware that the physical demands of past sports don't compare to the battles that you've recently encountered while fighting cancer, and the great thing is that you've won the battle and you serve as a role model that will inspire others to prosper as you did (and continue to do). I also know that during these most trying times in your life, you still managed to be a great father to your son, which is a full-time job in itself. In my book, you're an inspiring tower of strength, a model human being, and someone that God has brought to my life so that I may be a better person.

Thanks for being my friend.

Michael C. Myers, Power Houston, Toshiba UPS

Doc:

As I grew older I started to pay less and less attention to wrestling. I graduated college and wound up coaching college basketball at the

Division 1 level and thus spent my time traveling the country recruiting future superstars and such. After three years in the coaching business, I decided I had had enough with that life. Somehow I ended up in the concert business and starting working as a promoter for acts such as David Allan Coe, Willie Nelson, and others, and somehow found myself booking a few pro-wrestling matches! I had come full circle. I received a crash course in the business (if there is such a thing) and became hooked.

After a while my excitement stopped when I began to realize that most of the wrestlers that I had grown up watching (and now was booking) were nothing like what I had hoped they would be. I learned that the wrestling business had turned many of my heroes into some of the most unpleasant, unreliable, and unprofessional men I had ever met. Then I met Steve Williams. Not Doctor Death, but Steve Williams.

I had tried for the longest time to contact him to work one of my shows and finally had him scheduled to appear for my promotion. He worked a great match against Kamala and was extremely professional so I kept booking him again and again. It was cool because he would bring his son Wyndam with him from time to time, and the business started to become fun again. He was one of the only "boys" I ever dealt with who actually took the time to "teach" me about the business, and I never missed an opportunity to pick his brain whenever I was around him (most of the time I kept my mouth shut and listened)!

I also realized that he was truly respected by everybody in the locker room regardless of how big a star they were at the time. I had booked a huge show and had several "superstars" on the card: Buff Bagwell, Raven, Perry Saturn, Disco Inferno, and others were on the card. Thus, there were a lot of egos in back. I was running crazy dealing with production, ticket sales, and all the other fires that pop up backstage and had little time to deal with the extra issues that pile up when dealing with a card that loaded. But I can tell you one thing: when Doc entered the back, everyone stood straight and acted professional! There was no more BS because Doc would not tolerate it. He commanded respect and the miles he had traveled demanded it. He was "old school" and knew what that meant. That night

Doc worked with a slipped disc and could hardly turn his neck. While the other "stars" were trying to "work" me with their "phantom" injuries in order to get out of a honest night's work, Doc went out and made everyone look like a million bucks and delivered a great match in front of a packed house and led by example; I will never forget that. He was a stand-up professional when he didn't HAVE to be. That to me is a testament to his career, his reputation, and his legacy. He is one of the last of a dying breed and should be heralded as such.

I was devastated when I found out about the cancer. We had noticed his voice getting worse and worse but never suspected anything like that. To me, cancer is the worst word in the English language. Here was my friend and my hero who was also a father, a son, a brother, as well as a born-again Christian, and he was having the toughest fight he had ever had. Doc was booked to headline a show for me before the cancer had been found, and I assumed he would not be doing the show. After weeks of chemo, which had ravaged his body, Doc called me and said he was going to work the show! I thought he was crazy and did not want to let him do it, but he insisted and said he didn't want to let any of his fans down. The day of the show came, and I was worried to death about what would come, but my worries were soon laid to rest. Doc showed up, with his son right beside him, and was ready for action. This wasn't the same Doc we had seen time and time again. Doc had lost a considerable amount of weight and could hardly talk. He had no saliva due to the chemo and was noticeably weak, but assured me he would be okay. He asked me to go to the ring with him and talk to the crowd for him and I agreed. That night, in front of a few hundred fans in a small town in south Arkansas, I stood in the middle of the ring and raised Doc's hand in victory in what was his "last" match. I have the photo hanging in my home office beside pictures of me and Willie Nelson, Magic Johnson, and several others, and that photo means more than any of them.

God bless Steve Williams.

Mark Givens, Givens Entertainment

Steve:

Your newest crusade to be a motivational speaker is one you will make a HUGE DIFFERENCE IN THE LIVES OF OUR YOUTH. YOUR MESSAGE IS VERY POWERFUL AND HEARTWARMING AT THE SAME TIME.

We really appreciated you speaking to our wrestlers and football players at Green Mountain High School on April 20. You made an impact on at least two of the young men (they have told me to thank you for [coming] here).

If you are ever back in Colorado during HS wrestling season, please come watch our team at Green Mountain High School. We would love to have you here!

Take good care of yourself and continue doing what you do best! Bring the house down!!!

We really appreciate you and your STRONG MESSAGE.

Marchel Ray, GMHS Wrestling Team Mom
Mike Watt, GMHS Wrestling Head Coach

Steve:

When I heard you were diagnosed with throat cancer I had no doubt in my mind that if anyone can beat the battle, it would be you. You are a man's man, tough as nails, that enjoys life and would defeat your greatest opponent (cancer) with prayer and determination. You did just that!

Andy Vineberg, Former ECW and MLW employee

Doc:

I could not be more proud of you than ever before. You are an amazing man that does not know the words "I can't" or "I won't." You are a humble man that knows that God is full of grace and mercy and that you have been truly blessed by Him. You are one of my top heroes, because even through all the wrestling and winning, even while in pain sometimes, your biggest battle was with throat cancer. And you won ... again.

Not only did you get back up as soon as you could after the devastating cancer, you were determined to get back into that ring and at 46, YOU ARE BACK! You share your life story with all of those around you and at schools, to young men that are athletes and ... are totally in awe of this "giant hero."

I love you Doc, not only because you are a dear friend, but because you have helped me through a hard time. And no matter how busy you are ... you still remember where you came from and where you are going AND whom you serve.

You are a great man and I'm so blessed to call you a "dear friend."

Ruthie, A&R Scout for MLS-Arista and J Records,
Burnlounge.com Retailer

Doc:

My younger brother and I grew up during the glory years of Mid-South Wrestling and the Universal Wrestling Federation. Every Saturday we would turn on the old VCR and record each week's show. The one constant throughout all of those years was Doc.

Since I was in high school at the time and could drive, we made the hour-long trip from Pawhuska, OK, to Tulsa most every week to watch the best professional wrestling organization of its time. Steve Williams was a main reason and major factor in making the Mid-South/UWF go from a regional promotion to national popularity.

Some of my favorite Dr. Death memories include the dominance of the tag-team division a young Doc had with the veteran, Ted DiBiase. Steve was the young lion, producing power moves, such as the Oklahoma

Stampede, a devastating clothesline, and an explosion out of a three-point football stance. DiBiase was the technician. I remember seeing Doc and DiBiase go through legendary tag teams, such as the Rock-n-Roll Express, the Fantastics, and the Guerrero brothers.

One of the most memorable matches we witnessed was a bandelaro match pitting Steve and Ted against Chavo and Hector. It was a bloody brawl. It was also a match the Guerreros mastered. As Jim Ross would say, "Doc was busted wide open," but used his superior strength and explosiveness to throw the lucha libra stars all across the squared circle.

Williams and DiBiase retained their Mid-South tag team titles.

One of the things we really appreciated about Doc was that he never missed a night of work. He was tough as nails and when we made the trip to the Tulsa Convention Center or the Tulsa Fairgrounds Pavillion, we knew Steve "Dr. Death" Williams would be there to put on a show.

Matt Roberts

Steve:

I am writing this letter to express the grateful thanks to a man that gave … his time to make some elderly people happy. This is something that he did not have to do.

On March 13, 2006, the wrestling came to the Monroe Civic Center, and I planned, with the help of several organizations and many employees and friends, to take 13 residents to the civic center to see this event.

"Dr. Death," Steve Williams, was going to be the guest referee for the main match. Mr. Williams was just returning from a leave due to a major illness, a bout with throat cancer. I emailed Mr. Williams' fan club just to see if he could possibly take a few minutes to send some autographed pictures to some of the residents here at the West Monroe Guest House. Some of them do not receive mail and I, knowing that, thought that the mail … would make their day. I emailed him about the middle of the week, and that following Saturday morning, I received a call from Mr. Williams himself, and

he informed me that he would be arriving in West Monroe early enough on the 13th. … He could come by the nursing home and pay a personal visit to the residents and staff. My heart was overjoyed, not only because I was going to get to finally meet "Dr. Death" at 38 years old and after being a longtime fan of his, but because I knew what it was going to mean to the residents here at the guest house.

We kept this a surprise, and oh boy, were they surprised. I have never seen such excitement on faces as I did that day. Their hearts were overjoyed. They could not believe that someone of his standing would take time out of his busy day to come and spend a couple of hours with them. See, so many of these residents are here and never see anyone but us, the employees that take care of them. And they have so much to give, the unconditional love and appreciation they show for the little things in life is abundant. Each and every one of these residents makes my life worth living and I say that with the most appreciation to them, because in my heart, they are my family.

Dr. Death came in with a smile on his face and love in his heart and took pictures with the residents, signed pictures, and handed out some T-shirts, and that touched the lives of some very loving and thankful people. They still talk about that day and the night at the wrestling when "Dr. Death" looked out into the crowd and gave them what they call a personal and special thumbs-up from the ring.

Dr. Death is a very special man and is very much loved and thought highly of by all here at the West Monroe Guest House. His visit will never be forgotten, nor will he. We love you, Steve, and never forget how wonderful we here think you are.

I personally want to thank Mr. Williams and let him know he is in my prayers and will always remain in my heart. Thank you so very much for making that day special for my little residents, they are my world and you made it a little brighter for them.

One more thing, the residents here at the guest house watch the wrestling on Mondays and Friday nights. They would love to see "Dr. Death" do some commentating on those nights. They think he, King, and JR would make a wonderful team. As the Bible says, "When three or more gather!"

THANK YOU AND SO MUCH LOVE GOES OUT TO YOU STEVE!!!!!!!!!

Tommie Neathery (TJ)

Doc:

I am very excited about your book and many congratulations on it. I hope it lets the rest of the world know who and what you are, and who you have become. You mean a great deal to the "wrestling community" and now the fans can get a feel for that.

My favorite all-time story is the one I personally shared with you a couple of weeks back.

When I first began in Japan (1992–I think), we were working at Korekan Hall that evening and were arriving at the elevators. When the elevators opened there stood Dr. Death Steve Williams and Johnny Ace. I instantly stood up straight and stepped aside. I never did say anything other than "hello." It made that trip special because here were two of the men I watched and later hoped to be as big in Japan as both men are/were.

What a thrill so many years later to be working alongside both of you and actually getting to train with you and have you share all the wisdom with me down in Atlanta with Deep South Wrestling.

I have truly come full circle and I am very proud to call you "SIR" and "FRIEND."

God bless Doc, see you soon.

Billy DeMott

INDEX

INDEX

INDEX